CHURCHILL
AND TITO

CHURCHILL AND TITO

SOE, BLETCHLEY PARK AND
SUPPORTING THE YUGOSLAV
COMMUNISTS IN WORLD WAR II

CHRISTOPHER CATHERWOOD

FRONTLINE
BOOKS

FRONTLINE
BOOKS

CHURCHILL AND TITO
SOE, Bletchley Park and Supporting the Yugoslav Communists in World War II

This edition published in 2017 by Frontline Books,
an imprint of Pen & Sword Books Ltd,
47 Church Street, Barnsley, S. Yorkshire, S70 2AS

ISBN: 978-1-52670-496-2

For more information on our books, please visit
www.frontline-books.com,
email info@frontline-books.com
or write to us at the above address.

Printed and bound by TJ International Ltd, Padstow, Cornwall
Typeset in 10.5/13.5 point Palatino

Contents

Acknowledgements

As with everything I ever write, my first thanks are due to my wife Paulette, who is my constant companion, inspiration, support and muse. My thanks to her are profound and lifelong.

This book was made possible by two grants from the Winston Churchill Memorial Trust – a Traveling Fellowship in 2010 and an Archives By-Fellowship at Churchill College Cambridge in 2015. I am delighted to express my deep gratitude to two successive chief executives of that Trust – Major General James Balfour and Julia Weston – for the two grants that made everything financially possible. It should be added that they have not in any way chosen to vet or censor what I have written here. They know that I have not always been in agreement with Churchill's wartime decisions in some of my previous books, so the fact that I am utterly in agreement with the great man's policies in 1943 is happily coincidental.

I should add that members of the Churchill family whom I have the pleasure of knowing personally are refreshingly open to an honest appraisal of their ancestor's life, and they realise fully that hagiography of the kind that places Churchill as an icon not as a genuine flesh-and-blood human being does him no favours. I am grateful to one of his descendants for approving the grant – and neither he nor the Trust are responsible for anything that I have written in this book. Winston Churchill was entirely wrong to dispatch British, Australian and New Zealand troops to total defeat in Greece in 1941–1942, and entirely correct to back Tito and the Partisans as the best force to hold down German troops in Yugoslavia in 1943. He made both mistakes and also brave and intelligent rational decisions. The one in our book here was the right call and in this work, I am more than happy to defend him against the false charge of being a dupe, blunderer and all the other nonsensical accusations involved in his decision making in the complexities of war.

Everyone who writes about Churchill has, at some stage, to use the splendid Churchill Archives at Churchill College Cambridge – where I am writing this very page. Allen Packwood, the Director, was given a thoroughly well-deserved OBE during my research here, and he was characteristically modest in saying that it was a reward for his wonderful team during the research and initial writing of this book: Andrew Riley, Julia Schmidt, Katharine Thomson, Ceri Humphries, Gillian Booker, Heidi Egginton, Jana Kostalikova, Louise Watling, Natalie Adams, Natasha Swainston, Sarah Lewery and Sophie Bridges. All of them are the embodiment of helpfulness and patience in dealing with readers and their queries and I am pleased to include all of them in the acknowledgements. Allen has the gift of encouragement, and Andrew and Fiona Riley are a continuing joy and inspiration to their many friends. Sophie's hard work on the Deakin Papers enabled me to use them in a way that has transformed what I was going to write.

And it is thanks to Allen that my editor for this book is the accomplished historian in his own right, John Grehan, and that my publisher is that splendid company Pen and Sword whose publications have transformed our understanding of centuries of war. As ever, any controversies that have crept in are my responsibility – Allen is the embodiment of scholarly probity and neutrality in his position in charge of the UNESCO-winning Churchill heritage.

Dr Adrian Crisp and Professor Alec Boksenberg, both Fellows of Churchill College, and both with connections to the Archives Centre and/or the WCMT, have been instrumental in getting me financial support. Dr Crisp is an eminent hospital consultant and Professor Boksenberg a globally distinguished astronomer, and the generosity of these two delightful scientists to an historian, both on a professional level and also sheer personal kindness over the years, has meant a lot both to me and to my wife. Both of them make Churchill College Senior Combination [sic] Room one of the most enjoyable places in Cambridge with which to be associated.

Professor Christopher Andrew and his seminar on intelligence has been a source of much enjoyment and inspiration, and he was also kind enough to be a referee for my grants. As always, what I say here is my responsibility not his.

For three years I had the privilege of being a grantee of the Royal Literary Fund, a charity established under Royal patronage in the eighteenth century. I have considerable gratitude to the legendary Hugh Bicheno, himself a beneficiary of the RLF, in gaining this three-year grant. Hugh is a wonderful historian and unique character: one of the few former employees of MI6, which absorbed MI3 in 1945, to have his former status as a spy emerge in public. He was a true friend when my wife and I needed help the most and our gratitude to him is total.

ACKNOWLEDGEMENTS

Many friends have been splendidly supportive during the process of writing this book, including those who kindly gave me hospitality in Washington DC and Charlottesville VA during the research in the USA. In DC I am grateful to Mark Dever and his wife Connie (especial lifelong thanks there as they introduced me to a friend of theirs in 1990 to whom I have now been happily married for over quarter of a century), and to Sam and Jennifer Lam, Ricardo and Winnette Ambrose and to Deepak and Sarah Reju: a wonderful United Nations of friendship in one of the world's most vibrant cities. In Charlottesville Larry and Beth Adams transformed our lives for the better and Dick and Mary Howard gave their legendary hospitality. Sadly my wife's uncle, Lacy Foster Paulette Jr, a survivor of the Battle of the Bulge, is no longer with us.

As wonderfully ever, the Catherwood Support Team has been a complete joy in morale boosting, friendship, encouragement and more besides. My mother Elizabeth Catherwood has been her magnificent self, all the more so because she has spent not a small amount of the period out of action. She is the model for all those who survived the Blitz, the generation that lived through the war that this book describes. The same applies to Professor Geoffrey Williams, the opposite end of London for the V1 and V2 rockets than my mother, and like her still splendidly active and encouraging. Thanks to him and his wife Janice I have had the privilege of teaching delightful American students in Cambridge for a semester abroad, with World War II being an episode in the INSTEP history curriculum.

Other marvellously supportive friends during the process are: Andrew and Clare Whittaker (and their daughters, my god-daughters Charlotte and Rosie), Jonquil Drinkwater (and her parents, naval convoys veteran Geoff Drinkwater and his wife Gill), her husband Andrew Kearsley and their daughter (my god-daughter) Amalie, Richard and Sally Reynolds, Alasdair and Rachel Paine (and their daughters Lucy and Alice), Sam and Ana Mackrill (plus daughters Ele and Sophia and nephew Hugo), Nathan and Debbie Buttery, Simon and Susu Scott, John and Polly Stanton and the Cabbage Moor group, Christopher and Rachel Henderson, Hill and Chris Gaston, Nick and Liz Toop and their artist daughter Heloise, Betsy and Lamar Brandt, our god-daughter Lauren Marshall, her husband Tristan Pâris de Bollardière, and her parents Claude and Leigh Marshall and wider family, Don and Emilie Wade, Gill and Bob Smith, and many more besides, including at both Churchill and St Edmund's Colleges at Cambridge.

ACKNOWLEDGEMENTS

The staff at the Alderman Library in Charlottesville VA, those at the National Archives in Washington DC and the photographic staff at The National Archives in Kew, and at the University Library in Cambridge, have all been excellent.

Christopher Catherwood,
Cambridge,
May 2017

To

James Balfour and Julia Weston

Of the Winston Churchill Memorial Trust

And as always to

My Wife Paulette

Without the three of whom this book would never have happened

And with special thanks to the Academic **A** Team of

Adrian Crisp (Cambridge)

Alec Boksenberg (Cambridge)

Christopher **A**ndrew (Cambridge)

Alexander McCall Smith (Edinburgh)

And

Allen Packwood (Churchill Archives)

Andrew Riley (Churchill Archives)

Who bear no responsibility for the contents of this book

But without whom it would never have been completed.

Preface

In writing this book I have entered two minefields. One is that of writing about Winston Churchill, the heroic leader of his people during the Second World War, and the other is on the decision that he made in 1943 to switch British support from the Serbian-based Cetnik guerrilla band in German-occupied Yugoslavia to the Communist-supporting Partisans under their leader Tito.

For some, nothing less than hagiography of Churchill will do. Anything else is blasphemy; and for those for whom Communist rule over Yugoslavia throughout 1944–1991 was a disaster, Churchill's decision to support the Partisans is rank treachery, made worse by the fact that in the 1990s the breakup of that country brought back all the nightmares of the 1940s and who slaughtered whom. So a few words of explanation in this Preface are therefore necessary to explain the attempt I am making to be as careful as possible, in what is both an exciting and controversial subject even to this day, looking at events strictly in the context of their time rather than in retrospect.

In January 1965, I had the unforgettable honour of being among the thousands of mourning Britons filing past the casket of Winston Churchill, laid in state in the great medieval hall of the Palace of Westminster.

Fifty years on there was, as was fitting, much debate on Churchill and his place in history, with the perspective of half a century's worth of hindsight. One of the articles about the great man was unusual – by strongly Conservative columnist Simon Heffer in the left-leaning *New Statesman*. It takes someone impeccably on the right to deal effectively with what many are now calling "the Churchill myth". Heffer argued, cogently, that because we owe Winston Churchill everything in 1940 – not just the survival of Britain but of Western civilisation itself – that we fail to see the rest of his very long political career in anything remotely like the correct perspective.

The *New Statesman* kindly made my reply its letter of the week. In it I explained that for many Churchill is not really an historical figure at all, but an *icon*, a symbol of values that certain groups of people cherish, and who is therefore, as Heffer noted, somebody who exists above criticism, an infallible object on whom his enthusiasts project all that they want their own societies to be. Years after his actual death. Churchill worship – if one can describe it thus – is therefore significantly greater in the USA, for which country his finest years of 1940–1945 are often the sum total of knowledge of his decades-long political career. His opposition to appeasement has become symbolic of all those who wish to stand up to tyranny, from the Cold War down to Saddam Hussein.

In fact, as the historian Robert Rhodes James once demonstrated, in his book *A Study in Failure 1900–1939*, had Churchill died in 1939 he would indeed have been seen as a failure, albeit a magnificent one, rather than as the saviour of his nation that he became by living to 1965 and by saving his nation as Prime Minister in 1940.

In discussing Churchill, therefore, historians walk into dangerous territory. Years ago, as I told *New Statesman* readers, I once wrote a book questioning some of his wartime decisions and his earlier decision to create Iraq as a new nation back in 1921. (Sykes and Picot are innocent! It was Churchill!) For this, one of the main Churchill fan magazines has never forgiven me! Even a book of photos of Churchill's life, which called him with fullest respect our *Greatest Briton,* was dismissed because forgiveness for my earlier blasphemies could not be granted. As Heffer hinted, for some people only pure hagiography will do, and not to see him as without error is to hate him utterly: such concepts as nuance or historical balance being beyond the pale.

So it will be interesting to see what if anything they make of this book, which shows that a decision that he made in 1943, profoundly controversial both at the time and in the decades since, was unquestionably the *right* thing to do. And ironically some of those who defend Churchill zealously are often on the same side politically as those who regard Britain as having betrayed Yugoslavia, the subject of our book, in that year and ever afterwards. He must, they argue, have been deceived.

This of course is history with agenda, written very much in the framework of present-day anti-Communism, rather than looking at events in the context of their time.

And history with the conclusion already reached before the book has begun is an issue that frequently bedevils works on the Balkans, and on the savage events of 1941–1945 in particular. When Yugoslavia collapsed in the late 1980s/early 1990s all the barbarities of the Second World War came back with a vengeance, with scapegoats for the horrors of the disintegration of that country in recent times being sought in the decisions of the 1940s: history, in other words, read backwards. Since the earlier World War I had originated in an assassination in the Bosnian capital of Sarajevo in 1940, some looked for interpretation of 1990s massacres as far back as then, and even into other sanguinary events in the nineteenth century, back in some cases even to a Serb defeat at the hands of an invading Ottoman Turkish (and thus Muslim) army in 1389.

But in 1943 Churchill and his Chiefs of Staff had to make crucial military decisions, based upon ULTRA decrypts of Axis codes and the reports of MI3. This was because they had to work out how to keep as many German armies as possible out of Italy, where Allied troops were now landing in large numbers. And one can safely say that it is surely unlikely that who slaughtered whom in the fourteenth century was uppermost in their minds. Churchill had a very contemporary war to win, and preferably with as few Allied casualties as possible. As we shall see, as our book unfolds, the political complexities of which guerrilla band was doing the best to pin down the maximum amount of Wehrmacht divisions in the Balkans, was a matter of total irrelevance: which group of cutthroats was killing the most Germans was the sole criterion for decision making.

So therefore:

a) Churchill saved both Britain and Western civilisation from Nazi domination and barbarity in 1940: this is unquestionable and in itself allows us to call him the greatest Briton who ever lived, as a BBC poll suggested some years ago.

b) Despite being supremely right in 1940, his earlier career was sometimes chequered, with changes of political allegiance and a valid question mark against his judgement, as for example the debacle at Gallipoli.

c) In World War II he also made some strategic errors – writers as varied in status such as thriller writer Len Deighton and Sandhurst historian John Keegan have, for example, called his quixotic dispatch of troops to Greece in 1941, which resulted in a Gallipoli-style disaster, as the worst mistake of the war.

d) But he also made some brilliant decisions that saved countless and shortened the war – his realisation that only US entry could save the democracies, his effective use of ULTRA and other feats of military technology, and, in 1943, his choice of a Balkan ally against the Germans that saved thousands of Allied lives in Italy.

This therefore is a book that looks at Churchill *in the context of the need for the Allies to win the war against Nazi Germany*, one decision at a time. It also does not forget the key background fact that but for his holding-out against Germany in May 1940–December 1941, when the USA entered the war on our side, we would have lost and one of the worst tyrannies in history would have triumphed. And in 1943 Churchill put Allied victory first. He was no dupe, but a strategic genius, who saw that in the Communist Partisans, led by Tito, lay Britain's best chance of pinning down so many Germans in Yugoslavia that the Allied war in Italy could proceed with far better odds. Backing Tito saved British and Americans fighting the same enemy in Italy.

And when Tito took power in 1944–1945, many of his opponents were massacred either on his orders or those of his underlings. Yugoslavia in 1944–1948 was a Communist bloc country and as given to purges and brutality as took place on Stalin's orders in all the other Soviet satellite states. A close relative of good Yugoslav friends of mine was among those butchered in 1945. This book is therefore no wide-eyed apology for Tito or for Communism. I saw for myself the oppression in Iron Curtain countries in the 1970s and 1980s of those wanting freedom since my friends who lived there were dissidents, *especially anti-Communist* as a result.

But this is to look at history in hindsight. In 1943 Churchill had decisions to make. And he chose as a *British* Prime Minister acting in *British* interests against *Britain's* deadliest enemy the Third Reich. In that context he was surely right. That is what our book is all about.

And furthermore this book is unexpectedly for me far more than just about SOE. In discovering the treasure trove of the Sir William (Bill) Deakin archives in the centre at Churchill College where Churchill's own archives are housed, I found that there was massive evidence that it was the reports of *MI3*, part of military intelligence based in London and with access to the ULTRA decrypts of German communications, that made the crucial difference to how Churchill and his Chiefs of Staff perceived the war in Yugoslavia.

In other words, it was not SOE that *made* the decisions, but rather *confirmed* them, not left-wing conspirators based at SOE Cairo, but instead military intelligence officials in Whitehall with access to the Bletchley Park ENIGMA/ULTRA material, with a genuinely accurate view of what was happening on the ground. What SOE operatives, such as Deakin – a former research assistant to Churchill before the war – did was to affirm what the decrypts were describing to MI3 and to the Chiefs of Staff in Whitehall as well as, of course, the Prime Minister himself. Rather than shaping Churchill's views, Deakin, and later on Fitzroy Maclean, reinforced the opinion *already reached* by the Prime Minister and his military advisers.

So I ended up writing a book completely different from the original I intended, about Bletchley and MI3 as much as about the feats of daring of SOE. And as a result we have a much clearer picture of what Churchill decided in 1943 and why.

Chapter 1

A Truly Brief History of the Balkans

For Those Who Want to Know Who Was Killing Whom and Why

No event occurs in a vacuum nor is any conflict without its context, which is why the shocking scale of the slaughter in the break-up of Yugoslavia in the 1990s was a reflection, or continuation, of the subject of who killed whom back in the 1940s. Consequently, the period that is under consideration in this study remains a topic of intense feeling even to this day in that troubled region. People in the twenty-first century have car registration plates incorporating the date **1389** – a battle that the Serbs lost all those centuries ago but for many of whom, in Serbia and in the Serb immigrant communities in the USA, is even more important than what happened to them last week.

Not only that, but in today's world we have to ask the questions what and where is Yugoslavia? Look at a map today and you will not find it. But it existed as a country from 1918 to 1941, and again from 1945 down to the 1990s, when it disintegrated into a mass of warring countries, with borders that not everyone recognises even to this day. You have to be over thirty even to have heard of it, let alone know who lived there and how long it lasted.

Much was written during the later conflict in the 1990s of 'ancient hatreds' and of centuries-old rivalries, all in the attempt to explain to a baffled West European and US readership why, decades after the mass slaughter of the Second World War, after such carnage in any part of

1

Europe, people clearly still thought of each other in the most heinous and barbaric ways possible. Even in the twenty-first century NATO troops remain in parts of the Balkans, to keep peace and to prevent the kinds of massacre that were seen, for example, in Srebrenica in 1995. This was when over 8,000 innocent Bosnian men and boys were butchered by Serb forces, the kind of mass killing that the wider world had hoped had ceased with the Holocaust and the end of the Second World War in 1945. Feelings that arose in the 1990s were applied retrospectively to the 1940s, and so a genuine and contextual history of Allied involvement in the Balkans is now something filled with pitfalls and traps for the unwary.

For readers in the second decade of the twenty-first century, much of this has been forgotten as a result of the events of 11 September 2001, or 9/11 as that horror is now universally known. In our own time, there are still grisly tales of atrocities and large-scale slaughter, but they are now further from Western Europe and the USA, in places such as the Middle East rather than, as was the case with the Balkans, in Europe's own backyard. So perhaps it is now slightly easier to gain perspective, and to put the sad tale of the twentieth-century history of the Balkan Peninsula into a more objective light. One can hope that this is the case, but memories in that region are very long indeed – going back centuries – and so one cannot be as optimistic as it would be good to be.

One of the best properly historical accounts of both the 1940s and 1990s conflicts remains that by US academic John Lampe: *Yugoslavia as History: Twice there was a Country*, which was published between the Dayton Accords of 1995 that ended the Bosnia conflict, but before the war in Kosovo in 1999.[1] The neutrality of his writing has informed much of what follows, along with other works listed in the endnotes, including that of Marcus Tanner: *Croatia: A Nation Forged in War*.[2]

But not everyone sees it that way, and the Second World War is often seen through the prism not of its own time but through that of the 1990s conflict – reading history backwards if you like.

What follows therefore will be contentious, since participants in the struggle have fundamentally different interpretations from one another of what happened in the past and why. People died because of how others in the twentieth century saw events that took place centuries before. And lest readers in the West think this alien, did not millions of entirely innocent victims die in the 1940s at the hands of supposedly advanced and civilised Germans? How much in our own twenty-first century is similarly dominated by ways of seeing history, from

Northern Ireland to diverging interpretations of the Civil War in the USA? Flags can be as toxic in our present, for example, with all their symbolism, as they were to our ancestors, generations ago. We are not as different from what happened twice in the twentieth century in the former Yugoslavia, as we would like to think.

One of the biggest issues is what John Lampe calls 'pseudo-history'.[3] This even extends back to the time when Slavic tribes left their original homelands in the early centuries after the fall of the Roman Empire in the West. We think of 476 as being the end of Rome, because that is what it was for us in our part of Europe. But we forget that it was the *Western* Empire that fell, and the *Eastern* Empire continued down until 1453, with the Ottoman capture of Constantinople. Similarly, when we consider the Reformation in Western Europe in the sixteenth century, we also forget that the first split of Christendom took place in 1054, when the Eastern Orthodox Church split from Roman Catholicism.

To twenty-first-century minds this might all seem similar to the proverbial angels dancing on the head of a pin, the mockery of obscure scholasticism debating endlessly trivial issues of minor importance. But to millions these issues remain as alive and central as they have ever been, but in the West memories which our secular age forgets. The split between the Roman Catholic (and subsequently also Protestant) interpretation of the nature of the Trinity on the one hand, and that of Orthodoxy on the other was not merely a theological split. It became part of the very identity and self-image of its protagonists, since for most of the history of Christianity where you live determined both who you were and what you believed.

We recall this with the Reformation: England was Protestant and France was Catholic. England was effectively re-launched as a *Protestant* nation under Elizabeth I in direct contradistinction to *Catholic* France or Spain, the nation's deadliest enemies. In England at this time, as writers such as Graham Greene, and Evelyn Waugh, including the latter's biography of the Catholic martyr Edmund Campion, highlight to be a Catholic was to be a traitor.[4] Your country determined your faith, not your own convictions. Think, then, if you are British, of religious divisions in Northern Ireland. If you are Scottish, consider, the "old firm" rivalry of Celtic and Rangers, based upon Catholic/Celtic and Protestant/Rangers differences to this very day.

Nowhere is the fault-line between the two halves of the original split – that of 1054 – more acute than in the Balkans. And lest we think it an academic issue in our own time, it is one of the best explanations of what is happening in the Ukraine (the literal meaning of that name being 'borderlands') at the very moment this work is being written. The Ukraine is the disputed land between Catholic Poland to the west and Russian Orthodoxy to the east. Catholicism is the national religion and self-identity of Poland as Orthodoxy is to Russia again after the fall of the Soviet Union in 1991.

So we can remember this: no such country as Yugoslavia existed before 1918. (Strictly speaking, that year it was constituted as the Kingdom of the Serbs, Croats and Slovenes, but Yugoslavia is the name under which it existed for most of its history.) So, can anything that dates back to so recent a time as 1918 really be *ancient* hatred? Yugoslavia was a wholly twentieth-century creation, a land that no longer exists, just as the Duchy of Burgundy or the Austro-Hungarian Empire have similarly over the course of time vanished from the map.

But it is not as simple as all that. The ancestors of today's Slavic inhabitants of the Balkans came thousands of miles, from their original home on the Steppes. They did so, however, to a land already populated, by the name Illyria in Roman times. But exactly who may or may not descend from the original Illyrians remains actively disputed to this day, with potential for bloodshed as will become apparent.

Most reckon that today's Slovenes are their own people, Slavic but not having precisely the same ancestral root as the Serbs and Croats. Since when the fighting began in the 1990s few people of Serbian ancestry lived in Slovenia; Slovenes were of no real interest to the Greater Serbian nationalists of Belgrade, and so got swiftly forgotten. For centuries Slovenia was, in essence, the Austrian Duchy of Carniola – the entity by which that area was known down to 1918. The Germans, in the form of the Habsburg dynasty from 1334, who ruled it were Catholics, as were the Slovenes themselves. A city such as the present-day capital, Ljubljana, looks and feels Central European, and as we shall see, it was really only the events of 1918 that put distinctly Middle European Slovenia in the same nation as the very strongly Balkan states to its south.

Historically speaking it is likely that the Croats and the Serbs are actually *originally* the same people. While nationalists from both nations would today deny that they speak the same language, during the Yugoslav era – and thus during the Second World War – the essentially identical dialects were joined together as *Serbo-Croat*. Linguistically speaking this is correct, with the differences in reality no different from

4

the regional variations in English one sees, for example, in London on the one hand or Newcastle on the other, or the varieties of American-English between California and New York.

Under this neutral understanding, the Serbs and Croats are, if not the same race, very closely aligned one to another, certainly in terms of when their common ancestors arrived in the Balkan Peninsula after the fall of Rome. And then there are the Bosnians, again linguistically identical for all intents and purposes to the Serbs and to the Croats, but whose precise ancestry and course of history remains disputed today, again with much blood spilled over that issue as recently as the 1990s.

Each of these groups coalesced around various kingdoms in the Balkan Peninsula over the course of the next few centuries. But we need to remember who neighboured them in order to trace how they would evolve. For although they might have begun as variants of the same race each would develop in radically different directions over the millennium and more ahead.

Croatia and its Adriatic littoral Dalmatia was not far away from Venice, the great city-state and trading nation that would last as an independent entity down to 1797. The Croatians correctly perceived Venetian expansion as a threat to their own territorial integrity, and in 1102 they took the step of becoming aligned to the massive Hungarian kingdom to their north. In those days, Hungary included what is now Slovakia and the Transylvanian part of Romania, along with the Burgenland province of Austria. It was one of the mightiest kingdoms of its time. The deal with Croatia in 1102 proved to be the end of an independent Croat state right down to the 1990s, with Croatia being absorbed into the greater Hungarian realm, initially with some degree of autonomy, but never as a truly sovereign entity until our own times.

This made a permanent cultural difference to the Croats. They were part of a Roman Catholic empire under the rule of the Austrian Habsburg dynasty from 1526 down to 1918. Croatia, therefore, is part of the Balkans in a geographic sense, but culturally, spiritually and intellectually it is part of Central Europe, having been ruled from Budapest for over eight centuries. They may speak a language similar to Serb, but they have the Latin alphabet and hundreds of years of being ruled not by ethnically/religiously alien people but by fellow Catholics, the historic and psychological importance of which was already clear in the Second World War but even more so in the conflicts that erupted in the 1990s in that region.

We should not forget, that for hundreds of years, what is today the Dalmatian province of Croatia was quite separate from the northern, Hungarian-ruled part of the kingdom. Many ports on the Adriatic came under the sway of the Venetians, and soon so did much of the Dalmatian countryside, along with the Istrian peninsula. The Venetian architecture has survived, as have many of the buildings from Roman times, such as Diocletian's palace in Split. It was not until 1815 that Dalmatia came under the rule of the Habsburgs and, even then, it was ruled not from the Hungarian capital in Budapest but the Austrian capital in Vienna.

Not until after the First World War and the defeat and dissolution of the Austro-Hungarian Empire was the famous Dalmatian coast permanently united to the rest of Croatia. Even after 1918 some parts of the coast remained under Italian rule, and during the Second World War the Italians were still claiming suzerainty (as the heirs of the Venetians) over much of Dalmatia. Culturally the region remains strongly Italian in feel, and so while very much a part of the Balkans geographically, in every other sense it is closer to the West than it is to its Balkan neighbours, as the thousands of tourists who go there for summer holidays cannot fail to notice. Some of the most beautiful Italian architecture in Europe, and some of the oldest Roman remains, are in Croatia not Italy.

The main part of the kingdom of Hungary (including Transylvania, part of Romania since 1918) was conquered at the Battle of Mohacs in 1526 by the invading Ottoman army that only narrowly failed also to capture Vienna itself in 1529. Some of Hungary remained under Habsburg rule, and this included parts of Croatia, which thus also managed to avoid being crushed by Turkish domination. Other parts of Croatia, however, were like the rest of Hungary under Ottoman rule until the great reversals of the 1690s, when Austrian armies, under their famous general, Eugene of Savoy, began the fight-back against the centuries-old menace from Constantinople. So by the beginning of the eighteenth century, the kingdom of Croatia – minus the still-Venetian coast – was reunited, but still under Hungarian rule.

It was to be radically different for the Slavic peoples further down the Balkan Peninsula however, and this was to make a permanent mark on those regions that exists to this day.

For a while both Serbia and Bosnia were under the massive Byzantine Empire, which ruled much of the Balkans along with territory in present-day Anatolia. Interestingly, although we often remember the Byzantine-Seljuk conflict, between Byzantium on the one hand

and the Muslim ethnically Turkish Seljuk Empire, we forget that some of the former's greatest enemies were fellow Orthodox Christians in Europe, notably the Bulgarians. Not for nothing was one of the greatest Byzantine rulers, Basil II (reigned 976–1025) known by the gruesome nickname of Basil the Bulgar Slayer.

It was not until after his death that the Byzantines lost much of Anatolia to the Seljuk Turks, at the epic Battle of Manzikert in 1071. It was this devastating military setback that caused the emperors to make the huge mistake of turning to the West and requesting troops, an error that we know today as the origins of the Crusades.

The Crusades were theoretically intended as the West coming to Byzantine aid against the large Muslim empires growing in Anatolia and the Middle East. As we know from Western history, the Crusaders were to turn the request entirely to their own ends, with eventually disastrous results when Saladin launched a counter-offensive at the end of the twelfth century.

But far worse in many ways was the so-called Fourth Crusade, of 1204, which soon proved to be nothing of the kind. Encouraged by Venetian greed and venality, the Crusaders turned from the Holy Land to Byzantium itself, conquering the great city in 1204. While the Latin Empire lasted only a few decades, the damage done was colossal and eventually catastrophic. We are used to Muslims demanding forgiveness for the Crusades, but we forget that as recently as 2001, when Pope John Paul II visited Greece, the Greek Orthodox Church similarly demanded repentance for crusading foolishness.

Historically they have an excellent case. The Byzantine Empire restored in 1261 was a minute shadow of its former self, and was to be wiped away in 1453, to become the capital of the increasingly gigantic Ottoman Empire, the enormous superpower of its day. The Crusaders, in their greed, had destroyed the one power capable enough of resisting Ottoman conquest of not just the Balkans but perhaps of Europe itself. We forget how close a shave Europe had in 1529 and then again in 1683, when the Ottomans nearly captured Vienna, and thus the entry gate to the heartland of the continent itself. As the Hungarians and Croatians never forget, there were over 160 years of Ottoman rule in Central Europe as well.

Initially, however, other countries also benefitted from the Venetian lust for conquest. As those who know Shakespeare's play *Othello*, Venice ruled parts of the Aegean, including the islands of Crete and Cyprus, for over three centuries. And in what is today Serbia, a dynasty was able to create an empire of its own in the Balkans. These were the Nemanja kings, with their apogee under Stefan Dusan (reigned 1331–1355), who proclaimed himself Tsar or Emperor of the Serbs and Greeks in 1346. His empire spread over several modern-day states, including much of what is now northern Greece. His era is regarded as a golden age by many Serbs, as the time during which they were the greatest power in the Balkans.

Unfortunately, his legacy did not survive him. In 1389, a large Ottoman force invaded Serbia, and at the Battle of Kosovo Polje (the Field of Blackbirds) the Serbians were routed. To this day, Serbs still commemorate this loss, and in 1989, its five-hundredth anniversary, it was to prove a fatal clarion call to Serb nationalists that arguably set what was still Yugoslavia on the road to civil war, carnage and disintegration.

But while the greater Serb empire vanished, Serbia itself (and the scores of little principalities that grew up in the wake of Kosovo) was not finally conquered by the Ottomans until 1459. The small Bosnian state was vanquished similarly in 1463. It is no coincidence that these dates follow the destruction of the East Roman Empire, Byzantium, in 1453. The Ottomans had enjoyed a toe-hold in the Balkans for some time by these dates, but it was the fall of the Byzantine Empire that enabled them to finish off the job of conquering as much of South-East Europe as possible. One could say that from 1453 until their defeat in Vienna by the Polish forces of Jan Sobieski in 1683, that the whole of Europe, not just its southern part, lived in fear of Ottoman invasion and conquest.

In the nineteenth century, the Ottoman Empire was regarded as the 'Sick Man of Europe', after it had been so diagnosed by Russia's Tsar Nicholas I. The major European powers, such as Britain and France, argued that it had been in this condition since 1683, but it was not until the start of the nineteenth century that the major roll-back of their earlier conquests began in earnest. Slowly but surely nations that had been under the alien Ottoman yoke managed to regain their long-lost independence. Greece began the process in 1822, though even in the case of that country, the present-day borders did not exist until 1913, when Crete finally and legally became part of the mainland.

Serbia began its own tentative steps with a rebellion in 1817, with recognition in practice of its independent status in 1867, and formal acknowledgement in 1878. Even with Serbia, however, it also took until 1913 to gain roughly the borders that would eventually become permanent, until Kosovo with its majority Albanian population was able to escape in 1999.

Culturally and spiritually Serbia – and similar parts of the former Yugoslavia, such as Montenegro and Macedonia – were very different from Croatia and Slovenia to the north. Four-hundred years of Muslim/Ottoman rule left a permanent imprint, as the rulers were utterly alien from the ruled. The Ottomans allowed Orthodox Christianity to continue in what became known as the *millet* system. In essence, you were as much defined by your religion as by your ethnic origin.

Serbia was different. But suffice it to say, that with the dissolution of the Yugoslav state in the 1990s, who you *really* were became the very heart of the conflict. The Balkans have a group known in the West as the Vlachs. In reality they are almost certainly the descendants of the original inhabitants of much of the Balkan Peninsula before the advent of the Slavs. Wallachia, one of the historic principalities that now make up Romania, suggests this strongly, and any objective account of who they are would suggest close affinity to present-day Romanians.

But in the 1990s the 'pseudo-history' we saw earlier suggested that many of the Serbs in what is now Bosnia are in fact Vlachs who converted to the Serbian Orthodox Church in Islamic times. Needless to say, this is hotly disputed and is very unlikely, but in wars fought in Bosnia in recent times, this was not an issue of mere academic interest.

And who are the Bosnian Muslims? In medieval times, there were many in the region who converted to a religion now known as Bogomilism. This was a faith not dissimilar to the better-known Cathar heresy in southern France, and in both cases not unlike the dualistic Manichaean religions of pre-Islamic Iran, also known in the Roman Empire through the cult of Mithras. It was often argued that the Bosnian Muslims of today are the descendants of the Bogomils of the Middle Ages, but again there was no hard or objective evidence for this. Likewise, the idea that the Bosniaks (to use the current term) are either Catholic Croats converted to Islam (in which case Bosnia belongs to Croatia) or Serb Orthodox similarly converted (in which case Bosnia is rightly Serb), is all highly contentious and used to manipulate present-day disputes.

In fact, since the Bosnians, Croats and Serbs are effectively all originally the same, such differences would be, one would imagine, of little importance to the ordinary individual going about his or her daily life. But thousands of innocent people were slaughtered, both in the 1940s and in the 1990s because of how history was twisted in order to justify mass murder and conquest by one side or the other.

For a very short time in the Napoleonic era, some of the future Yugoslavia was ruled as a single province named Illyria, after the Roman original. Since the Habsburgs gained back their part of Illyria and also the formerly Venetian-ruled Dalmatia, nothing further happened. But in Croatia this brief flowering had a strong impact on many intellectuals, notably Bishop Josip Strossmayer. This was the period of romantic nationalism in Europe, and its Croatian equivalent was known as Illyrianism. This was the notion that the southern Slavs – Croats, Slovenes and Serbs – could come together and form a united southern Slavic state. Since the name Yugoslavia effectively means Land of the Southern Slavs one could argue that it was in Croatia that the concept of a Yugoslav state was born.

It would, though, take three wars and a foolish annexation for this to happen. Serbia was riven by many internal conflicts after independence, especially the dispute between the two dynasties that claimed legitimacy, the Obrenovic (which tended to be close to Austria) and the Karadjorjevic (or Karageorge, which did not.) In 1903, the Obrenovic dynasty was murdered out of existence in a military coup in Belgrade, and Peter (Petar) of the Karadjordjevic dynasty assumed the throne – theirs is the family that reigned for the rest of the monarchy, and which nominally held the crown during the Second World War.

The Serbs now had a policy of aggressive expansionism. This suffered a blow in 1908. Back in 1878 Austria-Hungary was given effective rule of Bosnia-Hercegovina but in the same terms that the British were to gain Egypt in 1882, nominally still under the suzerainty of the Ottoman Empire. But in 1908 the Austrians got rid of the pretence and annexed the province to the Austro-Hungarian Empire. Since Serbia regarded Bosnia (technically and Hercegovina but it is simpler to use just the first name) as part of Greater Serbia, this caused immense ill will, and intense embarrassment for the Russian Empire, which had regarded itself as the protector of all the Orthodox in the Balkans.

In 1912, however, a chance came for many of the Balkan states to come together to gain more territory, at the expense of the increasingly Turkish nationalist Ottoman Empire. In the First Balkan War of 1912/1913, Serbia, Greece, Montenegro, Bulgaria and Romania all joined together to conquer large swathes of Ottoman territory for themselves. But the winners fell out among themselves, and a Second Balkan War took place in 1913 in which Bulgaria lost out to the others. Serbia was able to make major gains in both conflicts, taking much land that was ethnically Albanian (today's Kosovo) and possibly Bulgarian (today's Macedonia, a state whose existence is still disputed, including by Greece.) And the Serb nationalists cast envious eyes upon not just Bosnia but on possible further expansion as well.

Croatia was still part of the Hungarian kingdom, and suffering since the strongly nationalist Magyars in control in Budapest were increasingly nationalist towards the Croat, Romanian and Slovak minorities within their realm. They only feared one person, the heir to the aged Emperor Franz Joseph, Archduke Franz Ferdinand, his nephew. Franz Ferdinand did not love the Magyars, and his morganatic wife Sophie was a Czech. His solution would have been to turn the Austro-Hungarian realm into a true Danubian confederation, under the Habsburg monarchs, but with far more ethnic groups able to rule themselves.

If he had not been assassinated by Serbian-backed terrorists in Sarajevo, the Bosnian capital, in 1914, and survived long enough to succeed his uncle as Emperor, history would have been radically different. For our purposes, the key thing is that he would have made Croatia separate from Hungary, and allowed the Croats to rule themselves for the first time since 1102. So instead of the Croats being obliged to look outside the Empire, to the Serbs, they could have had the best of both worlds, with effective independence but under the embrace of a still large but fundamentally altered Habsburg confederation.

But the murder of Franz Ferdinand and his wife in Sarajevo put an end to all these hopes. The Hungarians were zealous in their wish to hold on to Croatia, and the person who did succeed as Emperor in 1916, Karl, did so in the middle of a war that it was clear that Austria-Hungary would lose. By the time that he finally tried to implement the Franz Ferdinand confederation plan, the Empire was on the verge of both defeat and annihilation.

So, in 1918, it was the Illyrian solution that prevailed. The Slovene parts of Carniola plus a Croatia that now included Dalmatia were merged into the new state: the Kingdom of the Serbs, Croats and Slovenes, shortly after to become the Kingdom of Yugoslavia. Montenegro lost its independence, and Bosnia also became included in the new realm, as did greater Serbia.

The two biggest groups in the rather artificial entity now created, were the Serbs (the largest) and the Croats (the second largest). There were several other groups, such as the Bosnians, the Slovenes, the Macedonians (seen by the Bulgarians as Bulgarian and the Greeks as really Greek), the Albanians, and various smaller ethnicities including

Slovaks and Romanians cut off from their ancestral countries. It was, like many of the similar new states created in 1918, an ethnic mess, created by a mix of the destruction of the Ottoman and Austro-Hungarian Empires and the successful lobbying by ethnic groups of the American President, Woodrow Wilson.

The predominant ethnic group, the Serbs, held the monarchy, and during the early years of the new country they did all possible to stay in charge, being reluctant to share power with the Croats. The period 1921–1929 is often described as the 'Parliamentary Kingdom' and for much of that time the Serbian leader of the Radical Party, Nikola Pasic, was Prime Minister.[5] In 1921, the aged King Petar died, and was succeeded by his son, Alexander, who did not have a strong attachment to the concept of parliamentary democracy.

The people continued to vote for essentially ethnic parties, based on nationality, rather than ideologically-centred parties which had multi-ethnic appeal. This and the fact that the leadership came from aged pre-war politicians, both Serb and Croat especially, did not create the *Yugoslav* identity that was so important for the fledgling state to achieve a genuinely transnational identity. None of this made for internal cohesion and a sense of loyalty to the wider country.

As we will see later, the fact that Josip Broz Tito, the Communist Partisan leader, was half-Croat, half-Slovene made him a hitherto rare object – a true *Yugoslav*. While many historians divide Yugoslavia into two: 1921–1941 and then 1945–1991, there is surely a real case for saying that a *genuine* country only really existed in the latter time-period and especially during Tito's Presidency. There was a polity initially called the Kingdom of the Serbs, Croats and Slovenes and then called Yugoslavia, but, in reality, that suggests a far greater degree of cohesion and loyalty than actually existed.

So, the parliamentary experiment that existed within the nation, was riven from the outset. The leader of the Croat Peasant Party, Stjepan Radic, spent some of the 1920s in exile, in fear of his life. Because of the instability of the various governments, who ruled when, can be very complex and so outside the frame of a book of wider remit such as ours. In 1926 Pasic was forced to resign in a corruption scandal but the Radicals were able to cling on to power. Then in 1928 Radic was assassinated. None of this proved good for democracy, and to cut a long tale of intrigue and mayhem short, on 6 January 1929, the King organised a coup and granted himself dictatorial powers. The brief interlude with democracy was over. Of the very few groups that were genuinely multi-ethnic were the Communists, but at this period they were mainly clandestine and wielded precious little influence.

The years 1929–1941 could therefore be called dictatorial or perhaps authoritarian Yugoslavia. From 1929, until his assassination on a state visit to France in 1934, Alexander was both king and effective ruler of the country. And *Yugoslavia* was born as a name, as he changed what the country was called as well as abolishing democracy.

In theory democracy continued, but because so many people voted on ethnic lines, effective political opposition to the King was never really possible.

The new Croatian Peasant Party leader, Vladko Macek, continued the policy of his predecessors of non-integration with the government in Belgrade. It is important to recall that during this period it was the CPP (or HSS to use their Croatian language initials) that represented the ethnic Croats. The Ustasa, or fascist party, under the Zagreb lawyer Ante Pavelic, never had more than a mere handful of members, most of whom, like Pavelic himself, were in exile, plotting but absent. This is vital since the 1941 Independent Croatian State, the NDH, which was in power 1941–1945, was very much a Nazi/Fascist imposition, and pre-1941 had only the smallest of popular support. The idea, fostered later on, and especially by Serb nationalists after Tito's death, that the Croatians were all willing fascists simply does not bear up under scrutiny.

The other terrorist-style group was the Macedonian VMRO. Even today the exact status of Macedonians is unclear, except perhaps to the Macedonians themselves. It is normally called by the awkward name of 'The Former Yugoslav Republic of Macedonia' since to Bulgaria the Macedonians are western Bulgarians and to Greece they are northern Slavic-speaking Greeks. (In fact, a large percentage of present-day citizens of Macedonia are ethnically Albanian but that is another story.) The VMRO was active in terrorist outrages, supported not all that clandestinely by the Bulgarian authorities, and it was a VMRO terrorist who murdered both King Alexander of Yugoslavia and the French Prime Minister when the King was visiting southern France in 1934.

Alexander's assassination plunged the infant Yugoslavia into chaos. The country was already undergoing terrible economic difficulties caused by the global recession and the instability that now ensued made everything worse. The Regent was Alexander's cousin, the Anglophile Prince Paul, whose wife was the sister of the British Princess Marina, Duchess of Kent, so someone who had close personal ties to London. But the leading politician during most of the Regency was the ethnically Serb Prime Minister, Milan Stojadinovic. He was strongly Germanophile, and spent much of his Premiership integrating the Yugoslav economy into the growing embrace of the Third Reich. Some of this was to counter the danger that many Yugoslavs feared, rightly, was coming from Italy, since Mussolini had long coveted more territory in Dalmatia. But some of it also seems to have been ideological of a sort and this was to create a raft of problems for the Regent, who would have preferred the country to take a different direction.[6]

In 1939, the internal situation reached boiling point, as the clash between the two major ethnic groups – Serb and Croat – became dangerous. The answer of Prince Paul was to carve up the country into a part ruled by Croats and another under Serb authority. The agreement was named the *Sporazum* and it was a last attempt to deal with the issue before much of Europe spilled into war. In particular, Italy had invaded and conquered Albania that year and it was obvious that Mussolini was after Greece as well, not to mention parts of Yugoslavia itself. A drastic solution was necessary and the *Sporazum*, a Serb-Croat condominium of Yugoslavia, appeared to be the answer.

However, it proved problematic from the outset. The Slovenes in the north, very much a distinctive ethnic nationality of their own, with a long history of far gentler Austrian rule, were not happy at being relegated to a place under Serb authority from Belgrade. The Bosnians were ignored – as in the 1990s Croats regarded the Bosnian Muslim community as really Croatians converted to Islam centuries earlier, and the Serbs felt similarly: Bosnians were Orthodox Serbs who became Islamic in the Middle Ages. As before the large Macedonian and Albanian communities received nothing. The same applied to the minorities of German, Romanian or Hungarian ancestry. Furthermore some 866,000 ethnic Serbs were stranded in Croatia, a simmering issue that lingered until it exploded both during 1941–1945 and again in the 1990s.

The Croats were to be allowed a parliament of their own, running internal affairs, while Yugoslav issues such as defence and foreign policy would still be decided at federal level in Belgrade. And a *Ban* or Governor was to be appointed to represent the King. The man chosen was Ivan Subasic, an ethnic Croat, but someone who had served alongside the Serbs during the First World War when much of the Serb army was evacuated to Salonika (now Thessaloniki) in Greece, where many British and French troops were also based.

The elections never took place because almost as soon as the arrangement was signed, effectively creating two parallel states within a state, the Second World War broke out with the German invasion of Poland. Democracy, which was so agonisingly close for the Croats, never therefore had a chance. And Subasic, the *Ban*, was not elected but *appointed*, and, many Croats felt, because he was someone who had happily worked with the Serbs in the past, could be expected to do so again.

This is important since, as we shall see later on, the Americans took up Subasic later in the war, with the clandestine OSS (the precursor to the subsequent CIA) making him their man for Yugoslavia. To the USA he was, as he presented himself as being, the father of the Croatian people, their natural leader. But since his appointment came so soon before European war, he was never tested in peace. He was, in effect, a Viceroy rather than a ruler in his own right: no election had put him there. Significantly another major power also realised his potential as a leader, and about that we will wait until later in the book.

One of the few genuinely *Yugoslav* parties remained the Communists, the KPJ. But their adherents were tiny in number, and in 1939 it would have seemed utterly fantastical that only six years later they would be in power and ruling the country. When war began, though, they were zealous, but insignificant.

The Regency spent much of 1939-1941 attempting to stay neutral and to avoid the dangers of being invaded by Nazi Germany. From the British point of view it was vital for British strategic interests in the Eastern Mediterranean that Yugoslavia either remained a friendly neutral or, better still, joined the Allies.[7] But from the viewpoint in Belgrade, it was a highly dangerous option, especially after the fall of France in 1940. The USA was not in the war and at that time looked highly unlikely to join in – and precious few people apart from Churchill, who was half-American, had any regard at all for American military capabilities, especially since in 1939 the US Army was hardly bigger than that of Belgium.

The key factor, which we so often forget today, was the Nazi-Soviet Pact of August 1939. In the Balkans, it unhinged many of the national leaders very considerably, with good reason. If the Third Reich and USSR were effectively allied – which was indeed the case – and happily carved up Poland between them in the autumn of 1939 then who else might the Nazis and Soviets agree to invade next? In 1940 the Romanians, for instance, were forced by the Soviets to give up Bessarabia – today's independent country of Moldova – to the USSR and some major territory to both Bulgaria and Hungary. These steps were made with full German permission, which unsurprisingly scared rigid the Yugoslav leadership. Many predators wanted Yugoslav territory and any one of them might be in league with the Third Reich or Soviet Union to gain it at the country's expense.

It is clear that the British either never understood how terrified the Balkan states were *of the USSR as much as of Germany*. The only guarantee that the United Kingdom could make, therefore, was one that agreed to protect a nation against *Soviet as well as Nazi* attack. But this of course was utterly impossible for the British to undertake, especially in 1940, as their own survival hung by the slenderest of threads in the Battle of Britain, and against just Germany, not also the giant Russian behemoth as well. The fate of Poland in 1939, a country that both Britain and a still-undefeated France were pledged to aid but proved utterly unable to protect, showed that all too plainly. In 1940, the British were fighting for their own lives, so urgent calls to frightened Balkan nations such as Greece and Yugoslavia to join them against Hitler seemed to such countries as a guarantee of rapid conquest by either Germany or Italy.

So, what is extraordinary is not so much that the Regent Prince Paul finally succumbed to the Nazis on 25 March 1941, signing the Tripartite Pact with Hitler, but that he managed to hold out so long against Axis incursion. But the signature a few weeks earlier, of a pact between the Third Reich and Bulgaria on 1 March 1941, which gave Bulgaria considerably extra territory, was surely the nail in the coffin of Yugoslav resistance. The important fact is that German troops were allowed onto Bulgarian soil, and that put them right on the Yugoslav border. Until 1934 the Bulgarians had happily harboured VMRO terrorists, and they had long coveted Macedonia for themselves. Only a pact with Nazi Germany, Paul and others reckoned, could protect Yugoslavia against dismemberment.

However, on 27 March 1941, there was a coup in Belgrade, in which patriotic Serb officers overthrew the Regent, placed King Peter as head of state with full powers, and denounced the pact with Hitler. For Churchill, this was truly an heroic moment.[8] The Yugoslavs to him, as he told the House of Commons, had rediscovered their soul and defied the might of Hitler.

But as many of the cheering crowds in Belgrade realised, death was now upon them. Churchill was right to say that Hitler was furious, and German revenge was both unmerciful and swift. The Germans had already been deeply embarrassed at the fiasco made by the Italians in invading Greece, and now with Yugoslavia's defection to the Allied cause, a major military operation encompassing the entire Balkans was necessary. To the invasion of Greece, already planned, would be the destruction of Yugoslavia, two operations now able to merge into one.

For Britain, it was a case of be careful for what you wish. Churchill now had his Balkans front against the Third Reich, but it was to come at massive cost, not only to the wretched Greeks and Yugoslavs, who were swiftly overcome by the juggernaut of the Wehrmacht, but also of the British in North Africa.

The background to our story is now complete.

Endnotes

1. John Lampe, *Yugoslavia as History: Twice there was a Country* (Cambridge and New York, Cambridge University Press, 1996).
2. Marcus Tanner, *Croatia: A Nation Forged in War* (New Haven CT and London, Yale University Press, 1997).
3. Lampe, *Yugoslavia as History*, p. 207.
4. http://catholicism.org/evelyn-waughs-edmund-campion.html; accessed 24 November 2014; the book remains in print to this day.
5. For example, in Lampe, *Yugoslavia as History*, p. 125.
6. Argued by Lampe in *Yugoslavia as History*, especially pp. 173–83.
7. For a study of this, see Christopher Catherwood, *The Balkans in World War II* (Basingstoke and New York, Palgrave Macmillan, 2003).
8. Winston Churchill, *The Second World War III: The Grand Alliance* (London, Cassel and Co., 1950), pp. 140–8.

Chapter 2

Hail Caesar!
Britain, SOE and Yugoslavia After 1941

On 27 March 1941, the Government of the Regent Prince Paul was ousted in a coup, in protest against the Regent's deal with Hitler, and the British, it was claimed, were behind some of the plotters. The story is straight out of John Buchan and his character Richard Hannay, since Britain's MI6 (and later Section D) original man in place was a South African mining engineer named Julius Hanau – codenamed *Caesar* (which, as the historian of MI6 has commented is a rather unoriginal and easily-guessed codename; Julius and Caesar being somewhat inextricably linked). He in turn recruited two other Buchanesque mining engineers, Bill Bailey and Bill Hudson.

By the time of the coup, Hanau had been expelled from Yugoslavia. In the 1939–1941 period, the British had been keen to do as much damage to the Nazi war effort as possible, but had the acute problem that Balkan countries such as Yugoslavia and Romania were terrified witless of the Soviet Union, far more than they were of the Third Reich, and also that collaboration with Allied activities could bring the wrath of *both* the USSR *and* Nazi Germany upon them.

So how did we get there and what happened before the coup and as a result of it? We start by looking backwards to 1941 and then forwards to what happened in its aftermath, as Britain (and thus also SOE) had to recoup its position.

As Roger Moorhouse's superb book *The Devil's Alliance* on the 1939–1941 Hitler-Stalin alliance reminds us, we forget totally the period between August 1939, when the Ribbentrop-Molotov Nazi-Soviet neutrality pact was signed in Moscow, and the German invasion of the USSR in June 1941. We remember 1941–1945 when Britain and the Soviets were allies, but fail to remember the fact that for nearly a third of the Second World War Hitler's Germany and Stalin's USSR were friends, allies as Moorhouse reminds us, in all but name. And in 1940 Romania was carved up, with Nazi Germany supporting the annexation by the Soviet Union of huge swathes of Romanian territory – what was then called Bessarabia and is now the country called Moldova.

The attempts by the British to cause vast economic damage to the all-important River Danube trade between Romania and the Third Reich involved all sorts of plots, in many of which the forerunners to SOE were closely involved. This principally entailed blowing up the narrower stretches of the Danube at the Iron Gates gorge, that would have made river-based transport of vital goods from Romania to the extended territory of Germany either very difficult if not to say actually impossible. But had the scheme come to fruition – which in the end it failed to do – the neutrality of the Danubian nations of Romania and Yugoslavia would have been massively compromised. No Yugoslav ruler wanted their country to suffer the kind of dismemberment that the Romanians had inflicted on them and so, while profoundly irritating to the British, Yugoslav reticence at provoking Hitler was entirely understandable.

In Yugoslavia the person in charge – until the nervous Yugoslavs expelled him – was Julius Hanau, *Caesar*. His SOE file shows that he was by origin a South African Jew, someone who by definition would have had excellent personal cause to loathe the Third Reich and everything for which Nazism stood.

In the First World War, there was an attempt – mainly by the French but with a large number of British troops in aid – to launch an attack on Germany's allies Bulgaria and the Ottoman Empire through an Allied force based in what was then called Salonica (now the Greek town of Thessaloniki). Hanau served on this front, and after the war he remained in the region, becoming a businessman in Belgrade, now the capital of the newly created Yugoslav state.

In this, the official history of SOE adds, he was a success, "in the rather smoky atmosphere of business in the Balkans … He possessed a thorough knowledge of Yugoslavia and of the seamy side of Yugoslav affairs, much energy and ingenuity, real hatred for the Germans and an impish sense of humour."

Officially, in June 1939, he was put in charge of the pre-SOE Section D's skulduggery and mayhem-creating operations in Yugoslavia. As

SOE later related, he was so high profile that his cover was swiftly blown.

While of course utterly opposed to bribery and corruption back home in Britain, the Government was all for it if it would persuade local people to do the bidding of the United Kingdom – and the Allied cause in general. Here Hanau's expertise of the seamier side of Balkan corruption came in exceptionally handy, as he knew precisely whom to bribe.

Bribery to influence foreign elections is not a twenty-first-century phenomenon – Britain was active in such attempts back in the 1930s – and although Hanau's attempt judiciously to spread money is deemed to have failed because the expected Yugoslav elections of 1940 were delayed, he found that he could work with one of the political parties, the Serbian Peasant Party, with the aim that they would be active in supporting a pro-British policy in Yugoslav affairs.

Section D and then SOE was based upon the idea of doing as much clandestine damage to the enemy as possible. While the main focus of such activity was centred on the Danube's Iron Gates gorge which was in Romania, some of the other plots contemplated by Section D involved clandestine activity on Yugoslav soil, so Hanau was soon busy plotting. The Greben Narrows stretch of the Danube was entirely within Yugoslavia and the Kazan gorge was Romanian on one bank and Yugoslav on the other.

With the Kazan episode, Hanau did his best, and in November 1939 an explosion was briefly able to do some real damage to German shipping. But this drew the attention of Sir Ronald Campbell, the British Ambassador to Yugoslavia, and in turn to Sir Orme Sargent, one of the very highest diplomats at the Foreign Office in London, and someone who took a keen interest in the dealings first of Section D and then of SOE. Needless to say, the cautious officials were very wary of compromising Yugoslav neutrality, and as the Germans swiftly put two and two together in detecting a British hand in the plotting, then the whole idea was dropped.

By this time even the Permanent Secretary to the Foreign Office, the august Sir Alec Cadogan, entered the picture. He was warier still of such derring-do, and of the attempts by the French Government to undertake similar sabotage operations in the area.

The British Government, while officially doing all possible to get the Balkan countries to sign up against the Third Reich, was aware of the terror in which these countries beheld the Soviet Union, and thus of Stalin's friend Hitler. So, in May 1940 Cadogan pronounced – with backing from the Cabinet: 'No action must be taken which was likely to precipitate the armed occupation of the river or an early invasion of the Balkan States by Germany.'

So that, for the time being at least, was that Hanau had tried his best, but in June 1940 he was expelled, along in July with 'Bill' S.W. Bailey, one of the future key SOE personnel in the Balkans after 1943, and in 1940 someone with years of experience in the region as a mining engineer at the key Trepca mines. (Hanau later went on to represent Britain in West Africa, where he died before the war ended.)

When SOE was fully established by Churchill in 1940, its original leadership had therefore been exiled. One of the few still present was the Naval Attaché Sandy Glen, who had already made his mark as an explorer in the Arctic. But as we saw, Campbell, the Ambassador, was very wary of sabotage missions, lest the Yugoslavs leaning towards the Axis used British activity as an excuse for closing down ties with the United Kingdom. So, the dilemma the saboteurs faced – help the war effort and destroy German munitions but risk arousing the delicate diplomatic balance in the Balkans – continued to be an acute one.

Churchill, after becoming Prime Minister in 1940, famously wanted to use SOE to "set Europe ablaze". Clandestine links were begun as seen earlier with the Serb Peasant Party, but they were hardly major players in the murky world of Belgrade politics.

In addition, the stakes were now getting considerably higher. Back in 1939 the Italians had conquered Albania, under its wildly named King Zog, and on 28 October 1940 Mussolini decided to expand his Balkan empire further by attacking Greece, a nation which, like Yugoslavia, had remained studiously neutral. This action brought the war considerably nearer to the already nervous Yugoslavs, since it was now being fought right on their border. And with Italian troops being as militarily unsuccessful against the Greeks as they were proving to be in fighting the British in North Africa, the possibility of Germany taking an active part to shore up their accident-prone Italian ally, also loomed ominously on the horizons. Everything was becoming far too close for comfort – *and remember that the Third Reich and USSR were allies*, something we forget in looking at the history of this period but was very much at the forefront of every Balkan Government.

Also present in Belgrade, under diplomatic cover, was Tom Masterson, a man of sixty in a nominally junior post. He too had much

Balkan experience, destroying the famous Romanian oil wells at Ploesti in 1916, just in time to forestall their capture and use by the invading German Army in the First World War.

But despite the inspiring and skilled presence of both Glen and Masterson, the intrepid British agents were not able to accomplish much, even though the spread of war to the Balkans made doing *something* absolutely vital.

Then, on 27 March 1941, brave Serb officers undid the agreement the Yugoslav Regent Prince Paul had signed with Hitler, and declared themselves for Britain and the fight against Nazi Germany. As the official historian of SOE has to admit, one "cannot assess precisely the share of the credit to be given to SOE".

It took a very long time for Prince Paul to be forgiven by the British – if indeed he ever was by those who saw his peace pact with Germany as base treachery. But as the SOE history acknowledges, it was evident to the Yugoslav Regency that with Bulgaria and Romania now both very firmly in the Axis camp by this stage in 1941, and with Britain in no realistic position to aid Yugoslavia against German invasion, it was arguably in the country's "interest to compromise rather than to fight". On the other hand, from Churchill's viewpoint, this was in effect another victory for Hitler and as he put it, the coup really was a rediscovery of the true fighting soul of the Yugoslav peoples.

But all was in vain. On 6 April German forces invaded the country, with a blitzkrieg of duly terrifying proportions. In eleven days it was all over, with the new Government forced to surrender, and with the King and some of the key coup leaders fleeing to England; and the Germans began as viciously as they continued.

During the invasion, Wehrmacht forces occupied the Serbian town of Leskovac. That July, Communist guerrillas – the Partisans – sabotaged the railway lines nearby. German retaliation was swift and deadly: over 2,000 civilians in the town were promptly massacred. In October, some 2,700 more civilians were similarly butchered at another Serb town, Kragujevac. Resistance to the German occupiers was becoming rather costly. We look at this again in the chapter on MI3, since British reaction to how the resistance in Yugoslavia emerged would, by 1943, become vital to how the politicians and generals in London perceived the war – the key theme of our book.

After the successful Axis invasion of 1941, two guerrilla groups emerged. One, the Cetniks, was entirely ethnically Serb, and, importantly for Britain, represented the forces of the exiled King Peter, a cousin of King George VI. The other group, the Partisans, were less familiar.

Here we get into deeply controversial territory, for it became apparent to the British that the Cetniks and Partisans had rather divergent approaches to the savagery of the German revenge massacres.

It has not been put better than by Sir Fitzroy Maclean, Churchill's personal emissary to the Partisans from 1943, in his memoirs of wartime, *Eastern Approaches.* As he writes with sympathy: "To this [the massacres] and to subsequent disasters, Partisans and Cetniks reacted differently. In this difference of attitude lies the explanation of much that followed later." On the one hand:

> In the eyes of the Cetniks the results achieved by their operations could not justify the damage and suffering caused to the civilian population. Their aim was to preserve rather than to destroy. Henceforward they inclined more and more to avoid active operations; soon some even arrived at mutually advantageous accommodation with the enemy.

This last claim would create an enormous row after the war, with the sympathisers with the Cetniks accusing Maclean, as we shall see, of making false accusations against brave Serb fighters. But one can also say that while the argument on Cetnik/German collaboration still rages, ULTRA signals intelligence has rather proved the accusation's accuracy, and more importantly, it was the total passivity of the Cetniks *whether they collaborated or not* that was so to enrage the British Government back in London, especially come decision time, as we shall discover.

As for the Partisans, Maclean was surely right to argue:

> The Partisans, on the other hand, with true Communist ruthlessness, refused to let themselves be deterred by any setbacks or any reprisals from accomplishing the tasks which they had set themselves. Their own lives were of no account. As for the civilians, they too were in the firing-line, with the same chance of a hero's death as they themselves. The more civilians the Germans shot, the more villages they burned, the more enemy convoys the Partisans ambushed, the more bridges they destroyed. It was a hard policy, especially for the men operating in their own part of the country, but in the end it was justified by events and justified notably by the unwilling

respect which it imposed on the Germans, a respect which no amount of appeasement could ever have inspired.

It is of course very easy to say that their "hard policy" was justified, in the light of the thousands of civilian casualties that the German reprisal scorched-earth policy inflicted. And it is also easy for someone British to say that about the people of another country.

But Fitzroy Maclean and Winston Churchill, along with the Chiefs of Staff in London and commanders, from 1943, of Allied forces in Italy, were fighting a war to the death with Nazi Germany, one of the most savage foes since the Mongol armies of Genghis Khan swept across the Eurasian landmass centuries before.

And so, the moral dilemma – do you in pursuit of such a war support resistance to Hitler's Reich, pursued without regard to the cost? That was very much the case with Britain's and the USA's ally the USSR, in which *millions* of Red Army troops were poured into a killing machine that went all the way to Berlin, but with a carelessness for life surely without precedence in military history. As with Stalin, so with Tito, that of a war regardless of casualties, in order that Hitler and his Reich be defeated utterly once and for all.

It was thus a difficult decision, but one on which Churchill had, in effect, little choice, especially if death in the Balkans would, as he and his generals rightly calculated, save the lives of thousands of British and other Allied forces fighting the Germans elsewhere.

This is the dilemma that would continue down until late 1943 (officially until early 1944) when the British formally decided to opt for the Partisans. But until then they had to work out what on earth to do, since at this stage, in 1941, the Cetniks were at least a known entity whereas the very existence of the Partisans was distinctly shadowy so far as London was concerned, and whether or not Tito actually existed as a person, or was in fact an acronym, remained uncertain.

So, in September 1941 a brave thirty-year-old Serbo-Croat speaking former mining engineer, Captain D.T. 'Bill' Hudson was sent to Yugoslavia to find out the best he could about what was happening. He landed on 17 September by submarine, with two radio transmitters, neither of which turned out to be remotely reliable. It was at least a start, but sadly not a promising one, since he soon lost all communication with SOE, and was to spend several months completely incommunicado.

At least though he managed to find out that Tito was a real person, when he contacted the Partisans, and that Mihailovic and the Cetniks were the official opposition to the Germans so far as the Royal Yugoslav Government in exile was concerned. But it was also evident to him that a civil war between the two resistance groups was brewing if not already fully underway, and that of course was now going to be a major problem for the decision makers back in London.

In fact, according to Deakin, the civil war began on 2 November, with a Cetnik attack on the Partisans, near a place called Loznica.

In the end, pressure from Britain and the USSR created a brief lull.

But Hudson had, in his reports, let the cat out of the bag, and as he had to use Cetnik wireless sets he was rather limited in what he could say. As Deakin comments:

> The presence of Hudson as a witness on the spot, the basic military weakness of the small Cetnik bands, and the chance of Russian pressure on Tito, constrained Mihailovic, against his instincts … to refrain from further attacks on Tito's forces … But in reality there was merely a thin prospect of a temporary truce between rival factions. The personal relations of Mihailovic and Tito were irretrievably damaged.

In a message he was able to get through to Britain on 20 November, Hudson showed a true understanding of the actual position:

> My attitude to Mihailovic has been that he has all the qualifications except strength. At present the Partisans are stronger and he must first liquidate them with British arms before turning seriously to the Germans.

In other words, British supplies to Mihailovic would be used against Communist Partisans rather than the occupying German forces. This was not why Britain was fighting. As Hudson told one of the Partisans he met, the "British Government wants to know that there can be lasting agreement between Cetniks and Partisans."

Briefly, on 21 November, Hudson fleetingly led himself to hope that "Mihailovic has now agreed to recognize the Partisans."

This in turn led the British back in London to hope the same. But this was illusory. After some German action in late November Mihailovic was obliged to withdraw and, as Deakin puts it, "leaving Hudson as a lone fugitive in peasant clothes to pursue a bare and hunted existence … for the following months". For the next four in fact, in Deakin's words, he "dragged out an appalling existence, living mainly on potatoes, and, what must have been worst of all, entirely without news of the outside world." Not until 4 June was he in real contact with Britain again, and known to be safe at last.

But the key point is that at this stage in the war, when it looked to many in Britain that the USSR might not hold out, as *Barbarossa* was at this stage massively successful against the Red Army, there really was precious little that the United Kingdom could do to help anyone in Yugoslavia to combat the Third Reich.

So what the Chiefs of Staff wrote in November 1941 was crucial:

> Rebels are located in difficult hill country, whence they may well be able to keep movement in being for a long time, but probably only as a nuisance to the Axis and not much more. For revolt to develop into a nation-wide rebellion the movement would have to spread to the towns where in absence of British forces it would be quelled with extreme ruthlessness. This must be avoided. Our policy should therefore be to provide rebels with supplies necessary to maintain movement in the hills.

Considering how badly the war was going for Britain in North Africa against Rommel the prospect of any supplies at all reaching Yugoslavia was rather wishful thinking. While there were some both in London and in British headquarters in Cairo who were quite optimistic that supplies could be given to Yugoslav resistance, others, including SOE's Lord Glenconner, were more realistic:

> It is now evident that the C-inCs and Chiefs of Staff are opposed to diverting any of our forces to assist the insurgents, and we have, therefore, as usual, fallen between two stools, and are endeavouring to work a compromise between two opposite and conflicting policies because I am confident that, if the Germans were in our place they would either decide to back the revolt or leave it alone.

That conflict was to bedevil British policy until the end of 1943. But as the Official Historian of SOE, Mackenzie, is surely right to say:

> This aspect of the matter was much more fundamental at this stage than the question of whether to back Mihailovitch [sic] or

Tito. Unless substantial aid could be given, SOE's efforts would only result in a useless massacre.

Furthermore, since the civil war between the two resistance armies was getting worse, then the problem of who should receive any supplies was also purely academic.

In November 1942, Hudson was finally able to get through some serious thoughts to London. Deakin has called them "considered and perceptive" and soon – but not yet – they would be the view in Whitehall as well. In the light of criticism of the British decision to drop Mihailovic made long after the war, it is important to note that Hudson was pragmatic rather than ideological in his feelings about the ongoing inactivity of Mihailovic and his Cetniks. Some of the paragraphs from Hudson's long missive of 15 November 1942 bear this out:

> Mihailovic and [the Cetniks in Montenegro] are essentially opportunists and will not risk their, at present, comparatively secure positions for the sake of what they would call 'adventures'. Mihailovic remains opposed to undertaking sabotage against the Italians. He insists they will collapse shortly, when he expects to secure their arms and equipment, with which he plants to defend Montenegro [where he was then based] against the Germans. He argues that if he were to take action against the Italians now, the Germans would occupy Montenegro and he would thus lose the chance of securing Italian arms. He also fears that sabotage would lead to his losing the support of the people, who would blame him for Italian reprisals, as well as to the cessation of Italian food supplies for the Cetniks.

On the Italians, Mihailovic was several months premature; and when Italian surrender did come in 1943, it was of course Tito and the Partisans who managed to obtain the vast bulk of Italian supplies, as we see elsewhere in our book.

In addition, opposing Germans could lead to massacre, and this weighed naturally very heavy on Mihailovic's mind. Hudson was "personally convinced that these Cetnik groups" in Serbia which were moving on from Montenegro, "could organize derailments at points where the Germans were not able to take reprisals on Serb villages". As Hudson discovered:

No serious attempts however have yet been made to investigate the possibilities of carrying out such operations. The poor sabotage results obtained hitherto are due to lack of willingness on Mihailovic's part and to lack of energy. When I press for continuous large-scale sabotage, the General and his entourage reply that half a million Serbs have already been killed in the fight against the Axis and that they cannot risk reprisals; they emphasize that they will not depart from this standpoint for the sake of outside interest.

That "outside interest" was of course the Allied cause and Great Britain in particular, which in that month at El Alamein, saw a turning point in the war against the Third Reich.

So, what in the meanwhile? Hudson thought that when Allied victory against Germany was completely certain, he would finally move against the Axis, but "until then I consider him perfectly capable of coming to any secret understanding with either Italians or Germans, which he believes might serve his purposes without compromising him". And this would be confirmed by MI3 and Bletchley Park as time went by.

By November 1942, Hudson was by no means alone in terms of British SOE missions to Yugoslavia. One of these was the "Hydra" mission under Major Terence Atherton, sent in December 1941. Atherton was someone with excellent local languages, who had spent a decade in Belgrade as a journalist and had married a Muslim woman from the Bosnian capital Sarajevo. Unwisely perhaps, in the light of the fact that Atherton was supposed to find out about the Partisans as well as about the Cetniks, two Royal Yugoslav Army officers went with him when he landed. But by April 1942 Atherton was dead, killed in mysterious circumstances, with both Partisans and Cetniks blaming each other for his unexplained death, confirmed by Hudson around July that year, but with no more clue as to the perpetrators than anyone else. (Deakin had suspicions, but proof at even at that stage would be impossible.)

Other missions were then sent to find out what was happening, including one of Canadian Communist Croats, but no one of substantial enough knowledge really to make much of a difference.

However, Hudson and Atherton were both men of experience, and the decision of SOE to send them matched their qualifications. But Hudson's four-month disappearance – thankfully not death – and the murder of Atherton led people higher up in SOE to feel that what was wanted was a "senior mission to Mihailovic's headquarters, to establish the true state of affairs and to report … on the events of 1942".

So it was decided to send Colonel Bill Bailey, whom we have met before. He had not merely been a mining engineer at Trepca, in Serbia, but had also been, as previously noted, head of SOE in Belgrade. His qualifications were therefore considerable and, in late 1942, he went to Cairo, ready for a mission to Mihailovic to find out what really was going on.

His friend Bill Deakin has aptly summarised the background:

> His mission was devised at an unrewarding moment, in the face of complete lack of response from Mihailovic to British requests for active collaboration; in the knowledge that the Partisans were increasingly clashing with the Axis; and when the realities of civil war throughout Yugoslavia imperilled the unity of the country.

This is in fact understatement! As ever, this needs to be considered against the background of what the ULTRA decrypts were revealing simultaneously and what MI3 was piecing together in London. Bailey was profoundly experienced with the country into which he was due to parachute, but was not aware of what those like MI3 or indeed Churchill himself and the Chiefs of Staff were reading from Bletchley Park. Bailey and his mission were therefore not sent in isolation, but in the context of some of the people receiving his intelligence – those in London – knowing the *full* picture. As always, he would be in that sense affirming what was going on, rather than being the sole source of information, and that is something vital that we must always bear in mind.

In that context, in December 1942, the British policy makers in London were still hoping for a united Yugoslav resistance, the better to fight the Germans. They knew, as SOE operatives did not, that with victory at Alamein and with the war in North Africa now going the Allies way after years of setbacks, that the next target was Italy. For that to work Yugoslav resistance had to tie down as many German divisions in the Balkans as possible.

Therefore, as Deakin reminds us:

> Bailey's directive was a mixed one. He was to report on the military value of the Cetnik movement as a whole and persuade Mihailovic to undertake active sabotage. He was

also to study its political intentions and propose how British policy, still constructed in its original form of creating a united [i.e. joint Cetnik/Partisan] resistance front, could be implemented.

This was a tall order, and we should always recall that there were two quite contradictory wishes in play:

a) The wish of Britain for an *active* resistance.

b) The determination of Mihailovic to have as few civilian casualties as possible, and therefore to bide time until German defeat was inevitable.

This means that when Bailey landed in Yugoslavia on Christmas Day 1942, he was being asked to square a circle. When he met Mihailovic on Boxing Day, having parachuted in safely, he had a nigh impossible task ahead of him.

By early New Year 1943, he realised this, in his first stream of reports back to headquarters – this time, unlike Hudson, with his own wireless and independent radio operator. It was not long before he had to write back that his host, Mihailovic, was "determined to eliminate all rivals before attacking the armies of occupation, and was convinced that all Croatian guerrillas not under his command [many of the Partisans being Croat] were a hundred percent Communist and must be destroyed". In other words, the civil war had to be won first before Mihailovic would start killing the Germans.

So what next? For Bailey – in his thoughts of 22 January – the only way out was to draw a line of demarcation between areas in which the Partisans prevailed, and those in which Mihailovic and the Cetniks were in the ascendant. Britain could then support both sides but in different places.

As his colleague, Bill Deakin, summarised it: "The advantage of such a delimitation of spheres of influence would be to deprive Mihailovic of his principal excuse for not fighting the Axis, and at the same time the recognized presence of Tito in Western Croatia would create a source of trouble for the Germans in those regions".

So far so simple – or was it?

For the diplomats pondering such issues in London, there were a whole host of complexities. To begin with, the Royal Yugoslav government in exile had made Mihailovic their Minister of War in 1942, and anything that upset him would not go down well with them. The split could also create a Communist regime in those areas controlled by Tito, which was something that they were, understandably from their point of view, emphatically against.

We shall see how Sir Orme Sargent of the Foreign Office put it in the next chapter, but for now, as Deakin explains, they were in effect, "faced with evolving a cautious policy of support for both sides".

Long term this was naturally quite impossible, but then, on 28 February 1943, came an event that changed everything and would in time make Britain's ultimate decision a whole lot easier.

Chapter 3

A Conspiracy in Cairo?

Did Princess Diana die in a car crash in 1997 as the result of a deep plot by shadowy intelligence agencies, or because she was tragically not wearing a seat belt? Was 9/11 a dastardly Mossad/CIA conspiracy or genuinely the work of Osama bin Laden and Al Qaeda?

People all around the world believe conspiracy theories that purport to be the dark and hidden truth behind events that to most of us are obvious and easily explicable. The notorious nineteenth-century forgery *The Protocols of the Elders of Zion* was not only believed by many Nazis, who slaughtered millions of Jews as a consequence, but was taught in parts of the Arab world until very recent times. Some conspiracies are therefore very old and have lethal consequences.

What happened in 1943 is also part of a conspiracy theory. The decision to switch from Mihailovic and the Cetniks to Tito and the Partisans was a deliberate Communist fabrication, according to its believers, to ensure that there was a Communist government ruling Yugoslavia once war was finished. Key to this were the doctored reports from SOE's office in Cairo, led by a known Communist on the staff, James Klugmann.

In all the books that support the conspiracy version description of events in Yugoslavia, no one is more critical to their claims than James Klugmann, one of the notorious group of Communists at Cambridge in the 1930s, and the man who unquestionably helped the NKVD recruit university contemporaries as Soviet agents.

James Klugmann was born in 1912, to a middle-class Jewish family in London. He was educated at Gresham's School in Holt – also the alma mater of the Cambridge spy Donald Maclean – and then, significantly, at Trinity College Cambridge. Here he was the contemporary of the infamous "Cambridge Five" spies – Philby, Burgess, Maclean, Blunt and Cairncross. He himself was a very open Marxist as a student, and remained a wholly overt Communist the rest of his life, never concealing his true sympathies. From 1957 until his death in 1977 he edited the then very dour and slavishly pro-Moscow *Marxism Today*, after which a new editor Martin Jacques took over and made it into regular reading for the chattering classes beyond simply Communists and fellow-travellers.

In 1935, he embarked on a career that, with interruption in wartime, was wholly dedicated to the service of the Communist cause, initially worldwide and then within Britain itself. He would become the personification of the faithful apparatchik, obeying whatever line was issued from Moscow; and, after 1948, as we shall see, in a way that completely contradicted all that he worked for during the war.

From 1935–1940 he was secretary of a Moscow front organisation, in theory an international body of students, but, in reality, a Communist propaganda organisation designed to infiltrate universities across the world in the Marxist/Soviet interest.

During this time, he was not himself an active NKVD spy – the NKVD being the precursor to what became known during the Cold War as the KGB. But he was very much involved with Soviet intelligence in recruitment, in particular the "Fifth Man" of the Cambridge spy ring, John Cairncross, arguably the deadliest of the Cambridge Five since he would pass on extraordinarily confidential details to Moscow about the early years of the atomic bomb project. The talents for which he was respected by the Communists became valued in very different circumstances during the war, as we shall see below.[1]

Recent research has elucidated the report that Arnold Deutsch, the NKVD operative in London, would write on Klugmann back to Moscow (using the latter's codename 'Mayor'):

> Mayor (James Klugmann) is a party functionary who devotes himself entirely to the party. He is a quiet and thoughtful man. Modest, conscientious, industrious and serious. Everybody who knows him likes him and respects him.... He is known to the British police as an active communist. He is used to legal work and therefore incautious. But if his attention is drawn to this he will act as required.

In 1940 Klugmann was recruited to the Royal Army Service Corps, in the lowest possible rank, that of ordinary Private. But the organisational skills to which Arnold Deutsch, the NKVD clandestine operative in London referred, proved to be extraordinary, and it was this ability, to work hard and in a highly disciplined and focused manner, that drew him to the attention of many in the Army, who urgently needed such capable back-office administrators to run the logistical details of the war while others fought.

Another Old Boy of Gresham's School in Holt noticed these attributes, in particular. Brigadier (later Lieutenant General) Terence Airey who was working with military intelligence in Cairo, and fatefully recommended Klugmann to work in the headquarters of SOE in Cairo, which was responsible at that time for the Balkans and Middle East. So, in early 1942, Klugmann joined SOE as an officer, and soon began to rise in the ranks of the military as his service with SOE progressed. (It is worth pointing out that while Klugmann *was* at Gresham's with Cambridge spy Donald Maclean – who was an agent for the GRU, Soviet military intelligence, rather than for the NKVD – he was there years *after* Airey, being a different age.)

It is here that his very overt Communist sympathies made him suspect, although when asked *at the time* MI5 held nothing against him, even though, unlike the infamous "Cambridge Five" he had been totally overt about his political loyalties and views. A Government attachment to the MI5 file on him contained in the Deakin Papers in Cambridge suggests that any pre-war evidence against him had been destroyed in a Luftwaffe raid on MI5's temporary headquarters in the prison, Wormwood Scrubs. Many have believed this. As the war progressed, MI5 would eventually become very queasy about his employment in secret work in Cairo. But according to their own file upon him, it was not until January 1945 that they received irrefutable evidence of his Communist activities when with SOE.

Nevertheless, in 2005 the *Journal of Intelligence and Security* published an article that suggested that this view – the destruction of the files – while true of most of the files does not apply to Klugmann – *his* file survived the raid. What emerges from this alternative perspective is not conspiracy but blunder, with bureaucratic delays in MI5's ability to keep tabs on him, especially after he went abroad, to Cairo, and also because, by the very nature of things, the sheer chaos caused by war. In addition, this new evidence therefore suggests that Klugmann ended up "in Cairo more by luck than design", let alone in SOE.

But as to whether or not he was overtly Communist – something in which MI5 would be interested – there is no doubt whatsoever. As fellow SOE officer, Basil Davidson, in his memoirs *Special Operations Europe: Scenes From the Anti-Nazi War* makes clear, Klugmann could not have been more public about his Communism if he tried. (Davidson himself served with much bravery behind enemy lines in the Balkans and in Italy for SOE, and while no Communist was to become a well-known specialist on Africa with strong left-wing credentials.)

To Davidson, Klugmann in Cairo was nicknamed the "priest of Saint Rock", after the patron saint of dogs! Unlike most of the British officer corps in Cairo at that time, such as the legendary Patrick Leigh Fermor, the future travel writer, Klugmann hobnobbed not with fellow Britons in elegant cafes or hotels, but actually with ordinary Egyptians. This, in itself, was unusual, as were his – totally unhidden – Marxist views. It seems, Davidson recalls, that much of Klugmann's leisure hours were spent in giving improving talks with strong Communist perspectives to local people who "lived for his lectures".

By 1942 it was becoming clear all over Europe that the best resistance fighters in Nazi-occupied Europe were often Communists. There was an irony to this, since until June 1941 the USSR and Third Reich had in effect been allies following the Ribbentrop/Molotov Pact of August 1939, in which Stalin promised to be neutral to Hitler, and to carve up Poland and other parts of Central/Eastern Europe between the Soviet Union and Germany. In theory, this meant that loyal Communists in the wider world, who obeyed the decrees sent from Moscow, were not to fight with the Allies against the Germans, since to do so would be to break the terms of the agreement signed in Moscow, one witnessed by no less than Stalin himself. When *Barbarossa* began in 1941, however, that changed. A very considerable percentage of the French resistance, the *maquis*, were Communists, for instance.

What surprises many is that all the Cambridge spies (and presumably active Communists in countries such as France) stayed loyal to Stalin despite the Molotov-Ribbentrop agreement. Countless young idealists had been radicalised, to use a modern term, into supporting Communism in the 1930 because of the rise of fascism, and for many of them, the Spanish Civil War of 1936–1939, in which large numbers served as volunteers in the International Brigades. But for other Communists, the deal Stalin made with Hitler was an utter betrayal of the anti-fascist cause, a rude wake-up call to the truly perfidious nature of Stalin's thinking, and therefore reason to transfer allegiance from international Communism to British patriotism.

Klugmann, like the Cambridge spies, kept his pro-Moscow allegiance. Come June 1941 he was able to combine his ideology with patriotism, since both Britain and the USSR were now allies against the common Nazi enemy.

But to theoretical Marxists such as Klugmann, resistance, of the kind now being actively supported by SOE against the Third Reich, was a much wider struggle than the merely temporary battle against Nazi occupation in Europe. It was also a political fight against capitalism and a colonial one against Western imperialism. As he explained to Davidson in Cairo:

> You've got to see that this war has become more than a war *against* something, against fascism. It's become a war *for* something, for something much bigger. For national liberation, people's liberation, colonial liberation ... That's what the future now demands.

To Klugmann – and to Davidson, and others of not necessarily Communist but certainly left-wing sympathies – that meant supporting someone such as Tito in the struggle against Axis occupation in Yugoslavia. In terms of this kind of analysis, the Partisans were ideal because they were *against* fascism and *for* creating a new and idealistic/Socialist society after the war.

Needless to say, not everyone sympathised with Klugmann's rather overt Communist loyalties, tied as they would therefore have to be for support in Yugoslavia for the Partisans, on both ideological and military grounds. To SOE operative Bickham Sweet-Escott in his 1965 memoirs *Baker Street Irregular*, Cairo was filled with superb operatives, any one of whom could do great things; for instance, Patrick Leigh Fermor and Montague Woodhouse, both of whom became famous for their exploits in different parts of Greece. But there was, he recalled, "one cuckoo in the nest. One of the most efficient and hardworking men in the Yugoslav section was James Klugman [*sic*], now a leading member of the Communist Party of Great Britain."

As Klugmann was still alive at that time, Sweet-Escott was probably restrained by British libel law from saying more. But he was not alone in feeling as suspicious of the Priest of Saint Rock, both at the time and, clearly, decades later.

Was Klugmann a spy himself? And if he was, what was the truth about his impact? Can we really say that Churchill ended up dropping the Cetniks in 1943 and switching to Tito and the Communist Partisan forces *because of Klugmann*? This is vital, because it is possible that even if Klugmann was everything that the conspiracy buffs say he was, *his support of Tito made no difference at all* as to why Churchill made one of his most controversial decisions of the war.

We should in fairness quote from the conspiracy hunters first. David Martin's book, referred to earlier, not only made Klugmann the "Fifth Man" – erroneously as we saw – but also makes him *the* person responsible for Churchill's shift from Mihailovic to Tito in 1943. It should also be added that Martin was a lifelong supporter of Mihailovic, writing a book in the 1940s entitled *Ally Betrayed* and then again in 1978 with his book *Patriot or Traitor: The Case of General Mihailovich*. So, he is a strong protagonist of the Serb nationalist strongman.

He writes about Klugmann that he was a Soviet "mole whose great accomplishment was to falsify information in a manner that resulted in handing over a nation of 15 million people to Communist control".

Like other conspiracy supporters, one can argue that he considerably overeggs the pudding in describing what he argues to be the centrality of Klugmann's role: "I do not say that Klugmann did all this by himself, but I do believe that he was *primarily* [Martin's italics] responsible."

Martin also blames "muddle-headed liberals" who believed in the cause of progress, and for whom support for Tito overlapped between "Tito-mania" and "the conviction that the support of Tito served British interests in the prosecution of the war against the Nazis." But, Martin insists, although such people played a role, "none" of them "was as knowledgeable as Klugmann or had as much input into the shaping of policy."

According to Martin, Klugmann even influenced the Deakin and Maclean reports, which he says influenced Churchill:

> It is questionable whether Churchill was even aware of the existence of James Klugmann. But Klugmann's brilliance, his expertise, and his quite exceptional personality enabled him to win the support of other officers in SOE.... From Davidson and Keble it was only one more step to Captain William Deakin and Brigadier Fitzroy Maclean ... And from Deakin and Maclean it was only another small step to Winston Churchill.

Former SOE officer Michael Lees is much fairer to Deakin in his *The Rape of Serbia*, but he too grossly exaggerates the role played by Klugmann, giving him the "absolutely key position" in SOE Cairo (which Lees calls by its codename of MO4). But this is, as he admits, from *September* 1943 onwards – before Maclean's key report but well *after* the period in which, as we shall see, MI3 in *London* had already begun to change its mind in the light of the signals intelligence (Sigint) from Bletchley Park. It is interesting, that when he describes how, in his view, Klugmann conspired to be Brigadier Keble's amanuensis in Cairo, there is not a shred of firm documentary evidence. Perhaps he gives the game away when he writes:

> It is clear circumstantial evidence that Klugmann, either alone or through Keble, was able to switch the planes [to get British liaison officers out of the country] to suit his nefarious purposes.

Circumstantial evidence indeed!

We shall see in the chapters on Deakin and Maclean that this is an incorrect interpretation of the facts, and Martin admits fairly and fully that Maclean's dislike of SOE Cairo was an open secret. But the main point is surely that all this grossly overestimates Klugmann's *real* influence, not just in Cairo but, above all, in London, where he was not merely unknown but in fact totally irrelevant.

Klugmann, like others in Cairo, had access to locally broken Sigint – low grade German traffic – but not the much higher value grade ENIGMA/ULTRA material available thanks to Bletchley Park. Martin claims that Klugmann had access to *Most Secret Sources* but this is nothing to which he would ever have had access. This was ULTRA, and that is something that went direct from Bletchley Park to Churchill and the Chiefs of Staff, and, as we shall see, MI3, which was in London, not in Cairo.

The simple fact is that the material upon which Churchill and the Chiefs based their 1943 decisions did not involve Klugmann even remotely, and so the vast conspiracy of disinformation that Martin conjures up is irrelevant. There could, as Martin speculates, have been a whole host of other pro-Soviet moles in Cairo, working together with Klugmann, to spin webs of deceit and disinformation. But it would have made no difference to what Churchill and the Chiefs decided.

Furthermore, the MI5 files on Klugmann – KV2/791 – have now been declassified, and can be found both in The National Archives and in the Papers of Bill Deakin, Churchill's former researcher and one of the top SOE agents in Yugoslavia during the war. We, therefore, now know that Klugmann, a known Communist, was given a job in SOE Cairo over the strong objections of MI5, as Sir David Petrie of MI5 told the legendary Sinclair of MI6, rather late in the day, in August 1945.

Was this in itself sinister? The *Journal of Intelligence and National Security* examination of the relevant files is quite revealing at this point: although MI5 made their reservations clear as early as 1942, it "was not MI5's place to decide whether men like Klugmann should be barred from secret work. That was left to the judgement of the organisation concerned." This was SOE Cairo, who, this theory goes, knew about Klugmann's overt Communism, and, with the possibility of liaising with the equally Communist Partisans already in prospect, believed that his views "could be put to constructive use".

This idea is vindicated in what Brigadier Keble, Klugmann's boss at SOE, wrote in December 1942 to an enquiry about the latter's Communist views and sympathies, sent to MI5 via SIME (Security Intelligence Middle East) in the Middle East. Klugmann, wrote Keble, was "absolutely trustworthy". But the key passage is this:

> We are not interested in Klugmann's politics which concern this organisation but a little ... In any case, are we to stamp on Communism when probably our largest ally [the Soviet Union] is a nation composed of nothing but Communists?

As a result of this, many at MI5 decided that Klugmann was in the clear. Not until 1943, when a bona-fide Communist spy, Ormond Uren, was discovered by MI5 and successfully prosecuted, did MI5 realise the possibilities of Soviet penetration – and as we know, with what would end up as decidedly mixed results. So, they decided to interview Klugmann in 1944. But so genteel does the interrogation seem to have been that he was able completely to pull the wool over their eyes, just as Philby was notoriously able to do some years later. So, the report on Klugmann by Commander Senter of SOE to MI5 read:

> It is also material to note that much of his work in connection with Jugoslavia [sic] was done at a time when the official policy of HMG [His Majesty's Government] was to support Mihailovic: this did not appear to any of our officers to bring about any situation of divided loyalty so far as Klugmann

was concerned. Now that the policy of HMG is to support Tito, naturally no possible question of divided loyalty would arise, and it is not without interest to note that Klugmann has found value in some of his old Left Wing associations in Belgrade to be of value in connection with his work.

In fact, only until the bugged conversation below did MI5 really have the evidence it needed, and by then Klugmann was no longer in Government employment.

As MI5 knew, Klugmann was quite open at trying to get decisions favourable to the Partisans. MI5 had bugged a conversation between Klugmann and a top Communist Party official, Bob Stewart, and it's fascinating thirty-seven-page transcript tells it exactly as Klugmann wished the Party to understand his aims and objectives in Cairo.

Klugmann *as he saw it* controlled who went from SOE to the Balkans. As he told Stewart, he made sure that: "we recruited a number of British agents to go to Yugoslavia. All those Left Wing – or at least honest typical English – we were able to send to the Partisans; and certain Fascist and really bad elements we always sent to the Cetniks." From that he got to "the next stage to show that only in this [Partisan-controlled] area is work being done against the Germans". The consequence was Klugmann became "identified as a Partisan protagonist within the organisation" and as the Partisans did better, up went his personal prestige.

MI5's view of him, as expressed in August 1945, was:

> Throughout his time in the Yugoslav section, his dominant objectives were to gain information about, furnish assistance to, and finally gain British official recognition for the Partisans, at the expense of the Chetniks. To this end, he set about enlisting the sympathies of members of his own organisations although it is fair to say that he appears to have made no particular secret of where his sympathies lay, or of what he was doing. While as it later turned out, support for the Partisans was ultimately adopted as British policy, it must be pointed out that Klugmann entered on this task purely from Communist motives, and indeed in defiance of then British policy.

So, he was certainly what we call "an agent of influence". But was he, as Petrie and MI5 presumed, an NKVD spy as well? Did he try to doctor the information going to London to favour the Partisans at the expense of the Cetniks? If so, did it matter?

The key thing is this: Klugmann only counts if he was Churchill's principal source of information. If all he did, though, was to confirm what top signals intelligence from ULTRA and confirmed by MI3, was already telling Churchill, then Klugmann could have conspired all he liked but he would have made no difference at all to what Churchill decided and why. MI5 also realised that everyone in Cairo knew that Klugmann was an open Communist, and would therefore probably have taken his prejudices into account.

The main protagonist for the Partisans in Cairo was Brigadier Keble of SOE, who was someone with access to ULTRA material, knowledge of which was very highly restricted indeed, as we have seen elsewhere. The Cambridge Five spy whom Klugmann had recruited to work for the NKVD, John Cairncross, certainly did have ULTRA access, and passed it on copiously to his Soviet controllers. But there is no reason to think therefore that Klugmann had ever heard of it – which is ironic, since it was of course Sigint from Bletchley that was the *true* cause of why Churchill changed his mind.

What exactly was it that he boasted? The MI5 file tells us in some detail, but remember that this is Klugmann's own version of events. It is not even remotely an objective account of what actually happened in Cairo. It is Klugmann bragging to a fellow Communist about doing wonderful things for the Party, rather than a neutral narrative of how important Klugmann was in reality, rather than in his own rather grand estimation of himself.

Sir David Petrie, the Head of MI5, wrote to Air Commodore Archie Boyle of SOE in 1945. What he wrote was conclusive proof that Klugmann was indeed a Soviet spy:

a) Klugmann had carried out espionage tasks for the Soviet Union in the past – probably while employed by the Comintern before the war – and he had recently been approached again by a member of Soviet Intelligence.

b) Before he joined SOE, Klugmann had been carrying out Communist propaganda among Other Ranks in the Army.

c) Throughout his time in SOE's Yugoslav Section, Klugmann's dominant objectives were to gain information about, furnish assistance to, and finally gain British official recognition for the

Partisans, at the expense of the Cetniks. To these ends, he set about enlisting the sympathies of members of his organisation although he made no particular secret of where his sympathies lay.

d) Klugmann also manipulated the intelligence received on Jugoslavia [*sic*] by controlling the selection and destination of agents (e.g. the better ones to Tito); by the manner in which he briefed the agents (e.g. to look for what he wanted them to find), and by selecting or massaging reports so as to ensure that the Partisans appeared in a better light than the Chetniks ...

e) Klugmann established a personal liaison with Jugoslav communist officials in Cairo.

By the time that Boyle received this, however, Klugmann was no longer in SOE employment, so it was all rather late/; as Boyle noted:

I am never surprised when I hear of stupidities having been committed by [SOE Cairo] Middle East and whether Klugmann was taken on against good advice hardly matters at this stage ... Petrie's letter of course is rather one sided and one would think if one did not know the facts, that Klugmann had been responsible for the futility of Mihailovic and, against the better interests of the Allies, had brought Tito into power. Such an impression is, of course, entirely false.

As we saw, Basil Davidson knew Klugmann at the time in Cairo that the latter was an ardent Communist who lectured on Marxism to eager Egyptians, and who was, as everyone seems to agree, utterly overt in all his sympathies. But Davidson, a man of the left himself, albeit not in the Klugmann sense, wrote after Klugmann's death that the idea that a lowly officer could manipulate and deceive no less than the War Cabinet and the British Middle East Command into ditching the Cetniks for the Partisans was nothing less than a 'pitiful farrago of absurdity.'

But for Davidson, who, while with SOE during the war but not privy at the time to ULTRA, discovered, as others have done, the truth as we now know it. As he wrote, to rebut the conspiracy theorists who persisted in making Klugmann the centre of everything:

[The] archival evidence ... explains ... that the crucial decisions in and after January 1943 were taken from the analysis of Enigma decrypts (decrypted as Ultra) or else, in some cases, from decryption of other enemy signals, sometimes of Abwehr or Sicherheitsdienst material. That this material, available only to the Prime Minister and a handful of senior persons, could be fudged or faked (whether by Lt Klugmann or anyone else), is a quite dotty idea.

Britain was fighting hard in the Middle East, about to invade Sicily and needed effective allies. As Davidson recounts, this the Partisans provided rather than the Cetniks – killing perhaps as many as 100,000 Germans by 1945 and capturing some 200,000 more. As he concluded, "Any British officers who had a hand at all in helping that to happen were valiantly doing their duty".

The vigorous correspondence that ensued after Davidson's telling the truth about Klugmann showed that many who had been in Cairo at the time felt that the latter had indeed fudged not a few signals to London, and in the words of one former SOE officer (alas anonymous) that Klugmann had tried hard to cook the books. But does all this matter? That is what Davidson is trying to say: if ULTRA caused the change of tactics, then Klugmann's many and varied deceptions, if all true, made not an iota of difference to what Churchill and the Chiefs decided.

We can see this elsewhere in the Balkans. The historian of SOE in Albania, Roderick Bailey, makes some important points on this issue that apply as much to Yugoslavia as they do to neighbouring Albania.

As Bailey is correct to say: "The scale of Britain's wartime support for Tito was to confuse and to anger many, including several SOE officers who had fought alongside the Chetniks [sic]."[2]

Lees, of course, was one of these, and someone who, like virtually everyone else who worked with SOE in Cairo, knew that there were undoubted Communists in that organisation. But, Bailey adds, "Klugmann's accusers, however, have never produced a concrete case that confirmed he manipulated either policy or the outcome of events: all evidence was circumstantial."

This is another vital distinction. Klugmann may well have tailored his own reports, and was bugged by MI5 bragging on just that point, as seen above. But he did not alter policy in London, for the valid reasons that Bailey is right to remind us, because what was true of Yugoslavia also applied across the Balkans in general:

In recent years, however, the declassification of other wartime records, from Foreign Office policy papers and minutes of the

Chiefs of Staff meetings to secret transcripts of intercepted enemy signals [i.e. Sigint], has shown conclusively that Klugmann had much less influence than was long supposed.

Bailey is correct to show that it was Sigint that was all-important, for Yugoslavia as well as for Albania, the subject of his book. As he continues:

If junior SOE staff were keen to support the Partisans, so were very senior commanders privy to important intelligence to which SOE had no or little access. Recent studies of decrypted enemy signals demonstrate that, in March 1943, when they authorised SOE to contact the Partisans, the Chiefs were well aware from sources other than SOE reports, that the Partisans were causing the Axis serious problems.

In other words, what SOE were doing was to confirm what the Sigint had both independently and *already* made clear. The importance of this is critical, as it rather demolishes the conspiracy theorists who put everything down to spies and Communist agents of influence. As Bailey reiterates:

Top secret decrypts of enemy traffic had documented in detail, for example, the scale of a recent Axis offensive against the Partisans that stood as the largest anti-guerrilla operation Yugoslavia had seen for over a year. By June, when SOE was told to start arming the Partisans, decrypts also confirmed that Mihailovic's forces were less and less anti-Axis and were even collaborating.... Churchill, too, knew from the decrypts about Tito's superior activity and Mihailovic's failings. That July he noted from a long digest of intercepted material "the marvellous resistance by the followers of Tito and the powerful cold-blooded manoeuvres of Mihailovic." [Churchill's words]

As Bailey writes elsewhere, to confirm this, Klugmann's "efforts had little impact on policy makers, who, while not sharing [his] ... passionate commitment to the Communist cause, could clearly see a Partisan case for extensive and increasingly exclusive support". Once again, the Bletchley decrypts are the key. For indeed anything Cairo might have sent proved to be of little comparative importance compared to the clear and very direct evidence of Sigint.

This last factor therefore shows us that in a real sense many of the revisionists are asking the wrong question, however sincere and deep-felt their viewpoint might be, not to mention their strong dislike of Communism, and all the terrors that such ideology inflicted upon so many millions for so long. The main point is not that anyone was out to conspire to place a Communist regime in Yugoslavia after the war, even supposing that the Marxists in SOE in Cairo were hoping on ideological grounds for a Partisan-led country after the war. The truth is, as argued throughout this chapter, that the British wanted to divert as many troops from Italy as possible and they deemed the Partisans the best force to accomplish that in Yugoslavia. It really is as simple as that.

Roderick Bailey understands many of the dilemmas that the unfortunate Mihailovic faced, especially his very natural reluctance to sacrifice Serb lives to hideous German reprisals. This was something that everyone understood, including Maclean.[3] But since the Allies had a war to fight against the Germans, they had also to include what Bailey justly calls the "bigger picture".[4] Confirming what has just been argued in our chapter, Bailey explains:

> But in 1943, with the Allies busy planning the invasion of Italy and the Second Front, arguments for backing the Partisans as a means of tying down enemy troops went a long way to overriding long-term worries and dispersing sympathy for men seeking Axis help to settle domestic scores.

It was at Churchill's level, and that of the Chiefs of Staff in London, all of whom had access to ULTRA, that the decision was made:

> And the bigger picture revealed by the decrypts continued to provide Churchill and the Chiefs of Staff with strong enough evidence of the Partisans' superior worth and how compromised Mihailovic was becoming. In November [1943] the Chiefs of Staff advised Churchill that support for Tito should be increased. The same month, the Joint Intelligence Committee recommended that support for Mihailovic be brought to a close. By the end of the year, at the highest levels, frustration with Mihailovic was widely shared and Churchill had resolved to support only Tito.

This tells us what we need to know. Klugmann and other Communists in Cairo could exaggerate and dissemble all they liked, but in the end, it was London-controlled strategy, based upon Sigint of German signals, that made the decision. This was not conspiracy, but the need to win the war and reduce Allied casualties. For a democratic statesman such as Winston Churchill to decide to switch support from Royalist Cetniks to Communist Partisans must have been the result of solid reasoning, or because he was deliberately deceived by those secretly plotting for Communist domination. The idea that Churchill would have made his choice on the basis of clear British interests, to save Allied lives, knowing the possible political outcome in favour of the Communists – well, surely, such a thing is unthinkable? So a conspiracy by Klugmann *must* be true?

Theology comes in as well – the *scapegoat*, the innocent goat in Ancient Israel sent out to die in the Wilderness to atone for the sins of the guilty. Both Maclean and Deakin were scapegoated as the dupes of the evil Klugmann, and Klugmann's machinations make the innocent Churchill the scapegoat, the loyal defender of freedom and democracy duped into putting wicked Communists into power. As David Martin pleads:

> Let me make it clear that at this point I consider Winston Churchill, on the basis of his performance in World War II, to be one of the truly great figures of human history…. It may be no exaggeration to say that he was instrumental in saving the entire free world from Nazi subjugation. But even the greatest men commit blunders, especially when they are dependent upon others for information and advance. It is in this limited sense that I … examine Churchill's Yugoslav blunder.

Truth is often prosaic. Klugmann made no difference. The conspirators can spin all kinds of webs, but they are wrong. ULTRA decided everything, and to presume otherwise is to share in Klugmann's own delusion of his importance.

The historian Geoff Andrews has proved this in his 2015 biography of Klugmann: *The Shadow Man*. As he puts it:

> First, policy decisions over whether to support Tito were taken by higher government bodies than SOE. Secondly, Klugmann's objectives as a communist happened to coincide at this particular moment with the strategy of the Allies…. It was a visit by Winston Churchill in 1943 which proved crucial to the change in policy … Now German intelligence

reports intercepted by British intelligence had confirmed that the Partisans in Yugoslavia were strong while the Chetniks in some locations were found to be collaborating with Germans … Churchill, who had also received favourable reports on the relative superiority of the Partisans in Ultra decrypts from Bletchley Park was won over and from this point gave support to Tito …. [After the Maclean mission in November 1943] Churchill became further convinced that exclusive support for Tito was the best strategy in harming Nazi forces.

Of course, Klugmann was a Communist; overtly so. But as Andrews argues correctly:

During late 1942, Klugmann's political justification for allying with Tito's Partisans might have seemed unpalatable to the conservative ranks of SOE. Following Churchill's visit in January 1943, however, he could claim his argument had been vindicated.

When we look at the MI3 evidence it could be argued that it was later in 1943 – certainly by the summer – that the decrypt evidence had confirmed the shift in policy. But in essence Andrews is right; it was cold hard evidence that switched British policy not any kind of manipulation by Klugmann. Andrews thus concludes that, "we can exonerate Klugmann from claims that he acted as a Soviet agent and conspirator who subverted the just causes of the Chetniks in shifting Churchill to support Tito … His political convictions at this moment enhanced rather than obstructed the wider Allied military strategy."

So, there was no conspiracy. Klugmann was a Communist, but very much a bit player and certainly not someone remotely as important as the conspirators would have us believe. Sadly, for such views it is as simple as that. Diana died because she was not wearing a seat belt, the Americans really did land on the moon, Al Qaeda caused 9/11 – and it was the ULTRA decrypts and their analysis by MI3 and the Chiefs of Staff that caused Churchill to make his epic decisions in 1943.

Endnotes

1. The late David Martin, the distinguished American author of *The Web of Disinformation: Churchill's Yugoslav Blunder*, which came out in 1990, calls Klugmann the "Fifth Man", but Christopher Andrew's comprehensive

and authoritative official history of MI5 shows conclusively that it was Cairncross who was the "Fifth Man". Needless to say, conspiracy minded individuals dislike Andrew's book, even though he has seen all the MI5 files and they have not. Christopher Andrew has pointed out a serious error of Martin's book – the latter considers *Most Secret Sources* to be MI6 rather than what they actually were: Sigint from Bletchley Park. So he refers to one MSS, for example, on 24 September 1943 as a memorandum displaying "pro-Tito and anti-Mihailovic bias ... [and] evidence of a reckless and unrelenting bias". But it is a Sigint report of ULTRA decrypts of German material, straight from Bletchley Park to Churchill! It is a *German* field report! So, it was not written by 'ideological Marxists' but by German officers not realising – thankfully – that the British at Bletchley were listening in to all their communications. Needless to say, this misunderstanding does not help the case of the conspirators in their rewriting of history.

2. Ibid., pp. 131–2 for the quotations from this book.
3. Fitzroy Maclean, *Eastern Approaches* (London, Penguin, 2009), p. 336.
4. Roderick Bailey, *The Wildest Province: SOE in the Land of the Eagle* (Vintage, 2009), p.133 (and for the quotations that follow.)

Chapter 4

The Bletchley Park Sigint Unfolds

It was the Signals Intelligence from Bletchley that convinced Churchill that Britain ought to support Tito's Partisans in Yugoslavia rather than stick to the inactive Cetniks under Mihailovic.

Much has been written about how ULTRA (or Enigma or Boniface, the varying names given to the decrypts of Bletchley Park) shortened the war. We tend to think of this only in terms of battles, such as the struggle to achieve safe transatlantic passage for convoys bringing supplies from the USA to Britain, or individual events such as the D-Day landings in Normandy. But in fact, ULTRA or whatever term one gives it, played a much wider role, including in the decision making over who to back in the Balkans to divert German troops away from Italy after the invasion of Sicily began in 1943.

Leading SOE expert David Stafford makes this abundantly clear in his review in the international Churchill magazine, *Finest Hour*. Rebutting a conspiratorial interpretation of events in Yugoslavia in 1943, in the book *Hoodwinking Churchill* by distinguished film producer Paul Batty, Stafford writes:

> But many other sources, amongst them the Bletchley Park "Ultra" decrypts, demonstrated that Tito's Partisans were doing more to engage the enemy than Mihailovic, and SOE Cairo was hardly the deciding voice in the affair anyway.

How true this is we saw in the chapter on the response of MI3 to the intercepts. Here we can look at them with references to the sources that are available from The National Archives in Kew (in outer London) and can be ordered online for the curious who can therefore verify what follows personally. It is worth saying that *Hoodwinking Churchill* contains no references to MI3 or to any of the particular Bletchley Park decrypts that follow.

This is a puzzle, since they were available in 2011 when the book was published. Perhaps former Hut 3 codebreaker Ralph Bennett is right in his 1994 book *Behind the Battle*, on the role of ULTRA and other intelligence sources during the war to refer to the "passion and prejudice" of much writing on this subject. We can all agree that when it comes to the revisionists, although the passion and sincerity of their books shine out, the facts of what actually took place paint a very different picture.

To give a general view first, before going on to the details of individual intercepts, let us take a particular case. We have to remember that the idea that Brigadier Keble of SOE Cairo's revelations given to Churchill in early 1943 about Partisan activity against the Germans being greater than that of the Cetniks was in fact old news. What Keble possessed were decrypts of German secret intelligence organisation the Abwehr. These were codenamed ISOS and ISK and were in fact separate from ULTRA. His memorandum is supposed to have changed British attitudes to the Balkans, at least according to the revisionists who put great store in the supposedly all-important role played by SOE in Cairo.[1]

The truth, however, is rather different. As Bennett goes on to say, when Keble's memorandum, based on the ISOS and ISK decrypts of German intelligence codes arrived in London:

> It is plain … that Churchill had been made aware more than twelve months earlier of the Abwehr Enigma decrypts convicting Mihailovic of collaboration with the German occupying forces [so that] Keble's report can have told him nothing new… In the post-Alamein climate, still more after the whole southern shore of the Mediterranean had been cleared of the enemy in May 1943 and HUSKY [the invasion of Sicily] was being prepared, Churchill and the Chiefs of Staff were much less ready to be governed by old loyalties and much more inclined to support a side whose aims coincided with their own. A decision between Tito and Mihailovic was becoming urgent, quite independently of anything in Keble's report.

What emissaries from Britain such as Bill Deakin and later Fitzroy Maclean did, as we see elsewhere in our book, was simply to confirm what ULTRA was already telling Churchill and the Chiefs of Staff.

So, as Bennett recalls, from his own time in Bletchley Park in Hut 3 and as an historian, it was clear that ULTRA in 1943 became "a regular source of intelligence about the Balkans: signals were transmitted on twenty of thirty-one days in the month [in May] and this rate was maintained throughout the summer". Churchill and the Chiefs now knew precisely where all the key German divisions were and whom they were fighting. "For the first time too" he continues, "Ultra began to bear directly on the operations of the Partisans and the Cetniks."

This was of vital interest to London. As Bennett notes:

> At all events, the story of intelligence about wartime Yugoslavia takes on a new dimension in the summer of 1943, as Ultra begins to play a part in it comparable to that which it had been playing in North Africa for the past eighteen months.

ULTRA intelligence had helped Montgomery to beat Rommel at El Alamein in November 1942 and ultimately to drive the Germans out of North Africa by May 1943. Now with Italy next, the Chiefs of Staff fully realised the significance of the fact that "Ultra had down that over thirty German, Italian, Croat and Bulgarian divisions were in Yugoslavia, most of them engaged in operations against the partisans [*sic*]."

When Bill Deakin landed in Yugoslavia in May 1943, he and Tito came within a hairsbreadth of being killed, as we will discover when looking at the exciting account of Deakin's adventures in that country. But as we shall see, no fewer than 15,000 Partisans were able to escape the Germans and to live to fight another day. As Bennett, listening in to what was happening in Hut 3 at Bletchley, recorded later:

> The escape of the main body of the Partisans … from the pincer movement of SCHWARZ [the German attack] could be watched in successive Ultra signals which were often only twenty-four hours behind the events they described.

Needless to say, the impact on British policy was considerable, as Bennett recalled in 1989:

While this, the first thoroughly well-documented Partisan action with British blessing, was in progress, a new line of policy toward the Yugoslav resistance was being hammered out. The Foreign Office remained favourable to Mihajlovic [sic], but the Chiefs of Staff and the Middle East Defence Committee [MEDC] in Cairo (which asserted that "the Partisans are the most formidable anti-Axis element in Jugoslavia [sic]"), both with the benefit of Ultra, became increasingly hostile.

We shall quote from both the Chiefs of Staff and MEDC files later – all their comments also being found in Churchill's own files in his Prime Minister's office. But notice those words: "both with the benefit of Ultra". It was the Bletchley Park Sigint that made the critical difference, soon with so much coming in that, as Bennett groans to remember, he and the others at Hut 3 felt overwhelmed by the sheer volume of material. But all this points to the same thing – the change was caused not by people in Cairo but by the codebreakers of Bletchley Park.

Let us now backtrack to look at how the official history of British intelligence gives the details of individual decrypts that show the very precise role played by ULTRA in the unfolding story of Yugoslavia, starting slightly earlier than Bennett, in 1942.

From 1942, the activity by the guerrillas in Yugoslavia was so considerable that the Germans had drastically to increase the number of divisions placed by them in the country. In theory, their Italian ally was supposed to be active in crushing opposition but, in reality, Italy did not remotely pull its weight as proven by the file in the National Archives CX/MSS/T13 (Government Code and Cypher School: Signals Intelligence Passed to the Prime Minister). In some areas, the Italians even made deals with the royalist Serb guerrillas, the Cetniks, rather than trying to eliminate them.

This was seen in March 1943 during *Weiss II*, in which time the Germans were able to break Cetnik codes – something that was discovered by Bletchley Park. From this it seemed clear that the Cetniks wanted to collaborate with the Italians, in order to protect themselves against German attack.[2] The bauxite mines at Mostar (a city that would become famous during the later conflicts of the 1990s) were of vital economic importance to the Third Reich. So, they were naturally worried when, for example, during *Weiss II* that the Italians thought it might be an idea to use Cetnik forces near Mostar in order to eliminate any Partisan risk to the mines.[3]

The Germans did have local allies in the form of the utterly barbaric Ustase, the collaborationist regime that ruled over what is now both Croatia and Bosnia, and who committed atrocities often so vile that even the SS were shocked at the scale of the depravity inflicted upon the Serb victims. In Belgrade, the quisling Nedic regime also worked together with the Germans, and they had links of their own in parallel with the Cetniks, which did not go down well with the Germans, who hated all opposition equally.

So, by August 1943, Enigma showed that there were no fewer than seventeen German divisions in the former Yugoslavia.[4]

The key battles – *Weiss I* and *Weiss II* followed by *Schwarz* – were, as seen in the MI3 chapter, absolutely critical in persuading the Chiefs of Staff in London and thence Churchill that "the Enigma left no doubt that the fighting value of the Cetniks was greatly inferior to that of Tito's Partisans", as noted in London by the Joint Intelligence Committee and in the Enigma by DEFE 3/822/ML 5054, and the far greater level of Partisan casualties in CX/MSS/2782/T21.

It is worth adding that the decoders at Bletchley were also able to break Japanese diplomatic codes, so that they could find out what was happening in Yugoslavia from the Japanese embassies in Bucharest and Sofia, which confirmed what the decrypts of the German military and intelligence (Abwehr) codes were also telling them.

Then with the Allied invasion of Italy, the Germans were able to put into action their contingency plan for the Italian surrender to the Allies – the violence of which became famous in recent years with the novel *Captain Correlli's Mandolin* which describes the massacre of Italian troops by Germans on one of the Greek islands. In Yugoslavia some Italians quietly surrendered, others put up a brave fight but by October it was all over and the Italian forces there were out of the picture.[5]

But as we have seen, the Partisans made a magnificent effort to capture as much Italian equipment as possible, and to occupy all they could of territory hitherto held by the Italian forces. The Germans therefore had to send what has been described as "the largest force ever employed by Germany in anti-guerrilla operations" including no less than the First SS Panzer Army: the decrypts of which can be found in DEFE3/886-890 and elsewhere.

This was a desperate struggle, with the Prinz Eugen 7th SS Mountain Division and the Second Panzer Army also being deployed, all their decisions being helpfully decrypted by the codebreakers at Bletchley Park. And with great effect too – when the Germans decided, for example, to occupy the Dalmatian island of Solta, Allied air forces, using Enigma decrypts, were able to obliterate the German landing forces the very next day.[6]

And as the official history of intelligence then reminds us:

> These being the circumstances in which the Allies decided to step up supplies to Tito as a matter of urgency at the beginning of December 1943, it was the subsequent development of Yugoslavia into a theatre where Allied support to the Partisans could tie down substantial German forces which led to the decision formally to break with Mihailovic.

Indeed, increased Allied help to the Partisans soon brought active military dividends in the German inability to recapture large swathes of the territory that the Partisans had taken when Italy dropped out of the war. While the decrypts were proving Partisan success, many of the Cetniks were coming to the same conclusions and dropping Mihailovic for Tito.

Churchill's main concern was and remained the fighting in Italy, and the pinning down of as many German divisions in the Balkans as possible so as to prevent their transfer to Italy. Enigma had already shown that his hopes were succeeding – several of the German forces we just saw above, including the 371st Infantry Division had indeed been transferred from Italy to Yugoslavia to try to salvage as much territory as possible from the now advancing Partisan forces.

So Churchill's plan was working! And as David Stafford makes clear in his review of *Hoodwinking Churchill*, it was only natural that the great man would want to put *British* needs first:

> Maintaining the Anglo-Soviet alliance was an absolute imperative for Britain in the campaign to defeat Hitler, and Stalin's support for Tito was firm—and perhaps regretted by Stalin when Tito chose an independent policy after the war. To continue supporting Mihailovic would have been to throw dust in Stalin's eyes. Yes, Churchill was an anti-communist, and so was Mihailovic. But that was no reason for the former to support the latter. War is a dirty and often cynical business.

This vital fact is easily forgotten: Stalin and the USSR were our allies. Ideologically it was a strange alliance, and the emergence of the Cold War so soon after VE Day in 1945 proves this. But the circumstances of 1943 were clear: the Western democracies such as Britain and the USA were engaged together with the Communist Soviet Union in the defeat of Nazi Germany.

While this was going on, Mihailovic in his turn was now pursuing collaboration with the quisling Nedic regime in Belgrade – with active German encouragement – and with the SS in Croatia. The National Archives' CAB 121/529 file has decrypted situation reports from the Balkans, confirmed by Signit from Bletchley that Cetniks loyal to Mihailovic were now fighting alongside the Germans and Nedic supporting Serbs against the Partisans.[7]

This is vital, since as we see elsewhere it is at the heart of the revisionist thesis that it was material given by the Partisans to first Bill Deakin and then by Fitzroy Maclean that altered Churchill's mind, and that it must be the case that such material was faked by Tito to deceive the British.

On the contrary, however, it was this clear and unambiguous Enigma evidence that convinced Churchill beyond peradventure that Mihailovic was "in active collaboration with the Germans". In writing his account, in the fifth volume of his history of the Second World War, the Prime Minister could only refer obliquely to "all reports received" but we know from his telegrams preserved in his PREM files in The National Archives at Kew and in the Churchill Papers in Cambridge that it was to the Signit material to which he was referring.

Endnotes

1. *Inter alia* Ralph Bennett goes on to prove in *Behind the Battle, Intelligence in the War with Germany 1939–1945* (Faber & Faber, 2009), that the myth that Keble had ULTRA access in Cairo is in fact entirely erroneous, and therefore invalidates those who base their opinions on such mistakes.
2. The National Archives (TNA), CX/MSS/2152 and 2256/T10.
3. TNA, CX/MSS/2228/T10.
4. Director C/Archive 3808.
5. TNA, CX/MSS/3396/T1.
6. TNA, DEFE 3/8.
7. TNA, DEFE 3/7-12.

Chapter 5

MI3: The Unfolding Story

We have all heard of MI6, or SIS (Secret Intelligence Service) and MI5 (the Security Service). At one stage, there were as many as fourteen branches of Military Intelligence, down to MI14, which specialised, during the Second World War, exclusively on the main enemy, Nazi Germany. (MI17 functioned purely as a secretariat and not all the numbers were used.) We also know about MI9, the branch that dealt with escaped Allied prisoners of war.

But what was MI3, let alone its special division, MI3 (b), the part of military intelligence with which we are dealing here?

Originally, in 1914, at the outbreak of the First World War, MI3 was geographical information, with sections (a) to (e) dealing with different parts of Europe. MI3(b) included the Austro-Hungarian Empire, which broke up into several parts in 1918 and included the Balkan areas of what are now Croatia, Slovenia and Bosnia. By 1941, and the Nazi conquest of Yugoslavia, MI3(b) was interested in the Balkans and in intelligence of all kinds coming from that region.

The key facts about MI3 in all its parts, and MI3(b), our particular division, are:

a) They received ULTRA so knew everything the Germans were doing as discovered by the code-breakers at Bletchley Park.
b) Their reports went via the Director of Military Intelligence to the Chiefs of Staff and through them on to the Prime Minister himself.

In other words, they had full access to the most important secrets of the war and reported to those who made the decisions – Churchill and the Chiefs of Staff, the group that decided Britain's military policy.

This meant in turn that they were supremely influential. They saw the Bletchley material and that of MI6 and that of the Special Operations Executive, SOE. This in turn entailed the fact that they were several magnitudes more important than any field operative in SOE, let alone any of the SOE headquarters staff in Cairo. Any conspiracy theory that leaves out MI3 and which gives all the prominence to Communists in Cairo simply does not understand how British intelligence worked during the Second World War, and who made the crucial decisions and on what basis. The MI3-Bletchley axis alone had the full information upon which the Chiefs of Staff and the Prime Minister decided policy. It is as simple as that!

All of this has been known for some time – and also virtually ignored, especially in the conspiracy theory literature that seeks to exonerate the Cetniks from all blame and to refight the civil war of the 1940s all over again through the violence of the 1990s and reinterpret events of the Second World War through the prism of the Yugoslav break-up after 1990.

But in 1984, volume three (part one) of the official history *British Intelligence in the Second World War* was published, based upon archives many of which were at the time sealed shut. And while not referring specifically to MI3 as such – the simple term *MI* for Military Intelligence was employed instead – many of the documents that have now been released were used in the chapter 'Developments in Yugoslavia'. No names of MI3 officials were given, although those of the intrepid SOE operatives parachuted into the war zone were given, especially as many of them had by 1984 written their memoirs, notably those by Fitzroy Maclean and by Bill Deakin.

What Hinsley and the others wrote in the book cannot be clearer – published six years prior to two of the most influential conspiracy books. They say unequivocally that the decision in early 1943 to send people such as Deakin to Tito:

> Followed upon a considerable increase in Axis, and more particularly German, involvement against the Partisans, and was accompanied by firm evidence of a still more determined offensive against both of the resistance movements [i.e. both Partisan and Cetnik]. The evidence came mainly from the German high-grade Sigint.

They put in a footnote to the above paragraph:

Although the SOE liaison missions in Yugoslavia regularly submitted reports on Axis order of battle and military operations these were not usually received as promptly as the Sigint, nor were they always accurate or sufficiently definite to be useful for Allied operations.

Of the incontestable value of the Sigint seen by Churchill, MI3 and by the Chiefs of Staff in London, Sir Harry Hinsley and his colleagues make crystal clear:

The sole reliable guide to enemy resources and intentions, this had steadily increased in volume since the autumn of 1942 and was now becoming prolific as the German armed forces intensified their activities in an area where, in the absence of landlines, they relied entirely on W/T [wireless telegraphy] for their signals.

Could anything be clearer than this? Does this appear in either of the books by David Martin and Michael Lees that hatch disinformation efforts by Stalin's NKVD agents in Cairo? It does not – and actually also goes on to state that London, in other words Churchill, MI3 and the Chiefs of Staff, put more reliability on Sigint than they did from the reports from the agents of SOE, which tells you all you wish to know about any SOE infiltrators in whom the conspiracy believers put such store. (*Peter Babby's Hoodwinking Churchill,* published in 2011, takes a similar conspiratorial view and also omits the vital evidence from MI3).

When it comes to those who did go, such as Deakin and Maclean, they could not, for obvious reasons, talk about the true source of military intelligence information – the ULTRA decrypts. All of this had to remain unspoken and anonymous. And while both Maclean and Deakin knew of ULTRA at some stage in the proceedings, many others did not. The result is that those who knew the truth could not say how they knew it, and this allowed all sorts of weird and wonderful false trails and mistaken theories to emerge.

As the papers of Bill Deakin reveal, while MI3 saw SOE material, and passed on everything to the Joint Intelligence Staff (Military Intelligence, Naval Intelligence and Air Intelligence), there was not reciprocity – SOE could not see what MI3 was able to read and comment.

What is interesting is that as MI3's perceptions of what was happening in the Balkans changes, as a result of the 'Most Secret

Sources', the Bletchley intercepts, so too does British policy at the highest levels in London.

As we shall see as the story unfolds, this was to become a major problem, with some people knowing and others not, and as the Official History shows, when Britain had to make decisions based upon a source that for obvious security reasons they could never reveal – the ULTRA decrypts – those outside of the loop refused to believe the rationale given by the British Government because of the paramount importance of maintaining the ULTRA secret.

In February 1942 MI3 heard, via MI6, that Mihailovic and his Cetniks were doing their best to maintain some kind of resistance against the Germans. This of course, was not intercept evidence. Nonetheless the Chiefs of Staff were glad to hear that someone was attempting activity in the Balkans. And as MI3 and the Chiefs realised, there were no fewer than thirty German divisions in the area, along with a lot of through traffic coming up from Greece and down from other parts of the Balkans, as the war against the Soviet Union was not far away. In early 1942 the outcome of the war in Eastern Europe was still most uncertain, and anything that prevented German divisions from being transferred to the Soviet front was very welcome.

However, as early as March 1942, news came from Yugoslavia to MI3 that not all was as it should be, and that the situation on the ground was far more complex than London had realised.

As we saw, Hudson of SOE had reported upon the existence of Tito and the Partisans, but as he was often without radio contact and on his own in the mountains, he was not able to report back anything he saw to London and Cairo. However, with MI3 able to read German intercepts from the Balkans, they were slowly able to build up a picture of what was actually going on.

On 7 March Talbot Rice was able to record, through this knowledge, that the Cetniks were not so much fighting the Germans – which is what Britain naturally wanted them to do – but the shadowy Communist Partisans. Not only that, but within the civil war that was clearly emerging from German reports, the Communists were distinctly gaining the upper hand.

As Talbot Rice told his superiors in Military Intelligence, if that was the case, then Mihailovic "is far weaker than the communists and as he refuses to play second fiddle to them [and] fighting has broken out ..." to the disadvantage of the Cetniks. There was an obvious corollary to this: if the two main Yugoslav guerrilla groups were fighting each other, then they were not doing their job of fighting the Germans, which was thus bad news for Britain.

Soon the existence of the Communists was on the radar of MI6 as well. It is clear from the Deakin Papers that MI6's wireless transmitters in Yugoslavia had been captured and disposed of by the Germans after the successful invasion of 1941, so MI6 was in effect flying blind after that.

MI6 – SIS – was known to be hostile to the activities of SOE, since, by definition, SOE's mandate from Churchill was to create as much chaos and disruption as possible, and do so with whomever was causing the greatest disturbance to the Germans. This entailed – not just in Yugoslavia – wartime alliances with people whom Britain would not normally touch, especially Communists all over Europe, from France to the Balkans. Spies, contrary to James Bond novels, usually wish to operate as quietly and as under the radar as possible, to avoid any detection. Such a remit was naturally the exact opposite of that of SOE. However, MI3 was in an office in London, and so sharing information with the spies of MI6 posed no problem.

Correspondence between MI3 and MI6, all passed on to the Chiefs of Staff in memorandum form, noticed a crucial difference between the Cetniks and the Partisans, one that as time went on, was to become decisive.

The Cetniks were no friends of the German occupying forces. But they were naturally terrified of savage Wehrmacht reprisals. We can take one example: Leskovac.

In April 1941, during the German *blitzkrieg* through Yugoslavia, Wehrmacht forces occupied the Serbian town of Leskovac. That July, Communist guerrillas – the Partisans – sabotaged the railway lines nearby. German retaliation was swift and deadly: over 2,000 civilians in the town were promptly massacred. In October some 2,700 more civilians were similarly butchered at another Serb town, Kragujevac. Resistance to the German occupiers was becoming rather costly and this dominated Cetnik thinking. Here we can sympathise with the revisionists/conspirators, as these slaughters were truly terrible. As David Martin, one of the revisionist historians, has correctly observed:

> The massacre at Kragujevac became a symbol of the differences over strategy that divided the Partisans from the followers of Mihailovic. The question was not *whether* to fight but *how* and *when* to fight [Martin's italics].

61

That was simple from the point of view of the soldiers on the ground and their commanders. But Britain needed allies who *would* fight the Germans, and it was that factor that led to all the decision-making by Churchill and the Chiefs of Staff in London. That might have been unpalatable to Mihailovic and the Cetniks, who for reasons that we can all understand wanted to avoid massacres by Germans in their own territory. But Churchill could not decide British policy on the basis of what was or was not more convenient to the Cetniks. The lives of the brave British, American and Polish-exile troops in Italy were at stake, and the need to pin down as many German divisions in the Balkans as possible to reduce Allied casualties was rightly absolutely paramount in Churchill's thinking.

With the Partisans it was different – resistance should be taken to the enemy whatever the casualties. As the MI3/MI6 correspondence noticed, the Partisans wanted "an all-out permanent offensive, regardless of cost to combatants and non-combatants".

Decades later it is of course very easy to be judgemental, and say that we too would have opposed German occupation whatever the death toll. But for Britain – for Churchill and the Chiefs of Staff – in April 1942 the situation was desperate. Singapore had fallen to the Japanese in February, and Rommel was on the verge of capturing Tobruk, which his forces did in June. The USA was our ally, but as yet no US forces were fighting alongside that of Britain and its Empire. The situation of Malta in the Mediterranean was more than precarious. We know now it held out against the odds, but as the Chiefs of Staff reacted to information from the Balkans, what they needed was news of German divisions being contained, not of guerrilla fighters who, however rationally, seemed unwilling to fight. This meant that the politics of resistance were becoming complex.

As Churchill's military advisers realised, they had a dilemma: offering help to Mihailovic and the Cetniks would be to support the Royal government in exile, our official ally in Yugoslavia, with whom Britain hoped it would be dealing after the war was over. (Apart from anything else, young King Peter was a descendant of Queen Victoria!) On the other hand it was the Communists taking the battle to the Germans. Therefore:

> Apart from the political difficulties involved, the immediate result would be the loss of control over the revolt that could be exercised by ourselves or by the Yugoslav Government.

It would not however mean that resistance to the enemy would cease.

Britain had official links with the exiled Royal regime and none at all with the Partisans, Hudson's brief visit to the latter notwithstanding. Therefore it was only with the Cetniks, via King Peter and his officials, over whom the United Kingdom had any leverage. But this, as Talbot Rice told his military superiors in May, was also problematic:

> If we do not back Mihailovic, not only will we fail … but the military situation will develop into political anarchy. Not only will British influence and prestige in Yugoslavia be lost (possibly to Russia) but they will be seriously weakened throughout the Balkans and the Eastern Mediterranean.

By this time Churchill was becoming interested in precisely this question, with MI3 sending him a map of who seemed to control what in that very confused part of the world. Was Britain, in supporting their official ally, backing the wrong horse?

Furthermore the Chiefs of Staff were becoming equally interested in Yugoslavia with the hoped-for liberation by the Allies of Italy drawing near. On their way to the *Trident* conference with the USA, they held a meeting on 10 May 1943 on the *Queen Mary* and decided firmly that the Allies "should be prepared to exploit any weakening of the German position in the Balkans".

By the time that they arrived in the USA they advised their American colleagues at a joint Combined Chiefs of Staff meeting that:

> We do not believe that Germany can hold both Northern Italy and the Balkans without risking a collapse on the Russian Front. Even if she decides to abandon Italy and hold the Balkans, her task will be by no means easy … We should be prepared to exploit any weakening of the German position in the Balkans.

As we now know, this view of the Italian Front turned out to be wildly optimistic, though it is true that at several stages in the remaining two years of the war, Hitler was obliged to transfer troops from the Eastern Front to Western Europe whenever British and US pressure forced him so to decide.

But the key thing remains the same: Italy and the Italian campaign determined British Balkan policy. It was always pressure from the Chiefs of Staff to find an ally in the Balkans to tie down the Germans that motivated all of Churchill's thinking, and certainly not plots in Cairo.

In September, the intrepid Hudson of SOE had been able to report back, and as someone who had actually seen the Partisans was able to extol their martial values. So, did this mean that Britain should back the mysterious Tito and his Communist guerrillas? Or could the United Kingdom, as some thought, back both groups, with a territorial demarcation line designating who would fight the Germans where?

It was clear by now that Mihailovic and his Cetniks were doing virtually nothing to attack the Wehrmacht, and terror of vicious reprisals was a major factor in their decision to lie low. The other one was clearly political; if they conserved their forces until the Axis was beaten elsewhere by the Allies, then they would be strong enough to take on and beat the Partisans when victory came.

From a Cetnik viewpoint the logic of this was obvious. Who would want the kind of butchery that the Germans were happy to unleash, especially against innocent civilians? Some in MI3 understood this, noting: "In our opinion it would be dangerous to risk reprisals severe enough to cause estrangement among potential supporters." With this the Director of Military Intelligence himself agreed. The ghosts of Kragujevac were still, and understandably, haunting people's minds.

However, Cetnik inaction was conspicuous, albeit with the caution that ULTRA did occasionally report an anti-German action, such as the capture of the town of Foca in late 1942. ULTRA also revealed the considerably greater and indisputable amount of Partisan action.

What, in particular, began to change British opinion in London was the Axis assault in January 1943, with the Italian forces launching a full-scale attack on the Partisans, backed up by Luftwaffe bombing. And it was clear to MI3 that the Axis regarded the Partisans as the main enemy, as confirmed copiously by 'Most Secret Sources', the ULTRA decrypts.

Here the reaction "in Whitehall", as the official history describes all the different intelligence groups, becomes interesting.

SOE in Cairo did have access to low-grade German intelligence decrypts, mainly those of the Abwehr and Police. As we shall see in the Deakin chapter, Brigadier Keble of SOE Cairo did have access to the full ULTRA, but effectively on a personal basis, although as Basil Davidson's memoirs suggest, a very limited amount of people in SOE

Cairo were able to share the knowledge of complete ULTRA as delivered from Bletchley.

What the official history says is significant, in that it shows clearly it was in London and the Bletchley intercepts that changed minds about the Partisans, and that SOE in Cairo effectively played no role whatsoever in the epic change of direction that the Chiefs of Staff and Churchill were about to take.

As Sir Harry Hinsley and his co-authors wrote back in 1984:

> But it is noticeable that although SOE Cairo had not yet suggested that aid to Mihailovic should be stopped – only that aid to Tito should begin – discussion in Whitehall was increasingly concerned from February 1943 with the question whether or not to break with Mihailovic completely, and the explanation is to be found in the fact that developments in the Mediterranean, combined with evidence that the Partisans were a more effective military force, were lending persuasiveness to the military argument for aiding the Partisans. This is indicated by the change which took place in MI's response to the Sigint evidence.

This is an understatement, since the Sigint evidence was soon to become overwhelming, as the German assault on the guerrilla groups in Yugoslavia then unfurled, with almost more Sigint for Bletchley than MI3 and others could possibly analyse.

Allowing for translation time of the intercepts, the Sigint analysts at Bletchley, and the MI3 officers receiving the ULTRA decrypts, were what we would now describe as listening into the German *Fall Weiss* in as near to real time as was then technically possible.

And it was this, the clear and unmistakable evidence on the ground, from ULTRA, that began the major shift in opinion in London of what was actually happening in Yugoslavia, and whom the Germans perceived to be the real threat.

The importance of this cannot be overestimated. As MI3 informed MI14, "the activities of the Partisans must be causing the Axis considerable annoyance if it has been found necessary to mount an operation on such a large scale during winter". Snow and ice do not make ideal conditions for major operations yet so fierce had been the Partisan resistance to the Axis that the Germans felt no other option but to launch a full-scale onslaught.

As MI3 was picking up from ULTRA, soon no fewer than four *German* divisions were taking part in the operation – the Wehrmacht clearly estimated that so important was the offensive they could not leave it to their somewhat lacklustre Italian allies. Not only that, but as ULTRA also confirmed, no less than the SS Prince Eugen Division was dispatched to attack the Partisans, a specialist mountain fighting regiment consisting of ethnic Germans from the Balkans, and one that did not hesitate to commit atrocities, butchering hundreds of civilians in its wake.

But by February the ULTRA decrypts were telling MI3 that even the Prince Eugen Division was having difficulties in mopping up resistance, and was complaining loudly at the unreliability of Germany's Italian and Ustase (Croat) allies. It was clear from these sources to MI3 that: "This anxiety on the part of the Germans testifies to the skill of the Partisans in evading 'mopping up' even when a very considerable Axis force (seven divisions, with air support) is engaged on a methodical operation against them." The Partisans were fighting hard and against overwhelming odds – three Italian/Croat divisions in addition to four German and the full might of the Luftwaffe.

In March 1943 the second phase of *Fall Weiss* began. ULTRA revealed that the Italians were using Cetniks to fight against the Partisans – crystal clear evidence that Mihailovic and the Cetniks were actively collaborating with the Italian part of the Axis occupation forces. This, MI3 learned, was infuriating the Germans, who at this stage in the war regarded all Yugoslav guerrilla groups, whether Cetnik or Partisan, as hostile forces.

This complicated British policy – which group was really fighting whom? As Talbot Rice told his superiors:

> Partisan resistance continues to be strong, and their threat to the bauxite zone is unabated. The introduction into the already complex situation of Cetniks who are prepared to fight Germans, Croats and Partisans alike while preserving their understanding with the Italians, opens up every kind of possibility.

The earlier policy of backing the Cetniks now seemed to be unwise.

By the middle of March the Germans had decided to attack the Cetniks as well, a task made easier by the fact that they had managed to break the Cetnik codes; never of course realising that the British had broken ULTRA!

As the Director of Military Intelligence then wrote to the Chief of the Imperial General Staff Sir Alan Brooke on 17 March: "A remarkable situation or series of situations appears to be developing in Yugoslavia … In this confused picture two things seem clear (a) that the hands of all are against the Partisans and that (b) German-Italian relations are not good."

(In fact, on the latter point, the Germans were clearly very worried about the impending Italian collapse not just in Yugoslavia but elsewhere, so that contingency plans were put into place in case Italy surrendered to the Allies: Operation *Asche*. Needless to say, ULTRA picked up all of this as well.)

Again the significance of ULTRA intelligence from Yugoslavia cannot be overestimated. This was not Communist-mole inspired conspiratorial plotting from Cairo but clear evidence from ULTRA of the realities on the ground: the Partisans were the people fighting Britain's enemy the Germans. Communists such as Klugmann in Cairo could boast all they wanted, and delude conspiracy theory enthusiasts decades later that they were the hidden puppet masters manipulating the strings and fooling Churchill. But their bragging was pure fiction. Churchill knew the truth the information was from MI3 in London and from the ULTRA material from Bletchley, his beloved golden eggs.

In the words of the official history of British intelligence:

> In the course of these operations the Enigma left no doubt that the fighting value of the Cetniks was greatly inferior to that of Tito's Partisans.

Therefore, it was not some braggadocious self-promoting Communist in SOE Cairo but no less than the Director of Military Intelligence in London writing to the Chiefs of Staff who first started the epic shift in British policy, from Mihailovic's compromised Cetniks to Tito's unquestionably Communist but brave Partisans, when he told Brooke:

> Pending … further clarification regarding both Mihailovic's health and attitude towards us, and the outcome of various Axis operations in Yugoslavia, it is impossible to advise whether or not we should stick to our present policy of supporting Mihailovic and not the Partisans.

This was genuine evidence, ideologically untainted, and based entirely on military exigencies and criteria. While revisionists such as Peter

Batty have bemoaned the politically naïve British generals ignoring the future balance of power in Yugoslavia at the expense of short-term military gain for the Allies, what on earth were British commanders fighting an existential war against Nazi Germany supposed to do? Patriotism – to the United Kingdom – surely gave no option other than the one that Churchill's generals took.

And it is this that forms the background to the decision to take what Deakin and SOE were observing on the ground very seriously. All SOE knew from Bailey's visit to Mihailovic is that the Cetniks were demanding vast amounts of valuable British supplies and doing virtually nothing against the Germans.

When Deakin landed he was in the midst of a new massive German operation against the Partisans, designed to wipe them out: *Fall Schwarz*.

As we saw in Deakin's account, being under constant German attack was a truly scary experience. But what impressed the military back in London were the casualty figures, which Talbot Rice analysed in July, when *Fall Schwarz* was over. According to ULTRA, that is of course intercepts from *German* military sources, the Germans themselves had lost over 1,000 of their own forces, Partisan casualties mounted to at least 12,000-13,000, and Cetnik losses to precisely 17 people. Contrasting the 17 Cetniks with the 12,000-plus Partisans made it abundantly obvious who was bearing the brunt of the campaign against the Axis.

So, when SOE Cairo began to make its case, it was in this context that military intelligence, the Chiefs of Staff and Churchill himself listened to them. As Talbot Rice noticed in August, after Tito and the Partisans had managed to escape, Mihailovic and the Cetniks had done almost nothing:

> SOE are doubtful whether [Mihailovic] will ever be prepared to fight the Germans, even if the Italians collapse; and they propose in future to give their support mainly to the Partisans ... In view of [Mihailovic's] consistently unsatisfactory attitude we feel that SOE are probably justified from a military point of view in taking their present line.

This was, we must note, a military point of view. However, MI3 – and this is important once more to rebut the conspiracy theorists – and the rest of British military intelligence did not forget the political complexion of most of the Partisans, especially its leadership under Tito. As Talbot

Rice reminded everyone in an MI3 memorandum in September, when the repercussions of the Italian collapse for the Balkans were becoming clearer:

> The heroes of this period are undoubtedly the Partisans, who, taken unaware by the Italian armistice, were yet able to revise their strategy overnight and launch a successful drive to the coast. Except for [some ...] ports they succeeded in getting there first and now hold long stretches of coast and the principal islands ... Partisan military effort deserves all the support that we can give it. But their political aims are no less dangerous than those of EAM in Greece.

In other words, the British were not duped politically by Tito or for that matter by overtly Communist SOE staff in Cairo. They knew full well the implications of the Partisans, every bit as much as they were of the equally Communist EAM guerrillas over the border in Greece. They were making a military choice with their eyes politically wide open. In Yugoslavia Churchill chose the Communist Partisans; in Greece he opposed their ideological equivalents the EAM.

As MI3 noted, at the same time that Fitzroy Maclean was landing in Yugoslavia with the Partisans on his famous mission, it was obvious to notice, by analysing ULTRA, that one of the main reasons for Tito's success was that he was persuading Serbs and Croats to put aside their political differences and fight side by side against the common German enemy – whereas Mihailovic, a Serb nationalist, was doing or accomplishing nothing.

So how about direct German/Cetnik collaboration? Here, while Deakin's discoveries of such mutual aid made an impact, the precise ULTRA evidence did not exist. There was still room for doubt. While there was evidence that Mihailovic was happy to talk to his fellow Serbs in Belgrade, no less than Hitler's Foreign Minister, Ribbentrop, made clear to the quisling Nedic government there, that Mihailovic and all his followers remained very much the enemy.

Part of the reason for this is that the Germans simply wanted to wipe out all resistance groups, and this still included the Cetniks as well as the Partisans. But while the evidence of treason by Mihailovic remained uncertain, this was by no means the case with others. In 22 November ULTRA decrypted the treaty signed by the German commander in the south-east with Major Voja Lukacevic, one of the top Cetnik leaders. In return for not being wiped out by the Wehrmacht, Lukacevic agreed to cease all action against the Germans in southern Serbia, and to engage in joint Wehrmacht/Cetnik operations against the Partisans. As Bletchley decrypt historian John Cripps has noted, a "full copy of the treaty was sent to Churchill".

This is important, for as Cripps rightly goes on to explain, when the Prime Minister sent Maclean as his personal envoy to Tito, Maclean had not heard of the Lukacevic betrayal to the Germans when he formulated his famous report – but Churchill had. So, when the Prime Minister and the Chiefs of Staff (and MI3) read Maclean's *magnum opus* they were doing so in the light of the Bletchley decrypts showing major Cetnik collaboration with the Germans. When Maclean revealed what he knew of such links in general, it was not Partisan disinformation he was being deceived into hearing but confirmation on the ground of what ULTRA had *already* shown to be true to Churchill, even if the precise details of the Cetnik betrayal had not reached Tito's headquarters.

It is interesting that the truth as revealed by ULTRA shows that the growing Cetnik/Nazi/Nedic collaboration was in fact actively recruiting many Serbs. One of the most controversial episodes is the request made by Mihailovic to ask Major Radoslav Djuric, one of the key commanders in southern Serbia, to start collaboration with the Nedic regime. David Martin in his book rejects that Mihailovic ever asked for this – Djuric in fact refused unless ordered to do so by King Peter himself – but once again the decrypts are abundantly clear.

Significantly, Churchill received MI3 reports personally and direct from the Chief of the Imperial General Staff, Sir Alan Brooke. An example of this comes in now to our chronological look at the changing views of MI3 about events in the Balkans: the report they wrote for Churchill and Brooke on 27 October 1943, about how events were unfolding in Yugoslavia, and which was given by Brooke to Churchill the very next day. As always, the Prime Minister was given accompanying maps. It is significant that this particular file is in PREM3/510/9 in The National Archives in Kew, and anyone looking at Churchill's files as wartime leader could see full well that MI3 was briefing him and the key Army chiefs on a regular basis, and that it was this that was the source of Churchill's decision making along with the Chiefs of Staff. The revelations in this book are therefore those that could easily have been mentioned before, outside of the scholarly community.

MI3 was able to tell Brooke and Churchill that it was the Partisans who were able to take full advantage of the Italian surrender. As MI3 wrote:

With Italy's capitulation, six Italian divisions were disarmed by the Partisans, while two more went to the side of the guerrillas and are now co-operating with them. The Partisan potential was thus considerably increased.

Not only that, but it was also then apparent that as a result the Partisans had seized the strategic advantage:

At the same time, six further Italian divisions became ineffective, and with the Axis position thus weakened, the Partisans were able to take the initiative over practically all Yugoslavia.

The exact details, along with maps, were provided for Churchill by MI3. Large swathes of Yugoslavia were now under Partisan control. Not only that but the initiative taken by Tito in seizing so much Italian military hardware and territory changed the internal balance in the resistance to the Axis on the ground. Note that this was Partisan success and not related to British policy or to SOE: simply that Tito had the strategic vision to take advantage of the rapidly changing new climate created by the Italian collapse. In terms of the relationship between the Cetniks and Partisans, MI3 observed, for example:

In Montenegro new bands were organised, in territory which had hitherto been in the sphere of Mihailovic. In this area, the Partisans have in some cases established themselves peacefully, the followers of Mihailovic deserting to them as representing a more active body; in other cases they have come into open conflict with Mihailovic Cetniks.

This was a local decision made by patriotic Yugoslavs, better to fight the hated German invaders, the latter of which were naturally furious at Partisan expansion at Axis expense. This of course is why people such as Maclean found as they did; not subtle Communist misinformation at the expense of the brave Cetniks, but a summary of the plainly obvious facts on the ground, that guerrilla groups who wanted to take the battle to the Germans realised that only by joining with the Partisans would this be feasible and militarily possible.

Here again what MI3 discovered told Churchill all he needed to know. While some German counter-offensives proved successful, others were not. The Partisans now controlled much of the coast, for example, and posed a severe threat across all different parts of the country to the railway networks upon which the Wehrmacht relied.

Once again Montenegro proved symbolic of the changes, after the German attempts to regain lost territory petered out. As MI3 observed:

> Practically all the towns of the interior are in Partisan hands, and they appear to be firmly established there. Cetnik forces formerly in the area have in the main either been absorbed or have disappeared, with the exception of small bodies which are engaged against the Partisans. Mihailovic's influence in this area has completely declined, and even in Serbia proper Partisan popularity seems to be increasing. Mihailovic's forces remain inactive.

This could not be starker. There was now no need for the idea put forward by Bailey of SOE and others earlier in the year that the Partisans and Cetniks divide up resistance to the Axis between them. Now the Partisans were increasingly controlling the resistance even in the former Cetnik heartland of Serbia itself. While they were risking their lives to fight the Germans, *"Mihailovic's forces remain inactive"* and, as we see from the MI3 report, some of them were in fact fighting not the German enemy but their fellow Yugoslavs, the Partisans.

As MI3 summarised the extraordinary change in military balance between 8 and 27 October and slightly longer (in a report given to Churchill himself):

> In brief, active fighting has been in progress over the whole country for the last six weeks. There have been gains and losses on both sides, but on balance the Partisans have been markedly successful. Since 8 October (when the last special map was prepared for the Prime Minister) they have captured some 50 towns, and have kept interrupted more or less continuously practically all the rail routes and many of the roads of northern and central Yugoslavia.

What could be clearer? This quote is from War Office files, detailing MI3 reports and contained in the Deakin archives at Churchill College. But the WO originals and the PREM copies sent to the Prime Minister are all easily accessible at The National Archives in London.

MI3 concluded that with enough ammunition, the Partisans could achieve yet more still and keep the German lines of communication permanently cut. As their report to Brooke and thence Churchill ended:

> At present five to six German divisions are being contained in North-Eastern Italy and ten divisions in Yugoslavia itself. It may eventually be possible for the Germans to reduce the size of the former by one/two divisions, but it is most improbable that the latter commitment could be reduced; indeed if control of the lines of communication is to be regained, a larger concentration of forces in the area would probably become essential.

In other words, the Partisans, whom MI3 estimated at around 180,000 strong, would be tying down even more German divisions than they were already, something that someone in Churchill's office, if not Churchill himself, noted in the margin of the memorandum. No wonder that the Prime Minister and Chiefs of Staff were looking favourably on Tito and his Partisans.

The same date MO4 of the War Office reported to Sir Alan Brooke and to their colleagues at MI3 (with a copy to Churchill) about events in the Eastern Mediterranean. Partisans, they reported, had captured the town of Sanski Most (near Banja Luka in Bosnia). At the request of Churchill's staff, they added that an entire Croat (Ustase) regiment, commanded by German officers had been captured by the Partisans, with over 100 killed and also that "the booty was considerable and included over 1000 rifles and 66 LMGs".

But in Montenegro, MI3 reports were confirmed:

> In Montenegro German forces, assisted by Cetniks (followers of General Mihailovic) and Fascists have begun an offensive against the Partisans and the remnants of two Italian divisions who decided to resist the Germans. 300 of the enemy are reported (by a British Liaison Officer) to have been killed in the fighting ... some ten miles North of the Albanian frontier.

This too was incontrovertible evidence of Cetnik treachery, and this is War Office evidence, people with access to all the information.

To revert to the ULTRA narrative, when the code-breakers at Bletchley decrypted Mihailovic's order of 13 November to launch a major offensive against the Partisans, it was obvious to everyone in

London where Mihailovic's priorities lay. This enraged patriotic pro-Allied anti-German Cetniks, who now refused an order to kill fellow Yugoslavs to the advantage of the Nazis. Such loyal Serbs now began to defect in droves to the Partisans, considering Tito and his soldiers as what MI3 referred to as the "more active body".

Then on top of all this, on 19/20 November Britain heard that the Cetniks had allowed the 1st Panzer Division to be transported by rail from Greece to the Eastern Front in the USSR. This was through Cetnik territory, yet Mihailovic and his forces had done nothing to sabotage their passage. A report sent to Churchill suggested that this meant that there was now a "very strong case" for Britain "ceasing to supply" Mihailovic at all, an argument "made even stronger" by Mihailovic's utter inactivity in stopping the 1st Panzer.

This was the key difference. Mihailovic was letting Germans pass by unmolested, whereas the Partisans were actively engaged in fighting the Wehrmacht precisely upon such lines. Do we wonder why Britain looked more favourably upon Tito than on Mihailovic?

The data provided by MI3 enabled Britain to deal vigorously with the Royal Yugoslav government in exile. Anthony Eden, the Foreign Secretary, met up in Cairo with the exiles there around the time much of the MI3 material was coming in. The King was willing to contemplate pressure on the Cetniks actually to do something, but not the Yugoslav Prime Minister. As Eden told young King Peter on possible Soviet involvement in Balkan issues: "I explained that our difficulty was that the Russians would no doubt maintain that while Tito was fighting the Germans [Mihailovic] was not doing so. The King agreed."

The Prime Minister, however, did not, and so Eden had to point out the facts to him, which he possessed thanks to the information from MI3. When the former tried to maintain, as revisionists have done since, that the real fight was from Mihailovic, Eden was able to say:

> I told him that our information did not bear out this statement … Civil war in Yugoslavia now, for which we appeared to be rapidly heading, would benefit no-one but the Germans. The Yugoslav Prime Minister appeared to be chiefly anxious that M [Mihailovic] should conserve his resources for the post-German era.

By November intelligence was reaching Churchill through his aide Major Morton that Mihailovic and the quisling Nedic Government in Belgrade were collaborating in the area of Nis. The report – which Churchill received – was unambiguous, and is in his PREM files. It made clear that "collaboration with Nedic is impossible to condone. It is only one step from collaboration with the Germans themselves, and a very small step at that". Indeed it was the opinion of no less than the British Commander in Chief Middle East that the United Kingdom should "leave Mihailovic to rot and fall off the branch", but at this stage "not to push him off". Needless to say, a soldier's bluntness did not endear itself to the Foreign Office who announced that they were "not attracted" by such a statement. But not long later, as we shall see, the British Government, at Churchill's bidding, did indeed push Mihailovic and his Cetniks off the branch.

Significantly not all Cetniks were pro-Mihailovic: already some were thinking of deserting the Serb military leader and actually taking the fight to the Germans. SOE discovered that Djuric, the Cetnik commander in the area of Pristina, had heard conclusively that "Mihailovic had ordered Djuric to collaborate with Nedic Government in action against Partisans". However, these Cetniks were horrified at such a request. So SOE reported that "Djuric despite Mihailovic's order to contrary has already contacted local Partisans", although Djuric himself did not want openly to disobey Mihailovic.

Djuric has had a bad press. Pro-Mihailovic British writer Michael Lees called him "the ultimate nasty piece of work". Djuric was promoted by Tito, which earned him the suspicion of revisionist writers such as Peter Batty. Even Fitzroy Maclean wrote of him in *Eastern Approaches*:

> This amusing, somewhat cynical character seemed to have been received by the Partisans with open arms, although in the past he had always been known, even among the Cetniks, for the ruthless brutality with which he had waged the war against them.

But the key thing is that thousands of ordinary Cetniks were going over to the Partisans, not out of ideology but of patriotism, a desire actually to fight Germans. Djuric may indeed have been a man of violence but plenty of simple Yugoslavs wanted no more than to join an army that would liberate their country.

Through Sigint and MI3 the Deputy Director of Military Intelligence was able to brief Churchill's Chief of Staff, General Pug Ismay, about exactly where in Yugoslavia that Cetniks and Germans were actively collaborating. At this stage British Military intelligence did not want to swear blind that Mihailovic was actively involved in such efforts himself. But it was clear that ULTRA decrypts showed that in Kotor and the Sanjak such collaboration was demonstrably active.

All this caused despair among the British diplomats accredited to the Royal Yugoslav government in exile. As they wrote to the Foreign Office (with a copy to Churchill) that if this was verified, "it would put Mihailovic in a very different light ... On the military side, there would be an overwhelming case on security grounds for abandoning the attempt to make Mihailovic carry out a particular operation and a very strong case for ceasing to supply him." Even the diplomats knew that Mihailovic had given unfettered freedom of movement to the German 1st Panzer and this was without knowledge of the ULTRA confirmation.

Then at the beginning of December 1943, the Director of Military Intelligence wrote that Enigma decrypt intelligence had come up with the killer evidence – Mihailovic and the Cetniks were not merely inactive, but were in fact collaborating with the quisling Serbian regime of Nedic in Belgrade. Serbian nationalist loyalty was clearly trumping hostility to Germany.

He was not only talking to the Nedic regime in Belgrade. For there was: "an Abwehr signal of 1 December which reported that Mihailovic was negotiating with the SS in Zagreb."

This, from a British viewpoint, was sheer treachery. However Communist Tito might be, there was no question but to back him and not the Cetniks. Soon ULTRA was giving copious evidence of Cetnik bands loyal to Mihailovic "fighting with Nedic's forces and the German army against the Partisans in Croatia, Serbia and Dalmatia", with further Sigint reports being decrypted at Bletchley on 14 December.

Remember, this is ULTRA decrypt evidence passed on to Churchill via MI3 and Bletchley Park. This was direct proof. As Bletchley historian John Cripps has written, "Sigint had provided the facts which persuaded Churchill, on military grounds and military grounds alone, to chose Tito in place of Mihailovic." This article was published in 2001, but in revisionist accounts trying to excuse Mihailovic there is no sign of it in any bibliography.

Military intelligence was unequivocally clear. By looking at how MI3's views change as a result of the ULTRA signals intelligence we can also see why they changed their minds over the course of about eighteen months, and the evidence upon which that shift was made. No one was hoodwinking them or bluffing them into abandoning the Cetniks for a devious and scheming Tito. The military facts on the ground spoke for themselves. It is as simple as that.

As Cripps has put it, in "the space of six months, the evidence from Sigint had completely changed the view of Talbot Rice, and MI3b". This had been reinforced as early as July 1995, in a statement in *Intelligence and National Security* by Ralph Bennett, who worked in Hut 3 at Bletchley Park, Sir William Deakin, of whom we know much already, Sir David Hunt, who was an intelligence officer for Field Marshal Alexander during the war and had full ULTRA access, and Sir Peter Wilkinson, who was with SOE during this time.

They knew that on 1 November 1943, the German Commander in Chief South-East told both Hitler and the German High Command that "Tito is our most dangerous enemy", a statement that, through its ULTRA decrypt, reached Churchill, MI3 and the Chief of Staff in London. Significantly, the four of them and Sir Sandy Glen (then in Naval Intelligence and linked during the war to both SOE and SIS) all agreed that:

> In our opinion the reason for the change in sides can be amply demonstrated from German evidence available at the time ...
> that is to say, by a simple calculation of military advantage.

Churchill wrote in his wartime memoirs that at this point he was thoroughly persuaded "by all reports received ... [that Mihailovic himself was] in active collaboration with the Germans".

So their minds were changed. But how could this be put before the exiled King Peter, in whom Churchill still placed some forlorn hope, without making use of the ULTRA material that proved the British case beyond peradventure?

Deakin had to write the crucial memorandum for Churchill to use, and how he did his best to fulfil this difficult requirement, will be dealt with in another chapter. But remember it was not Deakin's evidence that turned the tide, but the subject of this chapter – ULTRA Sigint decrypts and the reports of MI3.

Chapter 6

Bailey and the Mihailovic Bombshell

Christening speeches are usually best forgotten, but on 28 February 1943, the Cetnik leader, Mihailovic, delivered a rant at one in the town of Lopovo that changed the course of history. (The official history of SOE is wrong to say that he spoke at a wedding – but it was a religious ceremony with other Cetnik leaders present, not that the exact venue matters.)

What did he say? According to SOE's Colonel Bill Bailey, Mihailovic proclaimed:

> As long as the Italians remained his sole adequate source of benefit and assistance generally, nothing the Allies could do would make him change his attitude towards them. His enemies were the Partisans, the Ustashi, the Moslems and the Croats. When he had dealt with them, he would turn to the Italians and the Germans. In conclusion, he said that he needed no further contact with the western democracies whose sole aim was to win the war at the expense of others.

Bailey was there himself, and the words of the speech were uncontested, since everyone accepted them as being genuine, including Mihailovic himself and the Yugoslav Royal government in exile. So angry was Mihailovic at Bailey for reporting the truth, that the British officer was exiled for six weeks, so that as Mackenzie, the in-house SOE historian, was right to say, policy towards Mihailovic was then taken without a British presence at Cetnik headquarters.

The Foreign Office received Bailey's report, and in their protest to the exiled Yugoslav authorities in London, they explained how Mihailovic in his tirade against the British had proclaimed that the Serbs were "completely friendless" and the "English were now fighting to the last Serb in Yugoslavia". No arms were getting through, so Serbs were now dying. The Allies were consumed with a "lust for fraud" and any friendship they might show to the Partisans would expose them as hypocrites.

On 11 March Churchill received details via ULTRA Sigint, in his yellow box, and returned it to 'C', the head of SIS. Whitehall was now put to work to find a solution for the treacherous anti-British outburst from Mihailovic. This was at the very highest levels of the Government, with Churchill and the Permanent Under Secretary at the Foreign Office – who was privy to ULTRA material – all involved in the deliberations.

To say that King Peter's ministers were embarrassed by this would be an understatement. They were horrified and wrote sternly to Mihailovic to tell him and in no uncertain terms. But at the same time, he was the official Yugoslav Minister of War. Yet however bad they felt, nothing officially changed, something not lost on the British.

People have argued to and fro about what on earth Mihailovic hoped to gain from this tirade. Sympathisers have suggested that he was fed up with the paucity of supplies – something as we shall see that the British acknowledged themselves in the discussions that followed. But here there is an irony. Until southern Italy was under Allied control, getting supplies to Yugoslavia was difficult. With the invasion and then successful conquest of Sicily and southern Italy a few months later, this became easier; but just at the very time when Mihailovic's stonewalling tactics enraged British opinion and turned them towards Tito and the Partisans, Mihailovic, on 28 February, also started to shift his opinion against the United Kingdom.

However, Mackenzie is probably right when he re-considered the issue just after the war:

> When he made the speech, Mihailovic calculated perhaps
> that the Partisans would shortly be eliminated by the Axis
> and that a little later the Axis would be eliminated in its turn,
> leaving him as the arbiter of the situation.

It seems, Mackenzie added, that Mihailovic thought little of Bailey – the mirror image of the contempt that the SOE Liaison officers had for the Serbian general and the fighting prowess of Cetnik forces. BBC confusion about which guerrilla group did what in Yugoslavia also did not help; as the official history rightly goes on to say:

> But this was the turning point in his [Mihailovic's] relations with the British: after this incident he broke contact with Bailey... [as above, for six weeks] while the battle with the Partisans was in progress on the Neretva front, and in the interval there was a decisive turn in British policy.

Now we know more than Mackenzie did, with our knowledge of ULTRA and the Bletchley decrypts, and the reports of MI3, we can add that seldom was truer a word written. Deakin, who discovered about ULTRA afterwards, considered that the issue of supplies was a ruse, as what it really amounted to was to give Mihailovic "the main pretext for collaboration with the Italians as an urgent alternative source of military aid against the Communists". Either way, Mihailovic's outburst was both treacherous and inexcusable.

Therefore, and not unsurprisingly, Churchill was disgusted. Officially speaking, in his protest to the government in exile, he told them that Britain was "becoming seriously disturbed ... and increasingly apprehensive". Privately via ULTRA, the Prime Minister was already beginning to hear of Cetnik/Axis collaboration, especially with the Italians. As he warned:

> You will, I am sure, appreciate that unless General Mihailovic is prepared to change his policy both towards the Italian enemy and towards his Yugoslav compatriots who are resisting the enemy it may well prove necessary for His Majesty's Government to revise their present policy of favouring General Mihailovic to the exclusion of the other resistance movements in Yugoslavia.

This was of course in fact only the Partisans, people who as far as Churchill were concerned were "men who at this very moment are fighting and giving their lives to free his [Mihailovic's] country from the foreigner's yoke", something that the Cetniks were singularly failing to do.

Churchill could not, of course, say that this was Sigint evidence from ULTRA, though that is precisely what it was. It should be noted that this was the London perspective, based upon decrypts, acting in unity with the SOE reports on the ground, in this case from Bailey. No Communist conspirator in Cairo was anywhere near the decision-making process, and, furthermore, this was entirely a Cetnik own goal; their own leader attacking the British at the same time as glorying in collaboration with Britain's wartime Axis enemies.

Yet the key factor that so many of the conspiracy theorists overlook, is that Churchill was the British Prime Minister naturally putting his own country's interests and those of the Allies first – you would hardly expect him to do otherwise; as he wrote:

> His Majesty's Government cannot ignore this outburst, nor accept without explanation and without protest a policy totally at variance with their own. They could never justify to the British public or to their other Allies their continued support of a movement, the leader of which does not scruple publicly to declare that their enemies are his allies – whether temporary or permanent is immaterial – and that his enemies are not the German and Italian invaders of his country, but his fellow Yugoslavs and chief among them men who at this very moment are fighting and giving their lives to free his country from the foreigners' yoke.

To understand this reaction is critical to our whole book. Britain was fighting the Nazis – and at this stage in 1943 their Axis ally Italy as well. This is what the war was all about. How could it possibly be different? For the core of the conspiracy/revisionist argument is that Britain under Churchill allowed Communists to take power in Yugoslavia when the Allies should have stayed loyal to their original Yugoslav protégé, Mihailovic.

Our book argues elsewhere that the notion that the Cetniks could in fact have prevailed in Yugoslavia, which is the crux of the revisionist argument, is historical wishful thinking and surely strategic fantasy of the highest order? But if Mihailovic complained about not getting British munitions, and then in effect makes it clear that such armaments will be used not to attack Germans and Italians but rather other Yugoslavs – Tito and the Partisans – to get military advantage in a civil war once the Germans had gone, then he was surely deluded at the very least on how the British would all too naturally react.

Several brave SOE operatives were parachuted into Yugoslavia into Cetnik-controlled areas to find out what in fact was going on – especially in the light of Bailey's banishment from Mihailovic's presence.

One of them was Major Neil Selby who was dropped into Western Serbia on 23 May 1943, the same month in which Deakin had the great good luck of landing in Partisan territory instead.

By August, Deakin recalls, Selby had discovered that the local Cetniks were more "pro-Fascist than pro-Allied". This led him to decide that if he was going to be of proper help, the best course of action would be to try to get to Partisan-controlled countryside, and therefore "do more in one week than all I have done in months".

Alas en route he was captured by "Serb collaborationist troops, and handed over to the Germans". He was a truly heroic individual. When in Gestapo HQ in Belgrade, he shot two SS Guards, before being murdered by them as he tried to escape. Other intrepid SOE operatives sent to Mihailovic territory met similar sticky ends almost as soon as they landed, with five British officers being slain in May 1943 by the forces of Germany's ally, Bulgaria.

As Bill Bailey shared with SOE in messages that got back to London, the situation with Mihailovic was not encouraging:

> The fact that he is willing to compromise himself in order to defeat the Partisans is a salient demonstration of the fear and hatred felt for them. He trusts that the general joy and relief at the end of the war will conceal and pardon his misdeeds.

From an internal Yugoslav perspective – who would control the country after the Axis had been defeated – one can just about see Mihailovic's point of view, as have many writers in sympathy with him ever since. But from a British viewpoint the whole notion is surely fantastical. Germany was Britain's mortal enemy, whose defeat was the absolute and utterly non-negotiable object of the war. Churchill therefore merely reflected the opinions of his countrymen.

The British *political* dilemma was fully discussed at the highest levels, however. As Sir Alexander Cadogan wrote to the Prime Minister, when Bailey's message via SOE arrived in Whitehall:

> Our policy hitherto has been based on the argument that, whereas it may be in our short-term interest to transfer our support from Mihailovic, who is doing next to nothing to help fight the war, to the Partisans, who are offering active resistance to the enemy, our long-term interests demand continued support of Mihailovic, not only in order to back up

King Peter and the present Yugoslav Government but also in order to have an armed force in existence to prevent anarchy and Communist chaos in Yugoslavia on the withdrawal of the Axis.

This was therefore British policy in March. As we shall see, the military situation on the ground and the increased ability of the Allies to supply guerrillas in Yugoslavia once bases in southern Italy became available over the summer, was to change perspectives. This was a slow process, though, as the MI3 discussions make plain elsewhere in this book.

The Secret History of SOE summarises the debates happening in London after Bailey first wrote his views on partitioning support for the various guerrilla groups between different parts of the country. As Sir Orme Sargent, the great sage of the Foreign Office, wrote, there were four options:

a) Unconditional support to Tito
b) Unconditional support to Mihailovic
c) Drift
d) Equal support for both parties

The balance was now swinging towards course (d) but the decision was hedged a little [by Sir Orme Sargent] for the present.

Britain's dilemma is reflected in the reply that Churchill wrote to Cadogan, on 29 March, along with the British quandary that, at that stage in the war, there was logistically very little that the Allies could do to drop supplies by air to anyone, let alone the Cetniks, in Yugoslavia:

I agree that Mihailovic's attitude is intolerable. At the same time, it is true that we can do practically nothing for him and his people, and he might naturally ask himself how he may keep alive … He is certainly maltreating us, but I believe he is also double-crossing the Italians, and it is not much use preaching to the "toad beneath the harrow".

What Cadogan proposed to Churchill would change everything. Being a diplomat, he cautiously referred to the "situation in Yugoslavia" as "very unsatisfactory". Furthermore, as for Mihailovic: "all his energies have for the past many months been devoted to waging war against

83

the Partisans". Like the Prime Minister, Cadogan knew from the "most secret document" they had both seen that in this civil war in Yugoslavia Mihailovic's "forces are working in close collaboration with the Italians".

Cadogan knew full well that the Partisans were Communists: it did not need conspiracies in Cairo to try to hide this. Nor did it require Klugmann, plotting near the pyramids, to get Britain to send a mission to Tito, but the very highest echelons of the British Government in London itself.

For as Cadogan, he suggested to Churchill on 23 March:

> We have now decided as an experiment to establish contact if possible with Partisan elements in Croatia and Slovenia through SOE. It is not going to be easy to do so, but if we can learn what is going on in these areas, we shall be able to judge whether we ought to send material assistance to one or another of these independent bands.

The irony was that it was SOE in London, and SIS (MI6) and its leader C, Sir Stewart Menzies, who wanted to keep contact with Mihailovic "notwithstanding his misbehaviour". But the fact that the Cetnik leader was now denouncing the British and overtly colluding with the Axis was something that, as Cadogan ruminated, had "clearly brought things to a head".

So please note: it was Mihailovic's own priorities, i.e. the civil war over fighting the Germans, and his anti-British tirades, that set in motion the discussion in London that was to lead to his being dropped at the end of the year, exclusively in favour of Tito's Partisans. No one in London was under any false apprehension that Tito himself was a Communist, with all the political implications that flowed from that fact.

The Foreign Office had, before the Mihailovic outburst, been essentially pro-Mihailovic, as revisionist writers love to show in quoting memoranda by Cetnik-sympathetic diplomats, most of whom, it should be said, were not cleared for ULTRA.

Churchill, in May 1943, was away having a conference with Roosevelt. Eden therefore sent him a Most Secret Cipher Telegram to update the Prime Minister with how the Foreign Office's thinking had begun to develop following Mihailovic's outburst. It had become apparent to Eden and the diplomats that the Mihailovic policy of civil war with the Partisans and active collaboration with the Axis Italians was not going to change and that even the thinking of the Yugoslav Royal government in exile was "woolly and not entirely convincing". Both the Chiefs of Staff and SOE in London recognised that things had to change, and that Mihailovic should be given tests if British support for him were to continue.

These were:

1) The aim of all his policy must be resistance to the Axis.
2) For this purpose, the closest collaboration with our own military authorities (to be maintained through Colonel Bailey) is essential.
3) All collaboration with the Italians must now cease; nor must there be any contact or collaboration with Nedic.
4) Special efforts must be maintained to co-operate with all other guerilla [sic] groups in Croatia and Slovenia.
5) Every effort must be made to reach agreement with the Partisans and no operations taken against them except in self-defence. In return for acceptance of these five points we offer Mihailovic our maximum moral and material support.

No one could argue from this that the British did not give Mihailovic a full chance. As Eden ended by reminding the Prime Minister, it was now up to Mihailovic to prove himself or face the consequences:

> If Mihailovic accepts these conditions, then we shall all be in a position to develop our collaboration on an ever increasing scale. If on the other hand he rejects them, we shall at least know where we stand, and shall have to revise our policy accordingly.

This is vital, as it was Mihailovic's own reactions and inactions that determined British policy rather than imaginary conspiracies in Cairo. Had he even at this late stage repented, things could have been different. But he did not and they were not. How Britain could realistically have supported both the Cetniks and the Partisans is an interesting question but also a moot point, as the issue never arose. Mihailovic stayed the same, the Partisans continued to fight the Germans, and both ULTRA decrypts at Bletchley and MI3 reports from both Sigint and other sources tracked both guerrilla groups accordingly.

On 29 May, however, the British Commander in Chief Middle East, General Wilson, took matters into his own hands. Here Deakin might be right to imply that in effect the Army was saying that politics did not matter, all that counted was the *military* imperative. This became known as the "Ibar telegram" after the strategic river in Yugoslavia where much of the fighting was taking place.

General "Jumbo" Wilson's frustration, and that of the British military, can be seen very clearly in its tone, written as it was with the invasion of Sicily and the Italian mainland now very close (Operation *Husky* beginning in July):

> The war in the Mediterranean has come to a phase in which the Allied offensive can be considered imminent. It is absolutely necessary that General Mihailovic now carries out the obligations which he accepted earlier, and that he co-operates fully at this time.

The British military – Wilson would have had ULTRA access – knew full well the truth of the situation on the ground. Therefore, Wilson telegrammed Bailey what was by then very obvious:

> Mihailovic does not represent a fighting force of any importance west of Kapaonik. His units in Montenegro, Hercegovina and Bosnia are already annihilated or else in close co-operation with the Axis; it is also difficult to say that his units exist in Croatia, Slovenia and Slavonia.

Not only that, but as was then also more than plain:

> The Partisans represent a good and effective fighting force in all parts where only the quislings represent General Mihailovic.

Bailey's instructions to pass on to Mihailovic were also direct:

> You are to advise Mihailovic that the British General Headquarters in the Middle East requests that he, as an ally, stops all co-operation with the Axis and that he goes towards the east into Serbia. There he is to establish full authority and personal influence in order to continue the attacks on enemy communication lines.

This was a command from General Wilson, speaking as only one military officer could do to another. It should also be noted, that while everyone was in despair with Mihailovic, no one could claim that he was not being given a chance. Indeed, Wilson was in effect addressing a junior officer when he added: "You will advise Mihailovic that he immediately go to Kapaonik with all his faithful officers and men; if necessary he is to force through with armed forces."

Predictably, this was met with fury by Mihailovic, who told Bailey the same day that he would go into exile rather than obey a British order. Ignore it he did, as both Bletchley Park and MI3 were to discover soon, when significant numbers of German troops went totally unhindered through territory under Mihailovic's supposed control, as we see elsewhere.

Where Wilson, with the lack of political nous upon which Deakin reflects in *The Embattled Mountain*, went too far was to agree with the Bailey view of splitting the fighting into zones; one Cetnik, one Partisan. This idea might have been considered in Whitehall, but not for long. Second, the implication was that Bailey would be in effect in charge of what the Cetniks did, as Middle East GHQ's intermediary. Nobody would tell a Yugoslav what to do! This was a lesson that the British would have learned fully by the time that they were sending missions to Tito, but to a blunt soldier such as "Jumbo" Wilson, matters were a whole lot simpler. For as he concluded:

> We want you therefore to explain this to Mihailovic and to represent these decisions to him as forcefully as may be necessary, and to attempt to obtain his immediate and unequivocal action in their favour. You and the whole British mission will accompany Mihailovic to Kapaonik and ensure that his co-operation remains genuine and effective.

The key to all this was, for Wilson, that the "closest possible co-ordination of action with the Allied powers is necessary in view of future operations in Southern Europe".

As just seen, this was *Husky*, the invasion of Sicily and then Italy itself. The Italian campaign is in some ways an elephant in the room in the light of how some have approached the fighting in Yugoslavia, as if one could view the Balkans in isolation from the hundreds of thousands of British, American, French, Polish, and even Brazilian forces being sent to liberate Italy from the Axis. In fact, this is surely ludicrous, for the Balkans, the resistance in Yugoslavia in particular, were very much integrated into the whole Mediterranean strategic picture.

Again, all this was clear from Sigint and MI3's reports. No Communist cell or secret pro-Partisan conspiracy was involved in the orders stemming not from SOE but from *British* GHQ Middle East.

This is made very clear in *The Secret History of SOE*:

> As regards the 'Ibar telegram', at least, SOE Cairo were explicitly covered by the authority of the Middle East Defence Committee; and the new line was not one which SOE Cairo in its corporate capacity had advocated. The origin of the break (which was scarcely an accident) must therefore lie outside SOE in the realm of General Staff policy, which looked for immediate action and military success ... The invasion of Sicily ... was now impending, and Middle East could contribute to the battle only by action in the Balkans.

Beyond SOE, in the realm of General Staff policy, that surely summarises it all: however enthusiastically Communists and fellow-travellers in SOE Cairo might feel towards Tito, it was the soldiers who were dictating policy, not the conspirators.

But would Mihailovic take any notice? It was soon evident that he did not, since his movements, which were closely monitored in London, made this very clear. As Bailey lamented, Mihailovic and the quisling Nedic in Belgrade were for all intents and purposes joined by a common purpose: "Both are policing the country for the Axis, and conserving Serbian blood." As Deakin recalled: "British relations with Mihailovic had reached a deadlock."

As a consequence, Mihailovic was set various tasks, which he ignored. With the change of emphasis in London, as the official SOE historian makes clear, "Middle East's 'Ibar' ultimatum was cancelled", with the request to see if the Cetnik leader would agree to take action against the Germans.

The inevitable consequence of all the discussion was the suggestion from Cadogan at the Foreign Office in London that an SOE operative be sent to Tito. Churchill was at an Allied leaders' conference in Algiers in June 1943 when he discovered, via his aide on security matters, Desmond Morton, that the SOE agent sent was none other than his former research assistant Bill Deakin. Thus, contrary to Klugmann's boasts, it was emphatically not a conspiracy in Cairo that sent Deakin. It was a decision in Whitehall, and it was obvious that he was the best person in SOE to find out for Churchill who Tito was and what was going on, as would prove to be the case.

Furthermore, his mission, *Operation Typical*, was not even an exclusively SOE affair. The decision to send him on a mission came very hastily to everyone in Cairo, as it was from London the summons came not a plot by anyone of whatever political leanings in SOE Cairo. For it was first a joint mission, with Deakin representing SOE and Captain William Stuart of Military Intelligence. Both SOE and MI6 (the part for which Stuart worked) were responsible not to SOE but, and this is crucial, to GHQ Middle East, to General Wilson and the British military high command.

Stuart was no novice, being a fluent Serbo-Croat speaker, and had served in the British Consulate in Zagreb prior to the German invasion in 1941 and in military intelligence since that time. As we saw in the opening chapter, he was tragically killed not long after landing, but importantly when the mission was conceived he was, as Deakin recalls, very much in joint charge and with his own set of instructions from MI6. Indeed, Deakin remembers:

> It was therefore his [Stuart's] task to assess and report on the military situation both on the Partisans and enemy sides, whereas it was for me [Deakin] to consult with the Partisan leadership on joint operational tasks and also to convey general impressions of the strength and structure of the movement. We each had a separate radio set and W/T operator linking us with our respective stations in Cairo.

This is important. Stuart had his own chain of command and communications and no Communist officer in SOE could manipulate his reports for clandestine purposes. Stuart and Deakin were also to have completely separate ciphers.

Of course, Deakin had been sent because London wanted it, unlike, for example, a group of Canadian Croat communists who had been sent earlier under the auspices and initiative of SOE Cairo.

Deakin's line of authority was made clear in his set of instructions. He was the "liaison officer with Partisan GHQ for Yugoslavia". Critically he was told: "you will represent yourself as the nominee of GHQ Middle East, under whose orders you have been placed". This demonstrates that while being a member of SOE, he was under the soldiers, not SOE Cairo.

Deakin was told what to say to Tito and the leaders of the Partisans, to explain: "the point of view maintained by GHQ Middle East, namely, that the war in the Mediterranean had reached a stage in which Allied offensives must be considered imminent and the synchronization of the Partisan effort therefore becomes desirable". In other words, while Tito could not be told of the approach of Operation *Husky*, the British military knew precisely of such plans, and that the co-ordination of Partisan action against the Germans in order to keep as many Axis divisions in the Balkans as possible now became imperative for Allied operational reasons in Italy.

This confirms the thesis of our book, that Churchill and the British, while keen to pin down German divisions in Yugoslavia, were always thinking not just of the situation in that region but the strategic big picture of the war in the Mediterranean in general. Yugoslavia was important to enable Italy to go well. Thus, the maximum disruption in Yugoslavia was necessary, as Deakin's instructions made apparent:

> [He was] to arrange for the Partisan forces to attack specific targets on enemy lines of communication with supplies and, if necessary, British personnel provided by us; to report on the military situation in the country and advise us on the selection of targets; and to convey the wishes of GHQ Middle East, to the Partisan GHQ and to report on the point of view maintained by them.

In more modern times this would describe as "joined up thinking" or getting all our ducks in a row, so that one operational theatre against the Germans – in this case Yugoslavia – could co-ordinate with the main one in Italy.

GHQ Middle East could not tell Deakin of the ULTRA decrypts sent from London, and of the MI3 monitoring of events in the Balkans. Nor could he be privy to Foreign Office reaction to the Mihailovic outburst and the hopeless response to it of the Royal Yugoslav Government in exile. Of course, ULTRA had revealed the full extent of Cetnik/Axis collaboration, but all that vital information was behind the next set of instructions to Deakin, as is obvious:

> In dealing with British relations with General Mihailovic you will be guided by the following considerations, which you will make clear to the Partisan GHQ in suitable form. His Majesty's Government was not until recently aware that certain of Mihailovic's commanders had compounded with

the enemy. As soon as this information became available His Majesty's Government had taken steps to express its complete disagreement with General Mihailovic in continuing to maintain relations with these commanders.

This paragraph alone upends all the conspiracy theorists' notions that it was a Communist plot in SOE Cairo, and the deliberate manipulation of reports by James Klugmann from Partisan HQ via agents such as Deakin, that turned London from Mihailovic to the Partisans and hoodwinked Churchill. For the fact is that Deakin was going to Tito because London already knew of Mihailovic's double-dealing and treachery and wanted to engage with the Partisans because ULTRA decrypts and MI3's reports had shown that it was Tito and his guerrillas that were actually bothering to fight the German enemy.

At this stage, however, Britain was still open to giving Mihailovic a chance, so long as he deigned to do something to disrupt Axis ability to move troops and supplies and actually begin to fight the Germans. So Deakin was informed:

> Meanwhile GHQ Middle East is of the opinion that certain of Mihailovic's units in East and South Serbia are in a position to render service to the Allied cause by planned attacks on enemy lines of communication. It is the wish of GHQ Middle East, that nothing be done to interfere with these plans, and that they will continue to support all elements in Yugoslavia who offer resistance to the Axis. GHQ Middle East therefore welcome this opportunity of co-operating with the Partisans.

This shows, Deakin recalls, that it was realised Britain could not be taking a side in the Cetnik/Partisan internal struggle. The "strategic position of the Western Allies in the Mediterranean theatre" was what mattered. As Deakin's own reflections state:

> The intention expressed in the directive that British Middle East command were sending the present mission [Typical] was confined to the working out of co-operation with the Partisan Headquarters, and there was no hint that a proposal implied the recognition of the Partisan forces as formal allies [and] there was also no explicit instruction that I should attempt to secure Partisan agreement to co-operate with Mihailovic.

That would come in due time, as we shall see, but not when Deakin and Stuart were actually sent.

A brief parenthesis is now necessary and interesting.

In the light of *The Man Who Never Was* and Ben Macintyre's more recent book *Operation Mincemeat*, Deakin suggests that the Allies wanted the Germans to think that the Allies were launching an attack not on Sicily but on Greece. Axis lines of communication from Germany down through Yugoslavia and thence to Greece were already vital to get supplies from the Third Reich itself down to northern Africa, where until May 1943 the Allies and Axis were fighting battles such as Alamein. But if the Allies were to attack Greece, destroying Axis rail links through Yugoslavia would of course be vital. In addition, if an invasion of Greece was the Allied plan, then of course they would greatly increase their activity in Yugoslavia as a necessary prequel.

As Ben Macintyre shows us, the deception plan worked magnificently well. It was Sicily that was invaded in 1943, not Greece.

But the real-life invasion of Sicily still made Yugoslavia vital, as we see throughout this book, to pin down as many German divisions there as possible to lessen the amount of Axis troops that the Allies would face in Sicily and then in southern mainland Italy. So, either way Yugoslavia was critical.

As we now know, Deakin and Stuart were shortly thereafter parachuted to Tito's HQ, with Deakin left alive to tell their exciting tale.

SOE in London, via the Minister of Economic Warfare, Lord Selborne, kept Churchill closely in touch with Deakin's reports on the ground. Details took a while to arrive at Downing Street; it was not until 29 June that Selborne told Churchill that Deakin had survived the German bomber strafe that had killed the SIS/MI6 spy William Stuart (misspelt by Selborne as "Stewart"). It is significant that Selborne was cleared for ULTRA, so he was able to tie in Deakin's reports from the field with the ULTRA Sigint reports that both Selborne and Churchill received. Interestingly SOE gave greater credence to Deakin's casualty figures of Partisan dead than those of the Germans, whom they felt were deliberately exaggerating Partisan casualties for effect.

Churchill's reasons for wanting to see Deakin were because of reports that he was getting from SOE Cairo (dated 1 June 1943) on the situation in Yugoslavia. As Churchill was told, it was "regretted that Captain Deakin cannot attend in person as he was parachuted three days ago to Partisan GHQ". These reports were sent by Richard Casey, the eminent Australian statesman who, in 1943, was the British

Government's Minister Resident in Cairo, and the politician in charge in the wartime Coalition of events in the Middle East.

Churchill, in wanting to see Deakin, a lowly captain, was doing what he had done throughout his political career, ignoring the chain of command and going straight to the person he trusted for innate wisdom. This undercut completely London SOE and its political component, the Ministry of Economic Warfare, and also, more importantly, the Foreign Office, who thought that they were supposed to be in charge of such important issues.

Desmond Morton, Churchill's right-hand man on such issues, was equally flabbergasted, and duly wrote to the august Sir Orme Sargent of the Foreign Office, trying to explain away Churchill's *faux pas* in consulting someone as formally lowly as Deakin.

So he told Sargent:

I do not know what political event may have prompted the Prime Minister so to telegraph [to summon Deakin for his views on the SOE reports], but I do know that Captain Deakin was a friend of his in peacetime ... and is a young don at Oxford for whose judgement the Prime Minister has a respect. It is possible that the Prime Minister's telegram was prompted as much by a friendly desire to see Captain Deakin as by anything else.

Deakin clearly later saw this letter, as it is referred to in his memoirs *The Embattled Mountain*. He had in fact done no more than write to Churchill to apologise for not being in Cairo when the Prime Minister would be there, since he was about to be parachuted into Yugoslavia. And as Deakin recalled, his message to Churchill "contained no hint of high politics, or that I was being sent to Tito. But its effect was unexpected and certainly unintended."

Deakin is surely right when he remembers:

This episode seems to have prompted these reports on the development of British policy in Cairo, and by a minor footnote, the personal interest of the Prime Minister was directed at a critical moment of decision to the Yugoslav scene.

This is perhaps being too modest by Deakin, who at the time would not have known the major impact Mihailovic's outburst had made upon Churchill's thinking. While the note from his erstwhile researcher might have triggered the chain of events in considering "high policy" on Yugoslavia, that country was certainly already very much on the Prime Minister's mind. The report Churchill eventually received was devastating.

Racial differences between the three major groups in Yugoslavia – Serb, Croat and Slovene – naturally made someone as strongly Serb-identified as Mihailovic to be a truly Yugoslav leader "impossible". Nor did SOE Cairo hide Tito's Communist sympathies, or Mihailovic's "fanatical hatred" of them.

These factors, SOE was surely right to point out, made it difficult for Mihailovic to be effective throughout the country. This was a statement of the obvious, which over the course of time would become more apparent to British decision makers, seeking as they should, a group that would harass the Germans in as many parts of Yugoslavia as possible.

SOE Cairo was perhaps too unfair on him, when decrying his refusals to disrupt German lines of communication in the country because of a fear of German reprisals – everyone in Britain knew how barbaric the Wehrmacht was in savage revenge. But SOE was surely correct in saying that Mihailovic was, in essence, biding his time until the German withdrawal, so that the Serb cause would prevail after the war. This was as we have seen a constant refrain, and hard to contradict. But politically, since Mihailovic was the War Minister of the Yugoslav Royal government in exile, this created a political problem, as he represented the lawful British-recognised King. For the United Kingdom to back the rival Partisans there would, inevitably be "difficulties" with the official Yugoslav Government.

So far as SOE in Cairo was concerned, since SOE London still supported the Cetniks, Mihailovic would have to change his ways. Four requirements should then be made of him (see the five requirements given earlier in May):

a) his primary object must be resistance to the Axis and he must not fight the Partisans in Serbia, except in self-defence

b) he must break off all collaboration with the Italians and have no further contact with General Nedic, the Quisling Prime Minister in Belgrade, except with the approval of the British and Jugoslav [*sic*] Governments

c) his plans for resistance must be co-ordinated with the requirements of [the British] C-in-C Mid East
d) he must make special effort to co-operated with the Croat and Slovene Partisans.

This was all arguably very fair, if Mihailovic wanted British support, especially as everyone from London to Cairo was now realising that the fight in Yugoslavia was of strategic importance and that to supply the region by plane from liberated bases in Italy was now possible.

Bailey, as had other SOE operatives dropped into Serb/Mihailovic territory, took the view that Britain ought to support Mihailovic in areas of Serb strength, and the Partisans in those parts of the country in which the latter were stronger. The merit of this decision is that it avoided final and exclusive commitment to one side or the other. But even to support the Partisans anywhere would of course be highly controversial. Mihailovic, after all, did represent the official Government however inactive he might be against the Germans. SOE Cairo realised this: "This plan is an important departure from existing policy as it will involve giving active support to the Partisans with whom Mihajlovic [sic] has been waging civil war".

Morton, with his usual acute political antennae, realised that the SOE reports – one brief for Churchill himself (the one quoted here) and one longer and more technical – were indeed "not in line with what I understood to be Foreign Office policy" which at that stage was certainly true. But as Casey had asked Churchill to see them, Morton felt that he could not "take the responsibility of suppressing these documents altogether". While the conspiracy theorists might wish that he had, Morton was right to let Churchill see them; and with profound consequences.

But attempts at suppression there certainly were. Churchill's own Prime Ministerial files in fact contain them. As the file notes, the SOE Cairo report was regarded by those in authority as "a very odd document" and seen by them as "misleading in conclusion and recommends a course of policy opposed to that agreed by the Foreign Office, the Yugoslav Government, SOE and the Chiefs of Staff." SOE here though refers to the London headquarters, and not at all their staff in Cairo, whose views were, as we have seen, rather different. So, London therefore tried to come up with a solution of its own.

But Churchill was not easily duped, not against Mihailovic, as some revisionist books of the 1990s would have it, but in favour of what he regarded as more important than anything else – what ULTRA was telling the Government about the facts on the ground: not high policy but actual military reality.

The Middle East Defence Committee, which met in Cairo, now added its ideas to the general mix, for London to discuss. These were military men, with their own view of what SOE and Britain in general, ought to be about in the Yugoslav imbroglio.

They were under the impression that the Cetniks had suffered worse losses than was in fact the case, and the Chiefs of Staff would in reply inform Churchill of this. So, like Bailey, the MEDC wanted to split Yugoslav resistance into zones – one Cetnik and one Partisan divided by the river Ibar (described as *Ebar* in their memoranda].

But they also knew of the internal Cetnik/Partisan conflict, and of Mihailovic's priorities. So, like everyone in London, the MEDC insisted that two further considerations must be borne in mind:

e) Maximum resistance to Axis is of paramount consideration and that both Yugoslav Government and Mihailovic must be induced to place operational considerations first.

f) Partisans now most formidable anti-Axis element in Yugoslavia and our support of them therefore logical and necessary.

Even though MEDC exaggerated Mihailovic's setbacks, its overall priority was the same as London's: operational considerations first. But supporting the Partisans at all still had political repercussions, and this therefore made the final policy decision one not for Cairo, but for London.

So Churchill's Private Office, revealing that he knew full well of the existence of the SOE Cairo reports, informed both the Foreign Office and the Chiefs of Staff (who were of course using ULTRA reports and MI3's interpretation of them) as follows (using a cover phrase for ULTRA):

> The Prime Minister has asked, quite apart from the attached papers which he has not yet seen, for a two-page Report on what is happening in Yugoslavia. He wishes to know how much is being done by the Partisans and how much by General Mihailovitch [*sic*], and how many supporters each has, and he would like a map to illustrate the areas in which they both operate. The Prime Minister asked for this after reading a yellow box, and asked that the Report should be obtained "from the Intelligence Services".

'Yellow box' and "intelligence services" are both code for ULTRA; and this makes abundantly clear how and why Churchill made the decisions that he did. This therefore negates all the conspiracy theories about Klugmann, and about whether or not Brigadier Keble of SOE Cairo – the author at least nominally of the controversial report – was trying to fix things in favour of Tito and the Partisans. For even when Churchill had seen the Keble/SOE Cairo report, he, the Prime Minister, relied on the actual ground evidence supplied by ULTRA more than anything else.

Not only that, but Churchill insisted that everything be co-ordinated with the papers simultaneously "being produced by the Chiefs of Staff". This too is vital, as their views are usually discounted or even ignored by those fixated on Communists in SOE Cairo. As argued throughout this book, military strategy was more important than anything else, eventually, as we shall see, than whether or not the post-war Government of Yugoslavia would be Communist. And as the PREM files from Downing Street show, the Chiefs of Staff were as influenced by "information obtained 'from the Intelligence Services'" or ULTRA as was Churchill himself.

Nevertheless, SOE London, led by its political chief, Minister of Economic Warfare Lord Selborne, did its best to defend the existing pro-Mihailovic policy – with no less than the Foreign Office and "C" of MI6 on Selborne's side.

As the Minister told Churchill, "My sympathy is definitely with Mihailovic who has kept the flag flying since 1941." Selborne also, erroneously as it turns out, thought that the German offensive against the Partisans had wiped them out. But even allowing that this was a mistake – which it was – Selborne and the consensus of SOE London and MI6, felt that the Partisans were in effect a flash in the pan:

> I believe that the Partisans represent a spontaneous national explosion against the Axis, but they are led by Communists (mainly for accidental reasons) and I think that it is very desirable to support Mihailovic as far as we are able. I feel that COS ... have not given weight to Mihailovic's difficulties.

For Selborne, the lack of aircraft to drop supplies weighed heavily. But for Churchill, this was nonsense. As he told his personal Chief of Staff General Ismay on 22 June:

> I understood when I was last in Cairo, that an additional number of aircraft were to be made available. I consider that

at least a dozen should be placed at the disposal of the SOE authorities, and that this demand has priority even over the bombing of Germany.

That SOE operations should have priority over the bombing of Germany demonstrates just how important Churchill considered the fighting in Yugoslavia to be. Even the Foreign Office was in agreement, with Anthony Eden outlining the shift in his department's views to Churchill on 27 June. This is worth quoting, as it shows how events were causing such a major change:

> Our policy, as you are aware, has all along been to support Mihailovic to the best of our ability. It has not always been easy to justify this policy in view of Mihailovic's comparative inaction, reports of his collaboration with the Italians, his own Pan-Serb and dictatorial tendencies and his skirmishes with the Partisans.

One might well ask that with all this against him, why Britain supported him at all? Eden now explained this to the Prime Minister:

> But taking a long-term view there was no doubt that our interest lay in backing Mihailovic and thereby enabling him to preserve Yugoslavia – or at least Serbia – from chaos and anarchy when liberation comes.

Until this time, mid-1943, Britain had not had the wherewithal to send much aid. This would change, as would events on the ground, as Eden had to recognise:

> There is no doubt that it is the Partisans who have been causing the Axis the most trouble and that they now constitute a military organisation to be reckoned with. The recent Chiefs of Staff request, therefore, that sabotage and other operations by guerillas [sic] and resistance groups in the Balkans should be supported and encouraged as far as is possible induced us to reconsider our policy towards the Yugoslav Partisans.

Up until then the Foreign Office knew little, and so the feeling there was that SOE should find out what was going on at ground level. But remember, only very few in the Foreign Office had ULTRA access, and MI3, which did, reported to the Chiefs of Staff, not to the Foreign Office; and it was the Chiefs of Staff, with their MI3 and ULTRA decrypts, who were asking for the change.

Eden told Churchill that the Middle East Defence Committee supported the views of SOE agents already with Mihailovic that Yugoslavia, for resistance purposes, be split between Tito in some parts and Mihailovic in others, as we saw elsewhere. But the Chiefs of Staff wanted action.

So the considered Foreign Office consensus, as outlined by Eden to Churchill, was that first, Mihailovic could get continued support provided he carried out the sabotage operations requested by the military. Second, Partisans could be given plenty of support, provided that they did not use it for the purposes of civil war against the Cetniks. Eden also had strong reservations about the Bailey idea of partitioning Yugoslavia up for resistance purposes:

> This would in my view have strong political objections. By dividing Yugoslavia into areas and recognising certain political elements as predominant in those districts we should be taking the first step to breaking up the unity of the country which it is our policy to maintain.

This eventually would lead to support for Tito, since he was, as well as an overt Communist, a genuine *Yugoslav*, with support from across the country, in a way that a confessed pan-Serb like Mihailovic could not hope to be. But that lay in the future. The key thing is that the Foreign Office was changing its mind:

> The principal change in policy with which I hope you will agree is that we are now recommending that the Communist Partisans and the Croat guerillas [sic] should henceforth receive our military support.

In effect, the Croat guerrillas were Croat Partisans, but that small detail aside, it was London that altered British policy, not Cairo and that it was the reality of the fighting on the ground that had made the difference. It was certainly not ideology since so far as that was concerned the United Kingdom's view had hitherto been that Mihailovic was the best hope of keeping Yugoslavia preserved for when the war ended. Military factors had caused the shift in policy and, in particular, the views of the Chiefs of Staff. With all this, Churchill minuted that same day: "I agree."

The Chiefs of Staff in London then sent in some thoughts of their own, based of course in their case, on Sigint from Bletchley Park and the reports of MI3. They made clear that "resistance to Axis is paramount consideration" and that the "Partisans now most formidable anti-Axis element in Yugoslavia outside Serbia". At this stage, they did not want to drop Mihailovic altogether either, but he would have to agree to British conditions of actual and active military engagement against the Axis occupiers. Like Eden they were unsure of Bailey's idea of partitioning Yugoslavia into Cetnik/Partisan zones, and that the civil war between these two groups had to stop.

From "resistance to Axis is paramount consideration" of the Chiefs of Staff, to Churchill's famous phrase to Fitzroy Maclean that Britain should support whichever group was killing the most Germans, there is very little distance. In fact, it is saying the same thing. Yet Mihailovic proceeded to ignore all pleas to step up guerrilla activity.

Therefore, Mihailovic's outburst had set in motion a chain of events that changed everything, and he was the author of his own fate. There was no conspiracy. But there was an imperative to tie down the Germans wherever possible and to save Allied lives in Italy. This was surely Churchill's goal, as indeed, as Britain's leader against the Axis, it had to be.

As Churchill told the House of Commons in 1944, after the decision to drop Mihailovic had been taken:

> The reason we have ceased to supply Mihailovic with arms and support is a simple one. He has not been fighting the enemy, and moreover, some of his subordinates have been making accommodations with the enemy.

Churchill was being gracious, as Sigint gave good reason to suppose that Mihailovic had been in touch with the Germans direct. But what was beyond dispute was his inaction, and *that* was what finished him with Britain.

Fitzroy Maclean summed it up well in *Eastern Approaches* (spelling Mihailovic with a j) on Britain's relationship with Mihailovic and the Cetniks:

> Thus ended a connection which from the first had been based on a misapprehension. With the help of our own propaganda

we had built up Mihajlovic into something that he never seriously claimed to be. Now we were dropping him because he failed to fulfil our own expectations.

Some may disagree, but that surely seems a fair statement of what happened. Mihailovic was never going to be an active resistance leader, for reasons that were both good and bad. Tito wanted to kill Germans. It was as simple as that.

Chapter 7

Mayhem and Massacre on the Mountain

On a warm summer's day in May 1943, two young British officers were sunning themselves on a balmy Mediterranean beach in North Africa. One was Bill Deakin, an Oxford historian whose job before war broke out was to help the politically exiled Winston Churchill spend his sadly extensive leisure time writing the biography of his famous seventeenth-century forbear John Churchill, 1st Duke of Marlborough. Come September 1939, Churchill had discovered that there were now more important things to do.

Like many a physically fit young academic with a thirst for adventure, Bill Deakin had joined up and found himself posted to be part of Churchill's great plan to "set Europe ablaze" by becoming an agent for the Special Operations Executive. Much of what he was now asked to do – all behind enemy lines – was deeply classified, so when asked what he did, he would reply simply that he was "some kind of bandit", which usually sufficed.

The other officer was Bill Stuart, also theoretically an Army officer, but like Deakin, a man of secrets. MI6, the Special Intelligence Service, had wanted SOE strangled at birth. Chaps blowing up bridges, kidnapping German generals, creating mayhem: all these activities made the simple and necessarily quiet act of traditional spying far more difficult. SOE might have been the war child of the spies, but it was unwanted and disliked. But here, in Egypt, the Axis was finally driven out of Africa on 13 May, so SOE and MI6 were going to collaborate; and Bill Stuart was MI6's man.

Our two beachcombers would have had much ground for optimism. The Allies had finally won the Desert War. The southern part of the

Mediterranean had been recaptured. Not even the seemingly invincible Rommel had been able to withstand them. Operation *Mincemeat* was at that very moment deceiving the Germans into believing that the Allies were now going to invade through the Balkans, while, all the time, Eisenhower and the British and American forces under his command were readying themselves for the invasion of Sicily. Thousands of miles away, and often overlooked, the Red Army was finally on the victory roll after destroying the invaders at Stalingrad. Hope was possible at last.

With Italy then the next target, the presence of Axis divisions in the Balkans became rather important. The more German and Italian armies that could be pinned down by guerrillas in a country like Yugoslavia the better. A Wehrmacht force trying to find and eliminate resistance fighters in the Balkans was a division denied that could not to fight against Allied troops in Italy. In essence, Yugoslav freedom fighters would save British lives.

So, while Yugoslavia had always been important to British strategy, now what happened there became vital in the Allied wish to win the war with as comparatively few casualties as possible.

Therefore, when the Communist insurgents, the Partisans, under the command of their still shadowy leader Tito, sent a request through to Britain to send a mission to help in the guerrilla campaign against the Germans, they were taken far more seriously than before.

On 17 May 1943, the Partisans signalled Special Operations Executive HQ in Cairo to tell them: "We regard co-operation with the Allies as logical. Let them send a liaison officer to our staff. He could parachute at once in Montenegro near Durmitor."

Therefore, just three days later, on 20 May, Deakin and Stuart and the others in their party got going, without asking for any further details.

Durmitor – the *Embattled Mountain* of Deakin's memoirs – was entirely surrounded by Axis forces. As the Germans made clear: "After the successful and complete closing of the ring, the Communists will attempt a partial break-out through the front. Order: no man capable of bearing arms must leave the circle alive. Women will be searched in case they are men in disguise." In other words, all were to be massacred.

We tend to remember those incidents in Western Europe in which the SS slaughtered scores of innocent civilians. When Heydrich of the SS was assassinated in 1942, some 340 people were murdered in the Czech village of Lidice, near Prague. Likewise, at Oradour in France, in 1944, 642 ordinary villagers were slaughtered by a division of the SS.

103

But in Yugoslavia such massacres had become almost commonplace. In 1941 at Kragujevac alone over 2,700 entirely non-combatant men, women and children were butchered in a single village, nearly three times the total of both Lidice and Oradour combined. Estimates vary wildly – and statistics have alas been heavily politicised – but perhaps as many as 7 per cent of the entire pre-war population of Yugoslavia was murdered in the four years 1941–1945.

It was into this cauldron that Deakin and Stuart were being dropped. On 24 May, the green light was given: mission *Typical* had begun.

Weather delayed the British team, and it was not until the 27th, at 03:00 hours, that their specially adapted bomber plane was over friendly Partisan territory, with ground flares showing where the parachute drop should happen.

The wind was strong, carrying Deakin and his party some distance from the landing zone. Through the dark, they had to stumble a path to what they hoped would be the right place. A shot rang out; Deakin feared the worst.

But it had come from welcoming Partisans. They were safe.

Not for long, however! They still had a 10 kilometre walk to safety, across perilously open countryside, with no trees to protect them and with the peak of Durmitor, some 7,000 feet high, always in sight, snow-capped and surrounded by forest.

The group eventually made it to the hamlet of Zabljak, in itself a place of no importance, but now a ghost village, since it had changed hands many times in recent months in the struggle between the Partisans and their German enemies. But no time for rest. The march continued, ever wary of Luftwaffe planes or Wehrmacht patrols, until they progressed into the forest and to a woodland glade.

> In the centre ... seated on a rough-hewn ring of tree stumps and fallen boughs, we saw a group of armed men in uniform. They rose to meet us. One of them stepped forward, with an air of natural authority. Slim and neat in a grey uniform with no badges of rank, he was wearing an army side cap and black riding boots.

It was Tito, the mysterious leader of the Partisans, in the flesh, at last.

Tito was the *nom de guerre* of Josip Broz, the founder of the Communist movement in Yugoslavia. Significantly he was of mixed Croat-Slovene parentage, and someone who had lived, until 1918, in the former Austro-Hungarian Empire. Allied victory that year had joined together nations that had never before co-existed since the Slavic peoples had entered the Balkans well over a thousand years before.

People have all too glibly spoken of 'ancient hatreds' in this region, but since no entity such as Yugoslavia pre-existed the twentieth century that is historically inaccurate. So, what began as the Kingdom of the Serbs, Croats and Slovenes and then developed into Yugoslavia (= Southern Slavs) was an entirely modern creation.

It united parts of the Balkans that had for centuries been under Ottoman Turkish (and thus also Muslim) domination, such as Serbia, which were Orthodox Christian and used the Cyrillic alphabet, with former Austrian and Hungarian provinces, today's Croatia and Slovenia, and the once Venetian ruled Dalmatian coast, all these latter areas being Roman Catholic with the Latin alphabet. Not until the First and Second Balkan Wars of 1912–1913 did some other parts of the Balkans gain freedom. Furthermore, Bosnia, which is largely Muslim, was under Ottoman rule until 1878 and only formally annexed by Austria-Hungary in 1908.

So, in 1918 all these ethnic, linguistic and religiously diverse regions were put together in what hindsight has revealed to be a profoundly fragile and artificial creation. But the key thing for our purposes is that Tito himself was happily Yugoslav, coming from two of the groups – Croatian and Slovene – and someone who as a Communist was able to transcend ethnic differences through the strength of his ideological beliefs. The Partisans, among whom Deakin and Stuart now found themselves, were no different. Many were from the predominant pre-1918 group, the Serbs, but in their case Communism trumped Serb nationalism, and it was a united Yugoslav state for which they were fighting. The critical importance of all this will become clear as our story unfolds.

The British group soon found themselves in another world. Not only was there perpetual rain and mist. As Deakin recalled vividly in looking back at that extraordinary voyage:

> Although trained soldiers, we were men of the cities flung in the space of a few hours into the long march of an army inured by instinct and tradition to the strains of warfare without quarter, fought for survival in the cruelty of mountains which would yield respite and refuge only to those who could scale and dominate them with more secret knowledge than the foe.

The German enemy was all around them, making every effort possible to close the ring and murder all those inside.

As Deakin realised, daylight belonged to the Wehrmacht and Luftwaffe. Planes circled constantly in order to spot any Partisans, especially wounded stragglers unable to catch up with more physically fit mobile groups. Artillery pounded anyone it could find. This was, in military terms, a *kessel* or a cauldron, out of which the Partisans were aiming to escape, and inside which the Germans wished to trap and kill them.

Since all movement was in the dark, fear of getting left behind dominated everyone's mind. "Nema veze" or "we have lost touch" was the permanent nightmare.

By 5 June, the Partisans had still not managed to escape the mountain. The ring was tightening, and the escape routes narrowing as a consequence. Whichever way out they chose, there would be heavy fighting. All heavy weapons now had to be dropped if there was to be any chance of breaking through enemy encirclement. Each group would have to be small and nimble if survival was to be possible. At many points the Germans were only yards away. By 8 June the group with which Deakin and Stuart were travelling – along with Tito himself – found itself close to the edge of the ring. Freedom was so close, but so too were the waiting Germans, now often within earshot. Hunger gripped everyone as well as fear since rations, including those of the British party, had long since run out.

But the British sense of humour could not be defeated. Forced to drink nettle soup, Bill Stuart quipped: "Not bad, but needs some salt". Then another member of the small British contingent found a tin of sardines. Should they open it and eat the contents? Debate ensued! Bill Stuart settled the issue: "It is better to open it and die with a full stomach."

British and Partisan alike were soon obliged to concentrate on survival rather than on food. There were Dorniers, Stukas and Henschels swooping low over all of them: their escape group had been spotted. So close were the planes that some pilots simply tossed grenades onto the scattering groups below.

"Take cover!" Deakin shouted to Stuart, "they are using explosive bullets!"

Stuart fled in one direction, Tito – and Tito's dog, along with Deakin hastened off in another. Deakin, Tito and the dog hurled themselves into a hollow in the ground. They were lucky, in a way. The dog was killed saving his master. Tito had a nasty splinter wound to the shoulder, Deakin a slight leg wound. But all around them lay the bodies of dead Partisans, strafed or blown to pieces. Then they found Stuart's body, his wish to die with a full stomach granted him. He had been killed by what was either a direct bullet to the head or by a major bomb splinter. His radio operator, a Jewish refugee nicknamed "Sargent Rose", was stunned but alive, his life saved by the pack of playing cards in his breast pocket.

Over one-hundred Partisans had died altogether, plus Stuart, who was given a burial among the rocks. Not many were now left to try to make the final escape through enemy lines.

Deakin and Tito eventually escaped out of the cauldron. But the Germans counted 5,697 Partisan dead in the battle for Durmitor. Axis forces murdered some 411 out of 498 captured Partisans. In the Durmitor district itself they massacred 1,437 civilians and another 1,100 in the villages nearby. Partisan nurses who had stayed behind to tend the wounded were all butchered. Fifty villages were burned to the ground.

> The mountain was wreathed in the flames and ashes of villages and settlements. The scattered dead lay, spilt in heaps, as if by a giant hand, across this landscape of the moon.

Deakin's adventures were just beginning.

So too was the role that he played in the events that unfolded in London and Cairo, which determined British policy towards whom to support in the Yugoslav imbroglio and why.

The conspiracy theorists' views on what happened in 1943 have included much about Bill Deakin, because of his pre-war closeness to Churchill. It is completely obvious to them, as much as to everyone else, that Deakin was, if anything, a small-c conservative and indisputably not a Marxist of any description, let alone a Communist of sinister interpretation. So, the notion that he was some kind of romantic public schoolboy overwhelmed by the radical chic of Tito – rather as many generations of students were to be decades later with Che Guevara or Fidel Castro – is the prevailing view in the revisionist camp.

But all this presupposes that it was SOE and its reports that made the critical difference to Churchill, and as this book shows throughout, this was emphatically *not* the case.

As Deakin wrote to a US historian in February 1991, when it came to decision making, especially in relation to Yugoslavia and whom to support and why in 1943:

> Such a grave policy decision depended solely upon the military evidence of the British Chiefs of Staff as assembled by MI3 (Enemy Intelligence) and passed to the War Cabinet office and the Prime Minister and accepted somewhat reluctantly by the Foreign Office.

As we shall discover, MI3 had access to the ULTRA decrypts, which provided objective evidence from the Balkans rather than the necessarily more subjective reporting by SOE agents on the ground, such as Deakin himself. Everything that Deakin wrote in his field reports on *Typical* should be seen in this light, as indeed should his influence on Churchill, who heard everything that Deakin was saying to him in the context of what he, the Prime Minister, already knew from the ULTRA decrypts and their interpretation for the Chiefs of Staff by MI3.

Deakin stayed on in the Balkans until the war was over, but when Fitzroy Maclean, Churchill's personal emissary, was sent to report on Tito in the autumn of 1943, Deakin's main role was over – he was now a junior player in comparison. But because of his close personal pre-war link with Churchill he remained important.

Those prone to see dark forces at work regard all this as somewhat sinister, but Deakin is surely right in his book *The Embattled Mountain* to play down his own significance. Churchill had tried to get hold of him in the summer, not realising that Deakin was already with Tito and under gunfire in the Balkans.

But in November 1943 it was time for Deakin to go to Cairo, with a delegation of Partisans selected by Tito to speak there with Churchill. Tragically the first attempt was destroyed by sabotage; most likely caused by a pro-German traitor in the camp – and with Tito's initial choice of chief delegate Lola Ribar, who was murdered in the explosion. His replacement, 'Vlatko' Velebit, was selected and the new delegation, the happily still alive Bill Deakin included, set off on 29 November for their indirect and perilous journey to Egypt. This time security was considerably greater, and the circuitous route to Cairo, via Allied Headquarters in Brindisi in Italy, proved successful.

On 9 December Deakin, now in Cairo, was summoned by someone from the British Embassy to attend an unspecified meeting there that night. With secrecy being of the essence, no further details could be given. It turned out to be far more "formidable" a gathering than he could have imagined. Churchill was there, all the Chiefs of Staff, the British Commander in Chief for the Mediterranean and other very senior officials. He was in fact meeting many of the most eminent British delegates to the recent Allied conference at Tehran. The aim, now that the decision had effectively been made to support Tito, to question any SOE team members in Yugoslavia, Albania and Greece to confirm their views.

Deakin was ushered into the dining room. There he met Field Marshal Smuts, formerly a Boer guerrilla against the British back at the turn of the century and now one of the British Empire's most distinguished statesmen, from South Africa.

> "And what do you do?" I was asked. I could only reply, "I
> think that I am some sort of a bandit." Smuts gave a wink.
> "So was I once," and we took our places at the dinner table.

Afterwards Churchill began to interrogate the young SOE officers, to make "personal reports on the situation in the territories whence we had come". Unfortunately, as Deakin recalled some years later, "I have no recollection of what I said." Equally regrettable is that there is no official record of this conversation either! But the report by Deakin – accompanied by photographs – is in the Churchill PREM files in The National Archives in Kew, and makes the close links between Mihailovic and the Germans very clear, along with Deakin's strong preference for Tito as the best ally for Britain to tie down as many Wehrmacht divisions in the Balkans as possible.

The next day Deakin, along with Churchill's personal emissary to Tito, Brigadier Fitzroy Maclean, were summoned to the villa in which the Prime Minister was staying. As so often with Churchill's unorthodox approach to meetings, it was in the Prime Minister's bedroom!

Deakin soon realised the vital importance of the session, since the basic decision to switch allegiances on the ground would have profound repercussions at the national level. Technically the British Government recognised the government in exile of the young King Peter and to support an overtly Communist guerrilla force in the Partisans had all sorts of complications and permutations. How could Britain support King Peter as the continuing Head of State while simultaneously backing Tito within the country itself? Churchill needed the advice of

Deakin and Maclean in order to brief the Cabinet accordingly on his return home to the United Kingdom. Things were complicated further by the fact that the Royal Yugoslav government had now moved to Cairo to be nearer their nation "in case the situation warranted". What should Churchill tell the young King?

> For nearly two hours the Prime Minister interrogated me as the officer mainly concerned with interpreting the evidence derived from captured German and Cetnik documents concerning the links between Mihailovic and his commanders with the Italians and the Germans. It was a miserable task.

What Churchill could not of course tell Deakin was that the key information had already reached Britain via Enigma, on 4 December, of the very close ties between Mihailovic and the Germans that were now unfolding. Deakin knew later on of course but not at the time. One of the reasons why he was subsequently so interested in the MI3 reports with their ULTRA references is that he was, through them, able to discover the background to what Churchill was quizzing him on that morning in Cairo:

> The questions were pointed and searched out every detail within the reach of my knowledge, and as I talked I knew that I was compiling the elements of a hostile brief which would play a decisive part in any future break between the British Government and Mihailovic. It was a formal occasion, and there was no personal or private dialogue.

In fact, all Deakin was doing was confirming from his own trustworthy observations on the ground the messages that had already reached Churchill and the Chiefs of Staff via Bletchley Park and MI3. But with the secrecy in which Enigma was enveloped, the young British SOE officer could not know that then.

Interrogation then continued in the villa that evening, and as Churchill was very much of a night-owl, to the exhaustion of those such as the Chiefs of Staff who worked with him regularly, "the relentless questioning was resumed into the early hours".

Churchill's interviews with Deakin and Maclean would have confirmed what the Enigma decrypts had revealed, so he told the two men – separately according to Maclean's memoirs – that Britain now knew about the "collaboration between Mihailovic and our

Marshal Tito, leader of the Yugoslav partisan forces, stands with his pet dog 'Tiger' near the entrance to his cabin in the Yugoslav mountains. (Historic Military Press)

Marshal Tito (extreme right) with his ministers at his mountainside headquarters during 1944. (Courtesy of the Australian War Memorial; P02018.283)

The cabin that marked one of the original main entrances to Tito's cave headquarters in the Yugoslav mountains about half a mile north of the centre of Drvar.

The entrance to Tito's cave as it appears today. Note the memorial to Tito and his partisans that can be seen in the brick wall.

Pictured at their base at Celone, Italy, the crew of an RAF Halifax squadron don their flying equipment and parachutes before taking off on a supply dropping mission to Tito's Partisan forces in Yugoslavia, circa 1944. (Courtesy of the Australian War Memorial; MEC1772)

A 148 Squadron Handley Page Halifax drops supplies to Tito's partisans during 1944. (The Andy Thomas Collection)

Winston Churchill shakes hands with Marshal Josip Broz Tito of Yugoslavia during a meeting in Naples on 12 August 1944. The meeting has held to discuss coordination of operations against the Germans. (Historic Military Press)

A Douglas C47 Dakota of 267 Squadron RAF pictured having landed on a remote airstrip in Yugoslavia, January 1945. At this stage of the war the squadron was undertaking supply missions to Tito's Partisans. Besides war supplies, food and clothes, the squadron also airlifted in soldiers trained in Italy to assist in the fight against the retreating Germans. The airstrip seen here was carved in the deep snow by hand. (Courtesy of the Australian War Memorial; MEC1834)

A still from camera gun footage shot from a North American Mustang Mk.III of 249 Squadron, part of the RAF's Balkan Air Force, during an attack on a goods train near Maribor, Yugoslavia, 3 February 1945. Steam can be seen escaping from the locomotive's boiler as cannon fire from the Mustang scores a direct hit. The aircraft was operating in support of Tito's Partisans. (Historic Military Press)

An unusual relic of the Battle of Neretva. As part of the fighting, at the beginning of March 1943 Tito ordered this railway bridge over the Neretva river to be destroyed, preventing a further advance by Axis forces. The bridge has been left as it was during the war. Note also the abandoned train to the right of the blown bridge. (Elzbieta Sekowska/Shutterstock)

Part of the memorial commemorating the Battle of Batina. Lasting from 11 to 29 November 1944, the battle, which took at the Croatian village of Batina in Baranja and heavily involved Tito's Partisans, was, according to some sources, the biggest battle, in terms of forces employed, intensity of fighting, and strategic importance, in Yugoslavia during the Second World War. (Shutterstock)

Marshal Tito of Yugoslavia salutes after laying a wreath at the Cenotaph during the first day of his six-day state visit to the UK in March 1953 – the first made by the head of a Communist state to Britain. The Duke of Edinburgh was a member of the welcoming delegation. (Historic Military Press)

enemies" and also about the wisdom of switching support to the considerably greater ability of Tito and the Partisans to take the battle to the Wehrmacht. Then, as a result, poor Deakin was lumbered with the task of breaking the bad news to King Peter himself, then also in Cairo, at a private lunch which would be with Stevenson, the British Ambassador to the Royal government in exile, King Peter and his English ADC.

As the Official History of British intelligence in the Second World War states, Deakin's memorandum giving clear instances of Mihailovic's treachery and collaboration with Nedic "could not make use of the Enigma sent out to the Middle East". While with Tito and the Partisans Deakin had picked up copious circumstantial evidence of such betrayals, but nothing absolutely convincing. So, Deakin was in an awkward spot, especially as it is likely that at that time he himself was not privy to the secrets of Bletchley Park.

As Deakin notes:

> It was perhaps characteristic of Mr Churchill that he would entrust to his subordinates [Maclean as well as Deakin] such tasks for which they themselves bore a direct responsibility. It was an unpleasing form of testing evidence, but it was a simple and tidy manner of proving the point once he as Prime Minister had accepted it.

So, Deakin had to break the bad news to King Peter, both about the Mihailovic/Nedic/German collaboration and the fact that Churchill had accepted the Deakin/Maclean evidence as being true.

Deakin concludes his reminiscence by stating:

> The young King persuaded me to curtail our discussion, which was more a monologue on my part. He asked me politely to call upon him again. The occasion never arose.

A difficult task had been accomplished.

The especially secret nature of ULTRA meant that, alas, Deakin's report was not enough to persuade the few ardent pro-Mihailovic supporters in the Foreign Office, most of whom, the Official History makes clear, would have been cleared to be able to know about and read the ULTRA material that so convinced Churchill and the Chiefs of Staff via Bletchley and MI3:

> Although summaries of Enigma decrypts were reaching the Foreign Office by the autumn of 1943 … it must be presumed that those who were handling the problem at desk level in the Foreign Office had not seen the evidence implicating Mihailovic … In doing so it [the Foreign Office] was unaware that the Enigma decrypts had confirmed the allegations.

Attempts that have been made to use Foreign Office doubters are therefore not reliable, since all but the Permanent Under Secretary of State himself (Sir Alexander Cadogan) and the Foreign Secretary Anthony Eden would have been allowed both to know the precise nature of the source, its provenance and accuracy. What the Foreign Office was allowed to see from the autumn of 1943 were the MI6 intelligence summaries that its head C sent to them, and of course used by the Joint Intelligence Committee as well as the Chiefs of Staff.

We will see in other chapters that when Deakin went to Tito's HQ, it had already been decided in London that a mission be sent to the Partisans because of what the British Government – those with ULTRA clearance – had seen from the decrypts. It was therefore not Deakin but ULTRA that formed Churchill's thinking.

This cannot be exaggerated.

The reason is that revisionists, such as the eminent media specialist Peter Batty, author of *Hoodwinking Churchill: Tito's Great Confidence Trick*, are convinced it was either Fitzroy Maclean or William Deakin (Batty goes for Deakin) that made Churchill change his mind at this time. There is no question but that these revisionists believe their case and are being entirely sincere, but they cannot be more wrong, even when they have read many of the key documents for themselves.

Batty attacks Deakin for not being a good historian, and for failing to realise as an historian that Tito was hoodwinking both Deakin himself and Churchill. But the irony is that one can say the same, alas, of Batty himself, who has evidently read both the Official History of British Intelligence by Sir Harry Hinsley and indeed Churchill's PREM files in The National Archives in London, since he quotes from them.

In his case, while he shows the usual grossly inflated supposed key influence of Klugmann – which our book reveals to be entirely exaggerated – or "reds under the bed", he goes on to agree with a new category suggested to him of "blues *in* the bed" [Batty italics], of political conservatives who favoured Tito over Mihailovic.[1]

So, as well as accusing Klugmann of doctoring the evidence Batty also suggests that people such as Deakin were duped by Tito into believing in the existence of forged documents manufactured by Tito that suggested a degree of collaboration between Mihailovic and the Germans which was simply untrue. This, in turn, according to this view, changed Churchill's mind:

> In making his fateful December 1943 decision in the heat of war, Churchill relied heavily on advice from close associates who depended largely on information passed their way by Tito. That they were duped by the Partisan leadership is now clear.

In fact, this is sadly inaccurate, as all the material did was confirm to Churchill what he already knew from ULTRA and what MI3 and the Chiefs of Staff were telling him in London. Therefore, even the doyen of Second World War history, Sir Michael Howard, was in error when in his obituary of Deakin in 2005 (quoted by Batty) he wrote that Deakin "as a young officer in the Special Operations Executive it was largely his experience and advice that persuaded Winston Churchill to support the Communist partisans in Yugoslavia". Of course all this presumes that the evidence given by the Partisans to Deakin – which is easily found in Churchill's PREM files in The National Archives – was false. But it was accurate because it tied in with what ULTRA was saying, as we shall clearly see in the rest of our book.

To return to our narrative, at the great Allied leadership conference in Tehran it had been agreed that the USSR would also send a mission to Tito's Partisan headquarters. Deakin was asked to brief General Korneev and other members of the Soviet delegation in Cairo on what he had discovered. But naturally he had the same problem as when he had seen King Peter, whether or not he knew the full story. Material gathered from prisoners of war or from captured Cetnik documents could be regarded as suspect.

By January 1944, even Eden, who of course knew about Enigma, was compelled to throw in the towel and admit that Mihailovic was not only collaborating with Nedic but the German occupiers as well. As the Chiefs of Staff had also made very clear to him and to the Cabinet, support for Tito alone and dropping Mihailovic as a consequence was a "matter of great importance to our whole European strategy." Not only that, they averred, but "even if the evidence of Mihailovic's treachery is incomplete, there is no doubt that he is doing nothing to help in the defeat of Germany."

So, case closed? It should be, except that those who still defend Mihailovic, often for reasons far more to do with the politics of the Balkans in the 1990s than with actual events back in the Second World War, still alas persist in ignoring the crystal-clear evidence of the decrypts. Search in such books for references to MI3 or to Enigma/ULTRA signals intelligence and you will seek in vain – they are simply not there. Present conflict still bedevils the study of the past, and nothing could be clearer than this very subject. The evidence is all there, in The National Archives, in the Deakin Papers above all and in similar material such as the preserved notes and correspondence of Churchill's emissary, Fitzroy Maclean. Except for the Deakin Papers themselves all this has been out there in plain sight for several years, but sadly ignored it has been nonetheless.

Endnotes

1. See how often phrases such as "no doubt selected by Klugmann" appear. There is no question but that the revisionists are sincere in their belief in seeing Klugmann's malign hand everywhere, but similar phrases such as "this suggests" or "presumably by Klugmann" rather show that what we are seeing is the belief of the author rather than proven facts.

Chapter 8

The Maclean Mission

With a jerk my parachute opened and I found myself dangling,
as it were at the end of a string, high above a silent mountain
valley, greenish-grey and misty in the light of the moon.

Such was the landing in Yugoslavia of Brigadier Fitzroy Maclean,
Churchill's personal emissary to Tito, on 18 September 1943. This is
taken from Maclean's memoirs, *Eastern Approaches*. Published in 1949,
it is significant that my quotation is from the 2009 edition, brought out
sixty years after the famous original.

But it has also become notorious, for reasons that are, in essence,
nothing to do with what he actually did in his mission to the Partisans,
1943–1945. So, to understand the book properly, and the real reasons
why Maclean went and decided as he did, we need to examine some of
the context in which, decades later, his daring mission is now seen, or,
as one can put it better, hideously misinterpreted.

Were the decades of Communist rule in Eastern/Central Europe
from 1945–1991 a good thing? Or over forty years of tyranny and
oppression by a totalitarian ideology not much different from fascism
and, in its Stalinist period, every bit as vicious and murderous, with
thousands put to death for political dissent, Yugoslavia included. All
this took place after Maclean's mission, but as with so much in this
period, history is deliberately often read backwards, with the politics of
the Cold War influencing how we see the events of 1939–1945.

Post-Berlin Wall in 1989 and after the fall of the USSR in 1991,
Soviet/Communist imperialism does not have a good name outside of
Russia itself, where Stalin nostalgia has become all the rage.

Yugoslavia itself ceased to be part of the Soviet bloc in 1948, when
Tito was uniquely able to escape Stalin's iron grip. From then until the

country disintegrated, it was always an exceptional Communist nation: as your author's many Yugoslav friends would put it, still a cage, but a very big cage, certainly in comparison to odiously repressive regimes such as that of the Ceausescu period in Romania.

But what has this to do with SOE, Winston Churchill and the mission of Fitzroy Maclean, the Prime Minister's personal emissary to Tito, in 1943?

In terms of the context of the time, the answer is surely "nothing at all". As this book emphasises in every chapter, all Churchill's decisions were made for British reasons, in the British interest, in the context of the war between Britain and its Allies on the one hand, and Hitler and the Third Reich on the other.

Although the decades of Communist rule in Yugoslavia after 1948, when Tito ceased to be a Stalin loyalist and no longer slaughtered people wholesale, were nothing compared with the far greater oppression within the Soviet bloc – remember Hungary in 1956, Czechoslovakia in 1968, Poland in 1981 – they were Communist all the same. For some people, the fact that decades of Communist rule were, arguably, a direct by-product of Churchill's decision in 1943, by definition therefore what he, and Maclean as his emissary, did cannot be seen without considering what happened next, between 1945 and 1991. In addition to which, is the carnage and bloodshed of the break-up of the country in the 1990s, in which tens more thousands were butchered just as in during the Second World War.

While some, as we saw elsewhere, attribute Churchill's decision mainly to Deakin, Maclean became far better known – the fact that his book has not gone out of print in over six decades being proof – and to many he, either on his own or together with Deakin, are seen as the dupes that allowed the Communists to seize power in Yugoslavia and to stay in control down to the 1990s.

Churchill was no Communist, and nor, as we shall see, was Brigadier Fitzroy Maclean, a Conservative MP, a former Foreign Office diplomat (with strong connections to MI2) and a brave fighter in North Africa with the founders of the SAS. In Greece Churchill backed the non-Communist guerrillas and sent British troops post-liberation to make sure that the Greek king was restored to his throne.

But is not all this history in hindsight? As we shall see, Churchill and Maclean were not oblivious to the possible political implications of their decisions in 1943 for when the war was over. After all, Churchill's sixth volume of wartime memoirs is entitled *Triumph and Tragedy.*

Some see the "tragedy" as being his loss of power at the 1945 General Election, but far more tragic to him in many ways was the Communist takeover of Poland in 1944–1945 by the Red Army. This crushed Polish freedom and forced the Poles to spend the next forty-four years under Soviet rule. Churchill valued Stalin as an ally , in fact from June 1940 until December 1941 our only major ally against the might of the Third Reich, until the USA came in after Pearl Harbor. But despite his many agreements with Stalin during the war, the idea that the USSR would hold sway over vast swathes of Central Europe such as Austria or Poland was wholly anathema to him.

It is significant though that in his infamous "Naughty Document", more properly known as the Percentages Agreement, with Stalin in Moscow in October 1944, while Churchill agreed that for all intents and purposes Bulgaria and Romania would be under Soviet post-war control, and Greece under British predominance, his original pitch was for Hungary and Yugoslavia to be 50/50 or effectively under dual Anglo-Soviet influence. Molotov, Stalin's Foreign Minister, bullied the British into making Hungary a Soviet zone nation, as they would tragically discover in 1956, but with Yugoslavia Churchill stuck to his guns. As a result, when in 1948 Tito escaped Stalin's clutches, Britain was able to take full advantage of the situation, such that Yugoslavia was officially neutral in the Cold War while remaining Communist, therefore a very different place from countries as oppressive as Romania or East Germany.

As we shall see at the end of this chapter, one of the reasons why Britain was so successful in 1948 is precisely because of Maclean's adventures and Churchill's response in 1943.

Eastern Approaches is a gripping account of how Fitzroy Maclean was dropped in between enemy lines, found Tito and the Partisans, and after many adventures, reported to Churchill on what was *really* going on in wartime Yugoslavia. (Much of the book is also about his extraordinary life pre-1943, but it is his mission for Churchill in 1943–1945 that concerns us here.)

Maclean is the kind of larger-than-life character that needs events as dramatic as those of the Second World War to be seen in his full colours. After his diplomatic career, he took advantage of an old law that enabled him to leave the Foreign Office and join the Army by standing for Parliament as a Conservative MP. Soon he was an active officer fighting for the SAS in North Africa, rising from the lowest rank of private to becoming a brigadier for his mission to Yugoslavia.

Eastern Approaches was published more than twenty years before the ULTRA secret could be revealed. Looking at Maclean's own papers it is evident that he knew all about the decrypts that were changing Churchill's mind and that of the Chiefs of Staff that proved that the Partisans were killing far more Germans than the Cetniks. But, of course, he would have been totally unable even to hint at their existence when he wrote his book.

(The distinguished SOE expert David Stafford suggests that Maclean did not know the *full* story in 1943, though the papers suggest that he was not in ignorance for long.)

So, for quarter of a century and more he was forbidden to give the full reason why he was sent by Winston Churchill to see Tito and report from ground level what the Partisans were up to in the struggle against the Third Reich. He was not so much there to discover what was going on – Churchill and the Chiefs knew that already from ULTRA – but to confirm what the decrypts were saying, from among the Partisans whose heroic struggle against the Germans was plain from all the decrypts reaching Bletchley Park.

In December 1990 Maclean was free to write openly of his experiences back in 1943, and the circumstances of his controversial mission to Tito and the Partisans. This is today in his papers at the Alderman Library of the University of Virginia, where they were sold after his death.[1] Now the ULTRA secret was out, and now that everyone could know that Bletchley Park had deciphered countless German signals on the fight between the Third Reich and the Partisans, Maclean was finally able to tell it as it was.

In the summer of 1943 he was asked to meet with Churchill, he recalls, to undertake a special mission. Churchill had already heard that the British Government policy to that date, that of supporting Mihailovic and the Cetniks, was no longer appropriate. They had discovered that the Cetniks were reluctant to engage the Germans, and that a group named the Partisans "might be the more effective resistance movement".

The fact that Churchill knew even before summoning Maclean to go to Yugoslavia was, as we saw in the chapter on MI3, as a result of the ULTRA information gained by the British Government through the decrypts at Bletchley Park. Churchill did have some knowledge of the Partisans through an initial SOE contact, but it was Sigint that was his major source. This is vital to understand, as alternative views of the British decision place great weight on the possible existence of Communist spies in SOE headquarters in Cairo at the same time, as we shall see later. Suffice it to say here that even if Cairo was awash with double agents, working for either the British or Americans and as spies at the same time for the NKVD, it was not on the basis of their feedback that Churchill's decision was made.

This therefore is the real background to Maclean's mission to Tito, his conversation with Churchill in London, and his decisive report in November that the British should give their support to the Partisans. In other words, the Maclean report came in a context in which it was obvious that regardless of tales of Cetnik/German collaboration, which Mihailovic supporters deny to this day, it was evident beyond peradventure (a) that Tito and the Partisans were *the* effective fighters against the Germans and (b) that the Cetniks were not.

In fact, when Maclean's report did arrive in London, making the still controversial assertion that the Cetniks were collaborating with the Germans, it was in the context of actual signals intelligence and similar evidence that precisely such collaboration with the enemy was taking place, and proof quite separate from Maclean's own observation on the ground. Not only that but it was also clear that the Cetniks, despite Mihailovic's denials to the British, were also collaborating with the Bulgarians, and with the quisling Nedic regime in Belgrade.[2]

When his report arrived, signals intelligence in the Middle East – not SOE – had deciphered Sigint that was so crucial that the British Commander in Chief Middle East formally recommended to Sir Alan Brooke, the Chief of the Imperial General Staff, that the British Foreign Office change their policy to the Cetniks as soon as possible. Sigint had shown very plainly that at the end of October 'Mihailovic had ordered all Cetnik units to co-operate with Germany against the Partisans.' Interestingly there was also a decrypt from the Abwehr in Belgrade on 7 November protesting against orders to find Cetniks with whom to fight together against the Partisans. Other decrypts were also suggesting a much more willing degree of German/Cetnik collaboration, that convinced even C, the head of MI6, that some collaboration had to be going on.[3]

Not only that, but the same month, November 1943, the Chiefs of Staff, meeting at the Anglo-American *Sextant* conference, unanimously felt that:

> The successful prosecution of operations in the Balkans depends much more on good organisation. The business had

got far too big for SOE, and should be taken over by a proper staff.[4]

This was precisely what Maclean was there to do, on Churchill's behalf. So, the documentary evidence shows that it was military factors that led the British to make their critical decision in late 1943 to switch support from Mihailovic to the Partisans, and what Maclean did was confirm what other sources made plain to the key policy makers in London. Maclean was there to confirm the Sigint intelligence from a ground-based perspective as Churchill's emissary, not to formulate the policy upon which the Prime Minister would make his decision.

As the historian John Cripps has written, when Maclean's report came to Britain, advocating support for Tito, this "had been the view of military intelligence since at least the end of September, when Talbot Rice's [MI3] report backed the Partisans, and had also very probably been the view of MI6 for some time".

Not long after Churchill was sending Maclean, Roosevelt wrote to the Prime Minister telling him that the "chaotic situation in the Balkans causes me concern. I am sure you too are also worried", which was indeed the case and why Churchill was sending Maclean.

As we shall see in the chapters on the OSS involvement in Yugoslavia, the Americans also wanted to influence events there, under the eagle oversight of "Wild Bill" Donovan, Roosevelt's chosen leader of the new OSS.

With Maclean already picked, Churchill wanted to keep things British. He admitted the "vexatious broils" of the Tito/Mihailovic conflict – and a similar one in Greece – but he talked up the various missions that the United Kingdom already had in Yugoslavia and the wonderful job that some groups were doing to tie down German divisions in the Balkans away from the battlefront with the Allies. He did though have to admit that, "the differences between Tito's partisans [sic] and Mihailovic's Serbs are very deep-seated".

It used to be thought that the Americans were pro-Mihailovic: the chapter on the intrigues with the Croat exile leader "The Shepherd" show that in fact Donovan, whom Churchill reluctantly admired, were in fact more than different than anyone had hitherto supposed. We can therefore revert to the memorandum of reminiscences that he put together and sent to a Yugoslav enquirer in 1990.[5]

Churchill now requested Maclean to go to Yugoslavia, to find out for himself, as Churchill's own 'Personal Representative' and Military

Mission Commander to the Partisans. We must here recall that Maclean was a former Foreign Office diplomat, had been in Communist-controlled parts of the Caucasus for MI2 in the 1930s[6] and spoke fluent Russian. He had also been a Conservative MP since 1941, so was someone who shared Churchill's own political sympathies.

It is clear from Maclean's pre-mission talk to Churchill that the whole basis of his trip and investigation was as a short-term military expediency. "Politics", Churchill told Maclean, "were a secondary consideration. What mattered was to find out who were killing the most Germans and help them to kill more."

The importance of this entirely short-term outlook cannot be exaggerated. It is vital to remember that the British concern was the war, and indeed only the war. People who have regretted the Churchillian decision to back a Communist guerrilla group always overlook this key factor.

By the summer of 1943, British troops were fighting the Germans in Italy, and so the strategic situation in the Mediterranean, referred to earlier, had changed. Now attacking the Germans in Yugoslavia via a suitable military force was essential to the war effort, and to diverting as many German divisions away from the Allies in Italy as possible. The effectiveness of whomsoever Britain picked in Yugoslavia to accomplish this task was the paramount consideration.

If they chose Communists because the Partisans were more militarily effective than the Cetniks, then it would be a Communist army they would chose. However tragic it was that post-1945 Yugoslavia would be Communist-ruled, that was irrelevant to what was urgent to Britain in 1943. The Germans were still undefeated and in combat against British/German armies on just the other side of the Adriatic, in Italy.

So, this chapter argues that completely short-term military objectives ruled every decision made by the British. If there were any individuals in Cairo or elsewhere who had political agendas of their own, then that was unfortunate for the peoples of Yugoslavia after 1945. However, it made no difference at all to Churchill and to those in London who commissioned Maclean to go to Tito's headquarters and find out for himself.

Maclean was made a brigadier, which represented a very steep rise in military rank for him. As a brigadier, he would be under the distant authority of the Supreme Allied Commander in the Mediterranean theatre, and "on the political side to Mr Churchill himself". It was essentially a British venture, though the presence of an American,

Major Linn Farish, whose very considerable significance we will see in another chapter, gave it the cover of being an Allied mission.

As Churchill wrote about him, on 28 July 1943, pressing for his appointment as soon as possible: "Mr Fitzroy Maclean is a man of daring character ... What we want is a daring Ambassador-leader with these hardy and hunted guerrillas."

Not long after, Maclean found himself with Tito. Sir Fitzroy's memorandum does not go into the detail of *Eastern Approaches*, but Maclean reiterated his very high opinion of Tito, and of the latter's clear grasp of the military situation. As Maclean does comment:

> I had been told by Mr Churchill that what mattered was who was fighting the Germans. There could be no doubt at all that the Partisans were doing this and doing it most effectively. Moreover, by their operations they were containing a sub-stantial number of enemy divisions which could otherwise have been used on other fronts against the Allies.

This sense of what the Partisans were doing is critical to what Maclean decided to recommend to Churchill and why. Every German loss in Yugoslavia to the Partisans meant Wehrmacht troops denied to Italy to fight Britain and the Allies in the latter country. The Partisans were not merely fighting the Germans better than anyone else, but in so doing they were saving British lives. Furthermore, as Maclean also noticed:

> With no outside help they [the Partisans] were already making a most important contribution to the Allied war effort. If we could provide supplies and air support they could be helped to make an even bigger one.

So far so good, one might argue, and it would be hard for anyone to doubt the massive damage being done by the Partisans to the German occupying forces in Yugoslavia. But the next thought expressed by Maclean is where the controversy starts:

> It was also clear from the evidence available to us that the Cetniks, whatever their original intentions, could no longer be described as a resistance movement. Indeed in many instances they were acting in direct collaboration with the enemy.

Maclean made full use of his ability to write direct to Churchill, and not via SOE Cairo or indeed anywhere else. For example, Churchill's PREM files have the following message for the Prime Minister from Maclean's mission to Tito, on 29 September just over a week after his arrival:

> It is apparent that during the past weeks the Partisans have won considerable successes in many different areas, and are causing the Germans great embarrassment. In particular, the attempted German move to the Adriatic coast has been badly hampered by the Partisans, whose activities have forced the Germans to leave large reserves guarding towns and lines of communication in their rear, with the result that they have so far failed to establish a firm foothold on the coast ... New arrivals are provided with the arms of six Italian divisions now disarmed by Partisans.

All this, as we see elsewhere in our book, was confirmed to Churchill by Sigint and by MI3. So, the idea that Maclean was over-egging the pudding is simply untrue. He saw with his own eyes what the Partisans were doing and his reports direct to Churchill were verified by ULTRA, so that the Prime Minister knew for certain that Maclean was telling the truth.

We can now look at the famous Maclean memorandum of 6 November 1943, in which Brigadier Maclean reports back to Churchill about his findings, if you like his official report.[7]

Very little had been known about the Partisans since they had begun fighting in 1941, and Maclean's first task was simply to explain to people back in Britain who they were and what they had achieved. As Maclean wrote:

> They followed traditional guerrilla tactics of attacking and harassing the enemy wherever possible, while never allowing themselves to be forced on to the defensive. By these means, they were successful in keeping their own casualties to a minimum, while inflicting heavy losses on the enemy ... The savage reprisals of the enemy are not taken into consideration.[8]

Like other Western – British and subsequently also US visitors later on – Maclean also noticed the totally egalitarian nature of the Partisans, all sharing the same risks and living quarters. The writer Evelyn Waugh, who spent time in Yugoslavia with the Partisans, was initially impressed but found it oppressive as time continued. Maclean simply states it as a fact.

One of Waugh's great jokes was that Tito, the mysterious commander of the Partisans, was in fact a woman, which when Waugh arrived in Yugoslavia to keep an eye on Randolph Churchill, in the country to work for SOE, made relations between Waugh and Tito somewhat tense when Tito discovered the joke. The reason for all this secrecy is revealed in Maclean's report:

> From the outset, the Partisan movement has been based on a common front, directed by the Communist party in the person of Tito ... Tito's identity is kept a secret. He is known to be a man of the people and to have worked underground as a Communist agent ever since the last war. It seems likely that he is, in fact Joseph Broz [in fact Josip Broz], a Zagreb metal worker, who after passing some years in the Soviet Union, was sent back to Yugoslavia by the Comintern in 1937... [he] is the dominating personality.

No doubt then, that the Partisans, while containing non-Communists, was very strongly Communist-led. No wool over people's eyes here. Support for the Partisans would be to back a Communist-dominated movement. As Maclean was surely right to observe, the "military and political structure built up by Tito and his followers in two years, from nothing, in enemy-occupied territory, with no outside help, is an impressive one".[9] As a result of all this activity, the "need for the rapid organisation and despatch of supplies by the Allies cannot be emphasised enough ... The first signs of Allied air support have been greeted with great enthusiasm by the Partisans".

Maclean gave details of how the Partisan forces were managing to engage the enemy through using semi-guerrilla warfare. But perhaps the key thing was:

> The attacks of the National Army of Liberation [the official name for the Partisans] are causing ever greater embarrassment to the Germans, who, with an enemy who presents them with no targets against which they can strike back decisively, with unreliable allies, and without enough

troops of their own to occupy the country effectively, have been obliged to confine themselves to garrisoning the larger towns and trying to keep open communications between them, while leaving the rest of the country to the Partisans. This much the Partisans have achieved practically unassisted. Were they to be provided with sufficient arms and equipment, the embarrassment to the Germans would be enormously increased, and it might be in time that the National Army of Liberation could force the Germans to withdraw from the country altogether ... I have no doubt that ... [Tito's] readiness to accept our guidance and suit his strategy to our plans will be in direct proportion to the amount of material help that we are able to give him.[10]

The importance of the basic tenor of this paragraph cannot be overestimated. Although he would go on to point out that the Partisans were indeed Communist led and dominated, the crucial issue for the British Military Mission was the war. Who could keep as many German divisions in Yugoslavia and away from Italy as possible? That mattered to Maclean and to Churchill more than anything else. Indeed, one could possibly argue that nothing else really mattered at all. British decision-making was completely strategic in nature, and if the Partisans were killing more Germans and tying down more Wehrmacht divisions than anyone else, then they were the people to support.

However, as Maclean fully understood, the issue had considerable local complications. The Partisans were Communist, with all that that implied.

But the important problem was the civil war raging alongside the war against the Germans, and it is this issue above all others that has caused controversy ever since, as a perusal of the Maclean Papers makes very apparent.[11]

One of the most critical issues, which supporters of Mihailovic, a Serb, often overlook is the complex issue of nationalities in the then Yugoslavia, which we considered in another chapter. Whatever Tito's faults, Maclean realised back in 1943 what has been referred to elsewhere in this book, namely that Tito was a Yugoslav. As he quotes Tito himself:

The struggle for National freedom and the question of nationalities in Yugoslavia are closely connected. Our efforts to liberate the country would not be so determined or so successful if the peoples of Yugoslavia did not see in them to-day [sic], not only a victory over fascism, but a victory over the old regime and over those who once oppressed the different races of Yugoslavia and hope to oppress them once again.[12]

Tito may have been a Communist. But he believed in a very different configuration – a federal one – for the post-war Yugoslav state. Subsequent discussion in the Maclean papers from the 1990s show that the revisionists seen below hope that Mihailovic too would have formed a federal state. But this is surely wishful and speculative thinking. Arguably any Cetnik victory over the Partisans would have followed a vicious internal civil war. At the heart of such a conflict would have been those complex nationality issues which had failed to be resolved pre-1941, and which were to emerge with massive violence and carnage again in the 1990s.

Not only were the Cetniks effectively a Serb rather than Yugoslav force, they were also collaborating. Again, this is a source of much controversy, but Maclean trusted fully what the Partisans told him. He almost in fact also gave away the ULTRA secret in his memorandum, that not only was there evidence on the ground, but particulars of this collaboration "have already been given by signal".[13] But the evidence of Cetnik collaboration was indeed known in Britain by the Sigint reaching Bletchley Park, which outlined it in much detail and which provided the rationale for Churchill sending Maclean to Tito in the first place.

Maclean knew full-well the high esteem in which the Partisans held the USSR. As he laconically put it, Britain, "as a capitalist and non-Slav state, we are at a certain disadvantage".[14] But what really upset the Partisans was the perceived British preference for Mihailovic, which to them was incomprehensible. As Maclean pointed out for the information of his colleagues back in London, on "the other hand there is, to my mind, in Yugoslavia a deep-seated liking and admiration for Great Britain which could easily be developed", and the same applied to how the reputation of the USA could also be enhanced.

In his final section, Maclean came to the key point: what should Britain do next?[15] Should they support both the Partisans and the Cetniks? Or drop Mihailovic and give "our wholehearted support" to the Partisans? For "of reconciliation, or of dividing the country into two spheres of influence, there can be no question", which was precisely the problem. Furthermore, in "matters of military effectiveness there can clearly be no comparison between the Partisans and the Cetniks".

This last view has proved contentious. But Maclean was not ruling out the Cetniks altogether. For what he says in that light is significant, and was the real influence behind British decision making:

> It might, of course, be argued that it is worth continuing to support the Cetniks in the hope that they may eventually turn against the Germans and thereby contribute something to the united war effort. This argument would carry more weight if the Cetniks were more numerous, less disorganised and less set in their collaborationist ways. As it is, it seems likely that they are only kept going by our moral and material support, and that, if we were to drop them, the leaders would fade away and the rank and file join Partisans, as many of them have done already. Apart from relieving the Partisans of a constant source of annoyance, we should, by withdrawing our support from the Cetniks, release arms of which the Partisans could make the best possible use.

So, Maclean was open to continuing aid to the Cetniks, if they got their act together militarily and stopped the – still disputed – aid to the Germans. It was still who killed most Germans that interested the British.

Supporters of a different option for the British are frequently strongly Serbophile in their outlook, such as the late Michael Lees, whose book *The Rape of Serbia* indicates its sympathies in its very title.[16] But Maclean makes very clear the dangers to Britain of supporting what was, in effect, an essentially Serb resistance force, which is just what Mihailovic and his Cetniks were. While of course it is natural that many would regret the imposition of Communism after the war, Maclean makes the other key point, noted elsewhere in this chapter, that the Partisan strength was such that their takeover of Yugoslavia post-victory was inevitable.

> Taking a long view, the case for the wholehearted support of the Partisans is equally strong. There seems little doubt that nothing short of large-scale armed intervention will drive them from taking power in Yugoslavia as soon as the Germans are finally driven out. In fact, they effectively control large

areas already. Furthermore, they can count on the powerful backing of our Soviet allies. Mihailovic, on the other hand, is thoroughly discredited in the eyes of most of the population, and, even in the most favourable of circumstances, would have no prospect of uniting the country. His policy is, in any case, Pan-Serb, anti-Croat and violently reactionary, and is therefore opposed to our own aims. The support which we can give him can only serve to prolong internal dissensions, and by it, we are, in return for no corresponding advantage, prejudicing our position with the Partisans and driving them more and more to the conclusion that the Soviet Union is their only friend.

Once more, the conclusion by Maclean in that paragraph cannot be overestimated. As suggested earlier, come 1948 he would be vindicated completely when Tito effectively ditched Stalin while continuing his wartime friendship with Britain.

Thus, Maclean was being both pragmatic (in terms of the fight against Germany) and prophetic (in terms of what would happen in the future) when he wrote:

On the other hand, were we to drop Mihailovic and at the same time substantially increase our material aid to the Partisans, we would not only further Yugoslav contribution to the Allied war effort, but we should establish Anglo-Yugoslav relations on a firm basis, which would do much to consolidate our position in the Balkans after the war.

So, we see the short-term aim of hitting the Germans and the long-term one of having a Balkan friend after victory; both of which Maclean's efforts achieved.

The Vice-Chiefs of Staff – the deputies to the Chiefs of Staff – wrote to both Churchill and the Chiefs of Staff themselves on 26 November. What they sent was no less than the views of the Joint Intelligence Committee on Maclean's report. This can be found in JIC (43) 488 (0) (final). The JIC saw absolutely everything, from MI3 to all the ULTRA material and from MI6 to SOE. Theirs was therefore definitive, and what the intelligence chiefs of the JIC had to say was consequently highly significant.

It was aimed at being in time for the Partisan delegation coming to Cairo – as we saw elsewhere, because of tragedy a rather different group than the one originally intended. As ever, remember that this is the JIC, with total SIGINT access, not some individual's opinion, whether Communists in Cairo or Maclean's personal views.

"We agree with Brigadier Maclean's estimate of the Military strength, Morale and Effectiveness of the Partisan forces", they began. Then, after a remark as telling as that, they continued in similar vein:

> We agree with his estimate of the support which the Population (whether CROAT SLOVENE OR SERB) give to the Partisan Forces in the area in which they operate. Partisan operations on the ITALIAN Border are engaging four divisions of the GERMAN Forces in North ITALY and in addition their activities seriously embarrassed the GERMAN garrison in Yugoslavia.

So, what Maclean was telling Churchill on the ground was confirmed by all the intelligence available to the British Government back in London, and passed on to Churchill himself. The JIC further commended Maclean:

> We agree with Brigadier MACLEAN that if as a result of further supplies the Partisans' strength was increased they would be more able and more willing to coordinate their activities with our plans. They would also extend the area of their operations though this might result in clashes with MIHAILOVIC'S forces as well as with those of the enemy.

Churchill had wanted an effective collaborator on the ground, and now the JIC agreed with Maclean that in the Partisans he had one.

The JIC outlined various means of getting extra supplies through to the Partisans and interestingly added that if "tactical air support from Italy were intensified and more closely coordinated with the operations of the Partisans from whom a large body of Intelligence is received". This, in itself, is interesting as it shows that not only was intelligence being gained from the usual sources but that the Partisans were adding to the store of intelligence helpful to the Allied war effort; and there was no time to lose:

> Unless the Partisans very soon receive increased supplies and air support not only will their activities which are already

weakening under German pressure, seriously diminish but the German hold of Yugoslavia may become so effective as to enable the Germans even to reduce their garrisons.

The effects of this on the Allied war in Italy are obvious. German divisions no longer needed in Yugoslavia could easily be redeployed against Allied forces fighting in Germany, with grave results. Furthermore, reflected the JIC (with the backing of the Vice-Chiefs of Staff):

> We agree in general with Brigadier Maclean's assessment of Mihailovic's military capabilities and intentions. Although up to the spring of 1943 his operations constituted a serious embarrassment to the Germans his recent activities against them have been negligible. He has come to regard the Partisans as his principal enemy. Indeed there is evidence that he is collaborating with the Germans or that his Commders [sic] is so weak that he cannot prevent them from collaborating.

The deal with Nedic and the quisling regime in Belgrade at which we looked in the chapter on MI3 is very much what the JIC had in mind. It was not all *carte blanche* for Maclean from the JIC, however. As they reflected to their military superiors (and to Churchill):

> We do not consider that Brigadier Maclean has taken sufficiently into account the Political and personal support which Mihailovic has enjoyed in Serbia itself. Although the present situation is confused and fluid, he has hitherto enjoyed the support of the majority of the Population as a Pan-Serb and Anti-Communist leader. In spite of some desertions from Mihailovic to the Partisans it is doubtful whether the Partisans would obtain as much support as Brigadier Maclean expects should they penetrate deeply into old Serbia. Much will depend on the attitude of local Chetnik [sic] leaders who are by no means unanimously hostile to the Partisans.

This was also reflected in the views of some of the American liaison officers sent by the OSS to Mihailovic, at whom we shall look elsewhere. This is important because it shows that the opinions given to Churchill and the Chiefs of Staff were no starry-eyed pro-Partisan one-sided propaganda: British intelligence chiefs were well aware of the political implications and angles that any final decision would have to take into account.

But the key point is the next one – even despite what they have just argued, the military logic regarding what Britain should do next was nonetheless inescapable:

> On military grounds we conclude that there is every reason to discontinue sending Supplies to Mihailovic, while he is encouraging, or at best failing to prevent the collaboration of some of his forces with the enemy. If supplies were continued, not only is it unlikely that they would be used against the enemy but they would probably be used against the Partisans with a consequent reduction in the offensive effort against the Germans in Yugoslavia.

The noose around Mihailovic was tightening, and Sigint was part and parcel of it, not just Maclean himself. This JIC report was awaiting Churchill in Cairo when he met up there with Maclean.

After time with Tito, Maclean returned to Cairo to see Churchill. The conversation he had with the Prime Minister there in late 1943 was to become infamous. But it would be the JIC report, based upon Sigint, that Churchill had in mind when the encounter took place, something we should never forget.

Maclean's own account of the conversation is surely definitive:

> I now emphasized to Mr Churchill the other points which I had already made in my report [quoted from in detail in this chapter, below], namely that in my view the Partisans, whether we helped them or not, would be the decisive political factor in Jugoslavia [sic] after the war and, secondly that Tito and the other leaders of the movement were openly and avowedly Communist and that the system that they would establish would inevitably be on Soviet lines and, in all probability, strongly orientated towards the Soviet Union.

> The Prime Minister's reply resolved my doubts.

"Do you intend," he asked, "to make your home in Yugoslavia after the war?"
"No, Sir," I replied.

"Neither do I," he said. "And, that being so, the less you and
I worry about the form of government they set up, the better.
That is for them to decide. What interests us is, which of them
is doing most harm to the Germans?"

Thinking of our conversation over afterwards, I felt convinced
that this was the right decision. In 1943, the turning point of
the war had been reached, but this was by no means as clear
then as it is now.[17]

Seldom have truer words been thought, as has become evident
in our book, with the all-important Sigint reports and those of MI3
the unspoken basis for all Churchill's decisions and beliefs. But the
conversation in Cairo would become one of the most controversial of
the war, because at the time the existence of ULTRA – and probably that
of MI3 as well – all had to be kept totally secret, indeed as we know
right down to the 1970s, decades later.

To show how notorious his account has become, his exchange
was reformulated by Evelyn Waugh's fictional account of his time
with Randolph Churchill as SOE operatives in Yugoslavia. His *alter
ego* was Guy Crouchback, the hero of the *Sword of Honour* trilogy. Guy,
in *Unconditional Surrender*, has just arrived in Bari, the headquarters in
recently liberated southern Italy for all the various special operations units
acting in Yugoslavia. He meets Brigadier Cape, in order to be briefed at
the forthcoming mission to Partisan-controlled territory. As the novel was
written long before the ULTRA secret was revealed, Waugh died nearly
a decade before its very existence was made public, it naturally has no
reference to it.

In the novel, the Brigadier tells Guy:

Now, remember, we are soldiers not politicians. Our job is
simply to do all we can to hurt the enemy. Neither you nor I is
going to make his home in Jugoslavia [*sic*] after the war. How
they choose to govern themselves is entirely their business.
That's the first rule of this mission.[18]

From the mouth of Winston Churchill in Cairo to the fictitious Brigadier
Cape in Bari, the message was the same, and in *Unconditional Surrender*
Waugh makes clear what the basic mission was all about and puts
British policy into an excellent nutshell: *our job is simply to do all we can
do to hurt the enemy.*

That is precisely what Churchill, Fitzroy Maclean, and others all wanted to do – to give the Germans the hardest time possible. This is what we saw in the chapter on MI3. In Waugh's novel, the imaginary Brigadier Cape summarised it with perfect accuracy: *all we can do to hurt the enemy.* What else would one expect a British Prime Minister to want to do? It was not only the first rule of this mission but of Churchill's entire wartime strategy. Only, as all too many historians do, if you look back at 1943 through the prism of the civil war in disintegrating Yugoslavia in the 1990s could you in fact hold any other opinion. The niceties of what was going to happen in that sad and divided country after Allied victory in Europe was strictly secondary to the main aim of destroying as many of the forces of the Third Reich as possible, especially if that strategy saved the lives of thousands of Allied troops fighting the Germans over the border in Italy.

As Churchill told Maclean, and as Cape told Crouchback, ideology played no part in what followed, and no matter how much has been written subsequently to suggest otherwise, that remains the case.

His conclusions to Churchill were thus very clear:

1) That support of Mihailovic should be discontinued.
2) That our aid to the Partisans should be substantially increased.
3) That, in particular, an efficient system of supply by sea should be organised on a large scale without further delay.
4) That suitable targets in Yugoslavia should be attacked from the air whenever possible.

This proceeded to be what Britain decided to do.

On 9 December, the Foreign Office sent its reactions to Maclean to the Americans, with a copy to Churchill. The FO outlined Maclean's report, but added that other material from Serbia showed conclusively that:

> Mihailovic is not only of no military value to the Allies but has also become a standing obstacle to any sort of Yugoslav unity either now or in the near future [and that] he is so obsessed with the communist menace that he appears openly to admit that the protection of Nedic and the Germans is preferable to submission to the Partisans.

The Foreign Office were not the hoodwinked dupes caricatured by some. They knew full well what a transfer of support to the Partisans would mean. While the diplomats still held out hope that King Peter could sack Mihailovic and redeem the day – surely by now an increasingly forlorn and fanciful wish – they realised that dropping Mihailovic and giving "our entire support to the Partisans ... [would provide] a considerable military contribution to the war effort both now and at a later stage of the war". But inevitably this would result in a "more likely prospect of Yugoslavia being unified after the war in the form of a communist state closely linked to the Soviet Union".

So it was not as if Britain did not know the consequences of switching support to Tito. But while the Foreign Office dreamed of a deal between King Peter and Tito – one shared by the Americans, in their intrigues outlined in "The Shepherd Project" which we examine in another chapter – facts on the ground and the need for victory enabled the military to see matters in starker terms.

In such a spirit, the British Chiefs of Staff, in early December 1943, decided to tell Eisenhower that:

> It was agreed at the "Eureka" conference that our support of Partisans in Yugoslavia, which now falls within the area in which you are responsible for Allied operations, should be intensified in order to increase their effectiveness ... We consider that this mission is of such importance that it would be best to be controlled on a regular basis by a special commander and joint staff.[19]

This did not happen as such – Maclean's mission remained in place – but the thinking of the Chiefs of Staff is very clear: a British decision made in British interests to help an Allied campaign against Germany.

Ideologically it is easy to sympathise with those whose distaste for Communism, in retrospect, was not so much reactionary as visionary, given what we now know to be the scale of Communist atrocities worldwide for so many decades. Queasiness on these grounds is thus comprehensible. But the idea that we should have continued to support an entirely Serb movement surely makes no sense. If what happened post-1945 is supposed to inform our view of what should instead have been decided during the war, in 1943, then surely the ghosts of the eight-thousand and more innocent Bosnian civilians massacred in Srebrenica in 1995 by Serb nationalists should also haunt us.

Maclean's subsequent report of September 1944, written while Waugh was also in Yugoslavia, not too far away, is also interesting.

This is both for how it describes the situation in the country when other Allied missions had landed, and also how matters had developed over the months in which Britain had been giving aid to the Partisans.[20] It seems that not only were Mihailovic's forces making life hard for Tito's forces, but that they were also collaborating with the quisling forces of General Nedic, Hitler's man in Belgrade. Thankfully the Partisans prevailed, and as a result, they were "paralysing German troop movements and, in particular" had the effect of "diminishing German prospects of a successful withdrawal from Greece". This was something which, as we saw, Mihailovic had utterly failed to do when he and the Cetniks were unable to prevent German Panzer divisions passing through Yugoslavia from Greece en route to the USSR.

It is this that has become the object of much political controversy since then, because it is Maclean's mission and recommendations to Churchill that supporters of Serbia have regarded as a betrayal of a martyred Mihailovic. But as we have seen, it was the clear and objective evidence of the Sigint that showed what the Cetniks were up to and with whom they were collaborating. The same signals intelligence had revealed that it was the Partisans who were the enemy so far as the Germans were concerned.

However, all is not always simple. Despite the clear evidence to the contrary, many, especially in the 1990s, when all these issues flared up again, decided that Britain had taken the wrong side in 1943, and that it was all a Communist plot in SOE Cairo.[21]

Sir Fitzroy Maclean, as he had then become, continued to take a profound interest in the region, and in 1992 remained in excellent health. He and fellow veterans from SOE kept in touch and corresponded on the subject. One of these was a near neighbour of his in Argyll, and also an old warrior from the early days, called Hilary King, who had acted as Maclean's signals officer during the war.[22] The correspondence they had is all preserved in Charlottesville, VA, and continues to make significant reading.

As King points out (in a letter he wrote to Maclean on 9 August 1992), those seeking to revise the past tended, in his view, to dismiss the ULTRA decrypts as fraudulent, and confuse this with the perhaps more subjective communications despatched from SOE in Cairo. But as King reminds his old SOE colleague, the "Ultra material from the enigma machine in Bletchley is a different kettle of fish altogether, and masses of it is now in the Public Record Office."[23]

King also wrote his reminiscences to a British journal that had published much revisionist material. As he informed them, the "decisive evidence" of the correctness of the British decision, and for the fact that there was clear collaboration between the Cetniks and the Germans, came "under two heads".[24] The first was "ULTRA material from Bletchley – decrypts of German military signals – much of it publicly available. Churchill kept a close eye on this. No-one can sympathise with the claim that it was fabricated or distorted by German sympathisers in SOE".

Second there was convincing evidence from Hermann Neubacher, who was Hitler's representative to the quisling Nedic government in Belgrade from August 1943. Neubacher was sympathetic to the Serbs, and to the dilemmas of loyalty that Mihailovic faced. Significantly, Neubacher was horrified at the atrocities being perpetrated by the Germans and their Ustase allies against the general population. It was this revulsion against the Nazis and their collaborators that, according to Neubacher, drove thousands of Yugoslavs "of all political persuasions" into supporting the Partisans, even more than British help to Tito.

King then makes what is surely two vital points, on both of which the revisionists, in their natural sorrow that Yugoslavia fell to Communism in 1945, often omit. The first:

> What mattered to Western policy makers at that time [1943] was the way in which the parties involved were using the manpower available to them. As for Field Marshal Alexander, in 1944, what mattered was not the precise number of Divisions, but the thought that any of them might become available for transfer to the Italian front. From the Spring of 1943, the rapidly expanding ULTRA output showed conclusively that the Partizans [sic] were presenting the greater threat to the Germans, and that most of the German Divisions in Yugoslavia were engaged primarily in operations against them.

This is the point that we saw in considering how the Chiefs of Staff reacted to the MI3 reports on Bletchley Park intercepts, that of siding with the Partisans saved British lives in Italy.

The second point is that we could not have changed the outcome in the internal Yugoslav civil war. This is vital to state, since one of the real problems, as alluded to elsewhere in our book, is that in the 1990s people who, for understandable reasons, were horrified at what was happening in the carnage of the break-up of Yugoslavia after 1991, read back their contemporary feelings into the past, and wished for a different outcome for the 1940s. There seemed to have been few better ways of doing this, as the Maclean papers now in the USA make clear, than attacking Fitzroy Maclean and people such as his signals officer Hilary King, in the 1990s for decisions that they made in the 1940s.

But as Hilary King continued:

> Thus, the military case for supporting Tito in 1943 was unanswerable. Longer-term political arguments were more nicely balanced. But all the reliable evidence pointed to a Partizan victory in the civil war, with or without our help, which the Allies would be powerless to abort without a full-scale invasion. But the record shows that we did not have the resources for this as well as for our intervention in Greece.

The Americans were entirely against British intervention in the Greek civil war. As we saw, in considering Churchill's so-called "naughty document" in which he and Stalin carved up post-victory zones of influence in Europe, Greece was allocated to the British zone and Yugoslavia was 50/50. Would Stalin really have allowed Yugoslavia to revert to being a corrupt monarchical and Serb-dominated dictatorship after the war?

One rather thinks not. Plenty of Red Army troops entered Yugoslavia in 1944–1945, which did not happen in Greece, but they did so in the knowledge that their fellow Communist Tito, and his wholly Yugoslav-based Partisan forces, had already liberated much of the country. If Mihailovic had won the civil war or been in a much more powerful territorial position in 1944–1945, there is surely little question that the Red Army would have allowed him to take over the country.

Yugoslavia would have been another Poland, where the patriotic Polish Home Army was allowed by Stalin to be crushed militarily by the retreating Germans, so that the Soviet Union could take over Poland after the war. The idea that a few more weapons to Mihailovic from the British in 1943 would have altered the post-1945 outcome in Yugoslavia is surely fanciful, however much it would have been preferable to save the peoples of that country decades of Communism.

Finally, looking at history retrospectively can work for the non-revisionist side as well, as Hilary King also made clear in the letter he copied to Maclean in 1992.

But come 1948 all that was to change, with Tito's switch out of the Soviet bloc and into what, after 1954 he and others called the non-aligned movement. While some of the "non-aligned" were arguably nothing of the kind, that was not the case with Tito – he really was not part of the Cold War between Capitalist West and Communist East. This, King argues, was because from 1943 onwards he was receiving British aid and that by March that year Tito and his fellow Partisan leaders had understood "that they could count on no help from Moscow beyond didactic exhortations".

Writing in 1992, with the perspective of the total collapse of the Iron Curtain in 1989, King was able to say that British aid to the Partisans in 1943 was in fact "the first crack in the Communist monolith". Imagine if during the Cold War the Soviet fleet had been able to enjoy the facilities of a warm water port on the Adriatic, on the other side of that sea from NATO ships based in Italy? All this was denied to them by Tito's switch in 1948. Tito had remembered that in 1943 his real friends were the British, not the USSR.

Furthermore, as King pointed out in Edinburgh in a rather heated debate in 1992,Mosa Pijade, one of Tito's top advisers, told his British friends:[25]

> When our fortunes were at their lowest ebb it was the Russians whom we expected but no help came. Let us not forget that it was the British who first sent a military mission, and began to help us.

Not everyone agrees with this. The late Michael Lees, an aristocrat who served in SOE during the war – in his case, significantly, with the Cetniks – did not believe this. His book, *The Rape of Serbia*, is filled with loathing and dislike of all who disagree with his perspective, and holds in particular contempt Sir William Deakin, one of Churchill's former research assistants and who, as we saw, was in 1943 one of the first and most important SOE operatives to go to Yugoslavia.[26] So much, to Lees, is pure left-wing propaganda – eminent academics of radical persuasion are robustly trounced – and everything is a result of Communist conspiracy in Cairo.[27] Anything written that supports the Partisans, or the idea that they were killing more Germans than the Cetniks, was simply no more than "received wisdom"and thus biased or untrue.[28]

But significantly, although he has read Sir Harry Hinsley's official history, and quotes from human intelligence reports (Humint) of quite possible biased origin, he does not quote from or allude to any of the Sigint outlined in such detail above in this chapter.[29] That is highly significant, for the point of what is being argued in our book is that it was the objective reports from signals intelligence that made the critical difference, and not the reporting from the ground, from SOE. For him, what happened in 1943–1944 was all "Churchill's charade".[30] It was also a betrayal of Britain's real friends, the Serbs.[31]

The judicial murder of Mihailovic in 1946 by the victorious Communist regime has remained a controversial event. Attempts have been made since the new conflict in the 1990s, by Serbs and those sympathetic to the Serb cause in the USA and elsewhere, to have his reputation rehabilitated.[32] But, predictably, this has not met with sympathy in Bosnia or in Croatia, where memories of Cetnik atrocities are still vivid over half a century later.

Lees also makes much of Klugmann's presence in Cairo, as do all the conspiracy theorists. We look at Klugmann specifically elsewhere in this book, especially using his now declassified MI5 file. As our chapter on MI3 and Bletchley shows, Klugmann's blowhard boasting to a fellow Communist stooge was in fact completely irrelevant to any of the British decision-making process, based as it was on the hard evidence of ULTRA breaking the German codes rather than on fantasist Communists in Cairo over-egging the pudding and grossly exaggerating their own roles.

Furthermore, a concentration on Mihailovic and the Serbs entirely forgets the other key nationalities in Yugoslavia at the time, not least the Croats. It is a libel on a whole people to say that all of the latter believed in the collaborationist regime of the Ustase in Zagreb. Far from it! Many of the Partisans themselves were Croats and Tito was half-Croat himself, and from Zagreb. If we look at what the revisionists tell us, we see that this is a vital omission.

Michael Lees in his memoirs-cum-philippic, well portrays the sensitivities of Serbs loyal to Mihailovic and to King Peter throughout his book. Towards the end of the work, he argues that without British aid, Tito could never have conquered Serbia.[33] At this distance, such a claim is impossible to prove either way. But one could equally argue that Mihailovic could never possibly have liberated Croatia and Bosnia from the Axis, as he would have been obliged to defeat both the Germans and the Partisans, something that he would surely have found impossible to achieve.

The point made earlier in this chapter is therefore crucial here: Tito was a Yugoslav. The Partisans, for all that they were Communists, were truly multinational, just as Tito had persuaded Maclean in 1943. Countless Partisans were Serbs as well. Croats, Slovenes, Bosnians, Macedonians and Serbs – all these groups had chosen in large numbers to back Tito and the Partisans.

So, any solution to the Yugoslav issue, needed the active support of the Croatians, the second biggest of the nationalities. Mihailovic, as a Pan-Serb, could not deliver this, and by as early as 1943–1944 it was the internationalist Partisans who controlled most of the west of the country, where the non-Serb nationalities prevailed.

Maclean's own reflections on the Croats, and the natural affinity that region had with the West, is reflected in the natural empathy that Waugh found himself enjoying, admittedly in his case with the non-Communist, overtly Catholic version.

Having outlined the historic fate of the various countries, such as Serbia and Croatia, that we saw in the overview of Balkan history earlier in our book, he goes on to comment on the effects that centuries of division had upon the different peoples in the Yugoslavia he found in 1943.

> Thus, although their language and racial origin were identical, the two groups of Slavs found themselves separated by the national frontier of the Great Powers and gradually grew apart culturally, politically and traditionally.[34]

One of the key ways in which this happened was, as Maclean confirms, in religion, and as he puts it, with the Orthodox/Catholic divide came a cleavage that "still makes themselves felt today" and, one could add, continued with a vengeance to do so in the 1990s and down to the present as well.

So, for the Serbs, they orientated themselves to Orthodoxy, to the Orthodox Patriarch in Constantinople, and, your author would add, subsequently to the Autocephalous Serbian Orthodox Church centred in Belgrade, and in a wider way to the Russian Orthodox Church based in Moscow.

However, it was very different for the Croats, under the Habsburgs and, strictly speaking, under Hungarian rule for the Croats and Austrian for the Slovene, but with Maclean's basic point being correct. Where Evelyn Waugh, the writer, was based during his time with SOE during the war, the Venetian/Italian influence was also very strong, much of the region having been under Venice down until 1797. As Maclean writes, with good cause:

The Croats and Slovenes, on the other hand, looked westwards towards Vienna … In religion they were, like their Austrian masters, Roman Catholics, Christianity having first come to them with the Teutonic invaders from the north. Altogether, they became in their outlook generally, in their standard of civilization, and in their attitude to life, a Western rather than an Eastern people.[35]

For the Serbs, Maclean felt, it was different, since "for their part, made under Turkish rule, but little progress towards civilization as it existed in Western Europe". While "Zagreb came to resemble a European town, Belgrade remained an oriental fortress."[36]

As with all generalisations, there is some degree of exaggeration in Maclean's summary, but hundreds of years under the rule of fellow-Catholics and fellow-Europeans for the Croats, and Islamic rule by Turks for similar centuries for the Serbs is bound to have left some mark upon the mind-set of the two peoples. As we have seen, even the alphabet is different, Latin in Croatia, Cyrillic in Serbia.

So, it is quite natural that those former SOE executives who found themselves in Croat areas, such as Evelyn Waugh, discovered congenial and familiar surroundings in Partisan-occupied Croatia. This is important to note: the Partisans occupied much of Croatia. As recent histories, written with the background of the carnage of the civil wars of the 1990s remind us, the situation during the Second World War was often far more complex than propaganda suggests. We must not forget the pro-Nazi Serb regime under Nedic in Belgrade while rightly excoriating the equally Fascist pro-Axis Ustase regime under Pavelic. Research by a Jewish historian, Philip Cohen, published by Texas A&M University Press, shows that the Serb quislings were as complicit in the Holocaust as the Croats under the Ustase regime in Zagreb.[37]

While no one could deny the sheer obscene scale of the murders carried out by the Ustase regime against defenceless Serb and Jewish civilians, we now know that Serbs were killing Jews and Croats as well, and with German knowledge and encouragement.[38] As historian Misha Glenny reminds us, not only was the Ustase regime the most genocidal of any of the quisling regimes, but its "uniqueness lay in its brutality",[39] so much so in fact that it even managed to horrify the Germans, which must have been something very difficult to do.

But many Croats were in the Partisans, and that makes a difference. For the Croats, 1941–1945 was in this sense a civil war within Croatia, with Ustase Croats fighting with Partisan Croats. The idea that the Serbs were virtuous and that the Croats were not is simply incorrect – there were anti-German fighters both among the Croats and the Serbs, and the group that united such people above all others were the Partisans.

The situation when SOE landed in Yugoslavia was thus far more complex than is often allowed by those who want to over-simplify the picture for their own ideological lenses. The British knew that and supported the side that stood for a wholly national solution, as both Churchill and Maclean realised. Churchill and Maclean were right after all.

Endnotes

1. Maclean Papers 11487, Box 4.
2. Ibid., pp. 152–3.
3. Ibid., pp. 154–5.
4. Deakin Papers 83 quoting COS minutes in The National Archives in Kew.
5. Maclean Papers, 11487, Box 4.
6. Now accessible to the public at The National Archives in Kew as FO 424.
7. R 11589/2/G – papers classified with G were always more secret than those with normal classifications. It is also in the Maclean Papers at the Alderman Library, 11487, Box 1, Folder 1943 and the British Military Mission.
8. Ibid, p. 1.
9. Ibid, p. 2.
10. Ibid, p. 3.
11. See a later footnote for why this is a dangerous issue to pursue in print.
12. Maclean memorandum of 6 November 1943, ibid., p. 4.
13. Ibid., p. 5.
14. Ibid., p. 6.
15. Ibid., pp. 6–7, for the rest of the quotations from his report.
16. Michael Lees, *The Rape of Serbia* (New York, Harcourt Brace Jonvanovich, 1990).
17. Ibid., but the paperback edition (London and Basingstoke, Papermac, 1982), pp. 402–3.
18. Evelyn Waugh, *Unconditional Surrender* (London, Folio Society edn, 1990), p. 144.
19. Deakin Papers 83.
20. Maclean Papers, 11487, Box 1, Folder 6; also, R 16067/8/G.
21. This is clear from the discussion that Maclean had in the 1990s with Hilary King, his former signals officer during the British Military Mission. However, the discussion brings into it material that would certainly be

libelous if particular individuals are still alive, and is thus not quoted in detail in the present book.

22. Peter Wilkinson, *Foreign Fields: The Story of an SOE Operative* (London, I.B. Tauris, 1997).
23. Maclean Papers, 11487, Box 8, Folder July–December 1992.
24. Ibid., from the same file in the Maclean Papers.
25. Ibid.
26. Lees, *Rape of Serbia*, for instance the comments on p. 297 and pp. 302–3.
27. Ibid., p. 295.
28. Ibid., pp. 127 and 308.
29. E.g. on p. 124.
30. Ibid., pp. 313–25.
31. Michael Lees died in 1992. How he was not sued for libel by that brave patriot Sir William Deakin says more for Deakin than it does for Lees, whose portrayal of Deakin, and of British academics such as the late Elizabeth Barker, is wholly unfair.
32. See for example: http://en.wikipedia.org/wiki/Draža_Mihailovi #Legacy accessed 9th January 2015.
33. Lees, *Rape of Serbia*, especially pp. 322–3.
34. Maclean, *Eastern Approaches*, p. 283.
35. Ibid., pp. 283–4.
36. Ibid., p. 284.
37. Philip J. Cohen, *Serbia's Secret War* (College Station TX, A&M University Press, 1996), especially pp. 63–84.
38. For an excellent account, see Misha Glenny, *The Balkans* (London, Granta Publications, 1999), pp. 486–506.
39. Ibid., p. 501.

Chapter 9

Lawrence of Yugoslavia: Slim Farish's Adventures

It was not just British liaison officers with SOE or from Churchill who went to Yugoslavia. By 1943 Americans, from the newly formed Office for Special Services, the OSS, were arriving as well.

The OSS was the precursor to the CIA – and was the equivalent of a mix of both the SIS/MI6 (cloak) and of SOE (dagger) during the war, as is its successor organisation the CIA today, also both cloak and dagger. Britain divided cloak and dagger into two separate organisations, MI6 and SOE.

Its founder, an American swashbuckler nicknamed "Wild Bill" Donovan, was determined to be his own man, sending OSS officers to Mihailovic, for example, deliberately so after the British had in their minds switched from supporting the Cetniks to Tito and the Partisans.

We shall see in another chapter that the idea that OSS backed Mihailovic is in fact misleading, as Donovan and the OSS had a candidate of their own to lead post-war Yugoslavia, recruited by them from the Croatian exile community in the USA. But at the key wartime Tehran conference in late 1943, Roosevelt decided in favour of Churchill, to back Tito and the Partisans, no doubt to the great delight of the third major Allied war leader in Tehran, Joseph Stalin.

He did so as the result of reading a report by an OSS officer with Tito, Major Linn "Slim" Farish, famous as the great American hero of Allied aid to Yugoslavia during the war, and often referred to approvingly as "Lawrence of Yugoslavia".

Even the conspiracy buffs like Farish, such as the distinguished American Mihailovic-apologist David Martin, who wrote that he was "one of those rare people who instantly command admiration and

144

affection ... one of the handful of Americans who acted on the conviction that civilization was at stake in World War II". But when he and others wrote in the early 1990s they did not know something that, if they had, might have radically changed their minds.

Why was it that he received so favourable a press? It is, as they note, that he wrote two reports, not just one. The first, when he was acting as the American Chief of Staff to Fitzroy Maclean, on 29 October 1943, was entirely pro-Tito, and it was this report that convinced Roosevelt utterly that what Churchill had been telling the Americans about the Partisans was true.

Of course, unmentioned by the revisionists, but unquestionably true, was that Roosevelt would also have seen the same Sigint intelligence from ULTRA as Churchill, namely that it was the Partisans who, in the latter's phrase, were killing more Germans.

In the report that went to the Big Three in Tehran, Farish wrote about the Partisans in glowing terms:

> The Partisans have created solely by their own efforts in the face of the Germans, Italians, Ustashe and Cetniks, a free area of no mean size entirely encircled by enemy forces. Within this area, Mohammedans, Christians, Serbs, Croats, Communist Party members, any person of any religion or political belief can express an opinion concerning the way in which he believes the affairs of the community should be conducted. The above situation is probably unique in all of occupied Europe.

In 1945–1948, with Tito in power and ideologically linked to Stalin, this would prove to be an idealistic fantasy. But after Tito's break with the USSR in 1948 it was to prove more or less true in Yugoslavia, comparatively speaking, than in any of the nations of the Soviet bloc. As quoted elsewhere, Yugoslav dissidents in the 1970s would say that while their country was a cage, it was a far larger cage than any other Communist nation in Europe.

While David Martin is right to call this Farish report naïve, it does reflect one key part of Tito's unique achievement, that all the US and British officers dropped into the country noticed in relation to the Partisans: they were Yugoslavs.

This seems obvious; but it is not. Take the Cetniks. To describe them as "Loyalists", meaning loyal to the exiled King Peter, is highly misleading. For although the King's uncle Prince Paul had signed a pre-war deal with the Croats, about which we heard in the first chapter, there is no way in which the Cetniks were anything other than Serb nationalists. Indeed, one of their claims for priority in support was that they controlled much of Serbia, the heartland of the pre-1914 kingdom. So their loyalty might have been a personal one to the titular King of Yugoslavia but in practice their real allegiance was to him as the heir to the historic leadership of the Serb peoples.

As will be argued later on, the idea that a Serb nationalist army could unite a nation in which, although the Serbs were the biggest single ethnic group, in fact possessed a majority of different ethnicities – Croat, Slovene, Macedonian, Bosnian, Albanian, Vlach – is surely ludicrous.

During the war, the artificial Croat kingdom created by the Italians also contained much of historic Bosnia. Many Bosnians not only fought with the ethnically Croat Ustase, but even for specially raised units of the SS. (Much of the killing of the 1990s was over who the Bosnians really were in the eyes of Serb and Croat nationalists. A book by Oxford historian Sir Noel Malcolm, *Bosnia A Brief History*, shows conclusively that they were actually Bosnians.) Bosnians converted, as we saw, to Islam in the Middle Ages, and so the old-fashioned description of them as Mohammedans while incorrect now does show that they were different from the mainly Catholic Croats and Slovenes and the overwhelmingly Orthodox Serbs.

In the Partisans, Croats, Bosnians, Slovenes and Serbs all fought together, Catholics, Orthodox, Muslim and of course atheistic Communists. This is the point that so many who visited them realised: if you were going to keep Yugoslavia as a single country after the war, the people to back were those who fought, thought and lived as Yugoslavs. With all the other groups in Yugoslavia pre-1914 nationality counted for more than anything else. Not with the Partisans though; they were Yugoslav through and through.

So while Farish was indeed naïve politically – Communism was nowhere near as pluralistic as he thought it might turn out to be once the war was over – in terms of the basic building blocks of the country he was absolutely right. Keeping the country together needed the effort of those who wanted to create a genuinely multi-ethnic federation, and while one can legitimately argue that Communism was not an ideal way of accomplishing this, it was surely a whole lot better than the aggressive and divisive nationalism that slaughtered so many in the 1940s and again in recent times in the 1990s. Tito, as Farish and Maclean correctly observed, wanted Yugoslavia restored, and in that he succeeded.

Farish was totally right about Mihailovic, something omitted by the latter's defenders in considering what Farish wrote in 1943. He told his OSS superiors, and through them Roosevelt, that:

> The Chetniks [sic] under Col. Mihailovich [sic] and other officers of the Yugoslav army fought for a time against the occupying Axis troops in conjunction with the Partisans. But Mihailovich made the fatal mistake of allowing his political beliefs and his plans for the future to overcome his better judgement.

A fairer description of Mihailovic and the Cetniks could not be found. Farish continued:

> He feared Communism more than he feared the common enemy. He and his leaders were more concerned with their plans for themselves after the war than they were with the actual ending of the war by defeating the Axis. Acting upon these misconceptions, Mihailovich ordered his Chetnicks [sic] to attack the Partizan forces, and thus commenced the bitter civil war which has become so savage that it is difficult to see how a reasonable understanding can be brought about.

Again a fairer summary of the truth on the ground could not be possible. Farish's assessment is one that anyone with knowledge of the local situation, including the Germans, would have concurred. Whereas, as Farish then went on to state, as a result of this, many Cetniks were defecting to the Partisans, thereby, although he does not mention it, making the latter group even more representative of the country's ethnic mix than it was already.

Then came his *second* report, on 28 June 1944, about which Michael Lees comments in *The Rape of Serbia*:

> In his second report, Farish eats his own words. He issues a desperate plea for the Allies to intervene and stop the civil war between the Partisans and the Loyalists [Lee's word for the Cetniks].

147

Indeed, this is what Farish suggests:

> The senseless killing of these people by each other must be
> stopped. It is useless now to endeavor [sic] to decide which
> side did wrong. Too much blood has been spilt, the feeling is
> too bitter, and too many men on both sides have uttered rash
> accusations and performed rash acts ... I, personally, do not
> feel that I can go on with this work in Yugoslavia unless I can
> sincerely feel that every possible effort is being made to put
> an end to the civil strife ... and the United States has a very
> definite interest in seeing that it is ended as soon as possible.

After 1945 Mihailovic was arrested by the victorious Partisan
Government and after a show trial was executed. Many Americans
supported him and testified to the extent to which many Cetniks
had rescued stranded American aircrews and managed to evacuate
them safely. For many in the USA, therefore, Mihailovic was a hero,
and to some like David Martin and Michael Lees in particular, who
did all possible to organise his defence. As Farish pointed out in his
second report, there was no question but that the Partisans were using
American manufactured weapons in the civil war against the Cetniks,
including those dropped by Soviet planes but of US origin, given to the
USSR as war materiel by the USA.

The civil war was indeed more than horrible, with thousands
slaughtered by each other on both sides, just as Farish observed in
his second report. The hatreds that emerged during that time went
underground under Tito, but emerged as if not a day had passed in
the 1990s when Yugoslavia broke up. Thousands more were massacred,
some supposedly in revenge for fathers or grandfathers who had been
murdered during the Second World War and its aftermath, as if that
were a legitimate excuse for genocidal frenzy.

But in fact the revisionists forget something rather vital about "Slim"
Farish, however much he changed his mind in 1944, and repented of his
earlier unquestioning support for Tito. This is that he was in fact NKVD
agent "Atilla" [sic], working for the Soviet Union as one of their spies.

This is thanks to the treasure trove of American intercepts of Soviet
communications known as Venona, a project that began in the 1940s
before the Cold War started and much of which was released when
it was over in the 1990s. It is in fact how the Americans realised that
Donald Maclean was an agent for the USSR working in the British

Embassy in Washington, DC – the only reason that he was not caught and prosecuted then was that the CIA/MI6 liaison officer there was none other than Kim Philby, who we know of course as another member of the infamous Cambridge spy ring.

So according to the Venona transcripts, Farish was an NKVD spy along with being an agent for the OSS! His reference is: Venona Message 1397.

Farish was killed in a aeroplane accident on 11 September 1944, and so we have no means of knowing what would have happened had he survived the war. Was he actually a Soviet agent? What does an appearance in the Venona decrypts actually mean? According to online discussions of Farish, those who knew him utterly denounce any suggestion that he was anything other than completely loyal to the USA, so that the idea he was actually working for the USSR is nonsense. But his name is there in the Venona decrypts nonetheless.

For the conspiracy buffs this poses somewhat of a problem! He is the good American, the man who saw through Tito, repented of his support for the Partisans, and who spent much of his time in Yugoslavia with ordinary peasants who wanted nothing more than peace and quiet. But then, after many of the revisionist books were written, came the bombshell of the Venona revelations. As one pro-Mihailovic website fairly and honestly admitted, this makes things rather complex.

The problem with Venona is that the case against many people is their appearance in the decrypts, and no other evidence to prove their guilt is available from sources that have been declassified. To take one case, the historian of MI5, Christopher Andrew, is highly sceptical of the notion that the distinguished British historian Christopher Hill was, in reality, an NKVD spy during his time in British intelligence and the Foreign Office during the Second World War. (In 1956 Hill denounced his Communist past and Party membership, while retaining many of his Marxist beliefs.) The only proof that he *was* a spy is his appearance in Venona, with the codename Scott, and the possibility that he confessed before his death. But no concrete evidence exists.

However, it is odd that there was not an Oxford spy ring or even a London University spy ring to go alongside the infamous one at Cambridge. So, in his foolish youth Hill might well have been a spy, and then of course recanted. Perhaps the same is true of Linn Farish. That he was an ideological Communist, like so many of his generation in the 1930s, when the USSR was still the great hope of the anti-fascists who had been radicalised by witnessing poverty at home and the horrors of the Spanish Civil War. Then, when older, they realised that they had made one massive, serious, mistake.

This is quite possibly the case with two of the Venona names – Farish and Hill – though there is no way of knowing for certain, especially as Farish died so tragically on active service in Greece. One cannot argue, though, that Hill is in Venona, so he is guilty, but Farish, while equally present in the files, is a hero. As the honest websites realise, it is a grey area. Perhaps in 1943 he was a true believer, his ideology backed up by the impressive display of Partisan military prowess he witnessed alongside the decidedly very Conservative Fitzroy Maclean. Then, by 1944, seeing how brutal the civil war had become, which is incontestable whatever side one takes, he had powerful second thoughts, and understood that Communism was not all it was supposed to be.

We will almost certainly never know. But as always we should not forget: it was ULTRA that convinced the Western Allies to switch sides to Tito in 1943, and not the reports of Fitzroy Maclean to Churchill and Linn Farish to Roosevelt. In that sense whether or not Farish was Stalin's man on the ground with the Partisans that autumn as well as that of the OSS, is of secondary importance. Neither of his reports – 1943 or 1944 – actually changed history. The truth did.

Chapter 10

The Real OSS Report on Mihailovic

Donovan had more than one report that changed perspectives. The one with which this chapter is concerned was from Lieutenant Colonel Albert Seitz, written at the same time as that by Farish, but from the mission to Mihailovic and the Cetniks, rather than that to the Partisans. Predictably, it comes to the "Yugoslav situation" from a very different perspective, from that of Farish, and nothing has ever been revealed that might indicate that Seitz was anything other than totally loyal uniquely to the USA.[1]

Seitz was fully aware of the mess into which the Yugoslav imbroglio had fallen. He hoped that some "outside moral effect might be transmitted to the violently-warring factions within the country and that post-war aims might be segregated long enough to have some harmful effect on the German occupator [*sic!*]".

Seitz thus showed that he was fully aware that the Partisans were as active in positioning themselves for post-victory as the Cetniks – *both* sides were guilty. And as he went on to say:

> I believe that the removal of Mihailovic as Minister of War is like taking the dynamite off a package of dynamite, it is still dynamite [*sic* for punctuation] ... The Communists broke with him over post-war aims and concentrated in the West ... but to the Serb in Serbia ... Mihailovic is the hero fighting for the country and the restoration of the King. It is debatable whether the action of Tito, in removing his forces from the original resistance group, showed a transcendent desire for

151

post-war authority or a privately-conducted war against the occupator [*sic*] as a means of promoting that authority. I believe that proper patriotism would have blended the efforts of the total resistance groups.

There is much in what Seitz tells us. Tito was surely out for Communist rule post-war, and any history of Yugoslavia always makes abundantly clear that a huge part of his legitimacy in the next thirty years was the fact that he had liberated his own country from the Nazis. But was it any different with Mihailovic? One rather thinks not.

Seitz outlined the geographic situation; Tito and the Partisans were active in the western part of the country, and the Cetniks in the east, where the locals were as anti-Partisan as they were anti-German. Since it was in the east, where Mihailovic's forces were concentrated, that the greatest number of Wehrmacht occupiers were also based, there was therefore a problem.

Seitz was well aware of the ethnic/religious differences in Yugoslavia as well, something that had been much aggravated by the partition of 1941 and the ensuing civil war. There were the Serbs, who were Orthodox, the Croats and the Slovenes who were Catholics. Significantly he does not mention the Bosnian Muslims, but spoke instead of that part of Macedonia that had been annexed by the Bulgarians in 1941, that could be discounted.

He gave the OSS readers of his memorandum a brief potted history of the Balkan region, with the interesting interpretation that while, like others, he made the natural link between Serbia and Russia, based upon common Orthodox faith, he also referred to "a pro-Turkish Britain", the United Kingdom under Disraeli in the 1870s having supported the Ottoman Empire against Tsarist expansion.

His understanding of Bosnian history was somewhat shaky, since he wrote that both that province, along with Croatia and Slovenia, had been under the Austro-Hungarian Empire "for so long a time". Croatia had been centuries under Hungarian rule, and Slovenia under Austrian. But Bosnia, as any consideration of the causes of the First World War reminds us, was under the Dual Monarchy only after 1878, until that Empire's dissolution in 1918.

So, based upon this unusual understanding of history, he speculated: "It is a question whether blood and religious ties with Serbia will outweigh the present communistic following of Tito, in the view of the fact that the majority of Partisans are admittedly non-international

[sic]." One presumes by "non-international" he means nationalist, but this is not clear from the text.

The only thing that he could safely predict was that the Yugoslavs would never want to go back to the corruption and "political chicanery" of King Alexander's time. So, he suggested aiding both Tito and Mihailovic, "the Partisans in the West, the Serbs in the East. The bloody ground between can perhaps not be helped". The idea that Tito could take on everyone – Germans, Cetniks, Bulgarians – was to him "well-nigh impossible and has every probability against it". Tito was strong in the West but to try to go further would "snap the rubber band".

Donovan in his turn shared the report with the Joint Chiefs of Staff on 26 November, making clear that what Farish said was the truth, as opposed to the views of those in the State Department.[2] They would also have seen the less coherent but equally strongly felt memorandum by Seitz.

Donovan had, he told the Joint Chiefs, spent a solid fortnight examining the situation. He arrived in Cairo in October 1943 and removed Major Louis Huot, who had hitherto been in charge of operations, and also the liaison officer with SOE.[3] (Huot was sent to Bari, to establish the forward base there, only to lose this job in November 1943.) In November Donovan was back in Cairo, this time seeing one of the senior British Generals, Sir Henry Maitland Wilson, and the executive head of SOE, Major General Sir Colin Gubbins. The fruits of the fact that Donovan saw people of such seniority will become apparent below.

In his report, Donovan outlined to the Joint Chiefs:

> Since the Italian armistice, the British-American position in Yugoslavia and Greece has deteriorated. Certain contributory factors are within the control of the Allies and, if dealt with frankly and firmly, the present trend to further disintegration can be arrested.

The British and Americans might be Allies, but Donovan felt passionately that the British Foreign Office, either directly or through SOE, were responsible for the mess. British policy had "been dictated by the considered long-range political necessity of the British in the Balkans rather than the immediate and vital military problem here of its relation to over-all Allied operations".

This of course presupposes that the Americans were wholly pure and neutral in their own objectives. But that is how Donovan saw the situation, as well as reflecting the view that the resistance movements on the ground in both Greece and Yugoslavia had felt neglected equally by both Britain and the USA. Furthermore, he told the Joint Chiefs:

> There has been no coherent and integrated direction from Cairo of guerilla [sic] operations; no fixed representation there of the guerilla [sic] forces; no tie-up which would unify resistance and give cohesion to an over-all operational plan.

Such missions as did exist were not, to use a modern expression, fit for purpose so far as Donovan was concerned. His report covered both Greece as well as Yugoslavia, but in the latter, he noted, Britain had fifty-one liaison officers with Mihailovic and the USA a mere three, and they had sixty-one with Tito, while the Americans had but three and another three in the wider Partisan-controlled territory. All the guerrilla forces needed urgent supplies by sea or by air, and now the occupation of Bari made possible the delivery of such vital war materiel.

But as he realised, and as the Joint Chiefs were fully aware:

> Of course a factor which the Allies cannot control in the way of unifying assistance are certain political and ideological differences that exist. These differences are accentuated by the conviction of each side that the other has collaborated with the enemy and by the determination of each to eliminate the forces of the other.

Donovan was innately suspicious of the way in which the British denigrated Mihailovic, which to the former was the reason why the Cetniks in turn distrusted the British so much. All the evidence given by the British (much of which was, as we now know, based not just on ground observation but also on ULTRA material) was suspect to Donovan, as he felt that the British had simply not studied Mihailovic or the Cetniks properly.

With the Partisans, Donovan admitted that "Tito is said to be a Communist" though he had a senior adviser who was not. But with the Partisans, he was forced to admit that the British, in telling of the strength of Tito's forces, might not be exaggerating in this case. Quoting Farish, Donovan told the Joint Chiefs that the "Partisan movement ... is of far greater magnitude and military importance than is commonly known to the outside world. The average Partisan is sympathetic to Americans and is steadfast in his belief that we will come to their aid. While the Communist Party has played a leading role in the organization of the movement, it has not been able to indoctrinate it along strictly Party lines".

Donovan had clearly swallowed wholesale everything that Farish had told him.

Perhaps the real reason for Donovan's strongly anti-British sentiment can be seen in what follows:

> Up to a week ago, OSS-SO [Special Operations] had been excluded from all the meetings of SOE, not only dealing with the internal politics of these countries but from a consideration of all plans and operations ... However, as a result of a very frank statement to SOE as to our right to be informed of any plan in order that we might determine whether it was coincident with the principles set up as a guide for our course of action by the Joint Chiefs of Staff, there has been a marked change and we believe that no such problem will arise in the future.

Donovan was clearly not a man to cross! It is interesting here, because in that area and at that time, SOE clearly had the numerical upper hand. After the war SOE was abolished, and the OSS mothballed. But in the case of the latter, the OSS was to transport itself into the CIA, which is certainly the dominant partner in relations with friendly countries, such as MI6 (more correctly the SIS, Secret Intelligence Service) in Britain.

So, Donovan proposed to the Joint Chiefs that a "joint SOE-OSS operational committee" should be established in Cairo, and, interestingly, "placing the accent on the military rather than the political". This was classic US policy, as also evidenced, for example, in General George C. Marshall's decision to back Eisenhower in letting the Red Army capture Berlin, rather than risk Allied lives in what would otherwise have been a purely political decision for the West to capture the German capital before the USSR.

All operational decisions would have to be vetted by this joint committee, and it would have to be in the general Allied interest rather than that of a particular government. Any guerrilla organisation with Allied backing would have to place "authorized representatives" in Cairo. In addition, the Soviet Union should have a proper liaison procedure with the OSS and SOE. This last statement was unwittingly ironic since as we now know that not a few OSS operatives were also working for the NKVD, and so the Soviets would know what was happening anyway.

He ended by reminding the Joint Chiefs:

> [That], recognizing the temptation to the political leaders of Yugoslavia and Greece to play off America against the British and both against Russia, which tendency is intensified by our present attitude of telling them nothing, we forthwith make clear to them that the Moscow Conference has bound all three nations in their military effort and that the Balkan countries must temper their demands to the requirements of that joint effort.[4]

This sounded very proper, but how was one to enforce ammunition being used solely against the Germans, as opposed to the internal enemy in the civil war?

In January 1944, the OSS composed an internal summary of where things had reached in the rapidly evolving situation in Yugoslavia.[5] The King, it observed, was a "virtual prisoner" of "fanatic Great Serbs" which was naturally unhelpful to the Allied cause, and playing into the hands of his enemies. Because of the exclusion of all independent views, many hitherto loyal Yugoslav statesmen were now making common cause with Tito to form a new government in exile, one of these people being none other than Subasic, "the Shepherd".

Tito was now getting the bulk of the Allied supplies, his policy being "to fight the enemy everywhere at all times ... despite severe losses". The Americans then discovered that British policy was to drop Mihailovic and focus fully on collaborating with Tito. An American source at a meeting given by Churchill confirmed that for the British "Tito is very much in our favors [sic]". To Churchill, the Partisans were "fighting magnificently". Overtly, the British were telling their American ally the basis of why they had made the switch from the Cetniks to the Partisans – this was, we now know, ULTRA material, but this could not be revealed to the OSS.

The Partisans in touch with the USA were very open about being active Communists. The British told their OSS counterparts that while there was no indoctrination going on, "many of the best officers are Communists".

In other words, the overt Communist orientation of much of the Partisan movement was obvious and not concealed – both the USA and UK were going into their new relationship with Tito with their eyes wide open. Although some clearly, from what we have seen, denied that Tito was going to create a Communist state after the war, it is also plain that he was the man in charge and the head of the group responsible for killing the most amount of Germans. It was this short-term need, to hold down or wipe out as many Wehrmacht divisions as possible, while Allied forces slowly made their way up the Italian peninsula, that held most weight with the Allies. It must be remembered that this was US policy as well as British, so those inclined to suspect Communist moles in SOE in Cairo as the cause,need to take into account the USA as well as Britain.[6] The Allies were not being hoodwinked, and knew full well what they were doing. While there is little question but that there were active Communists among those working for SOE in Cairo – whether active NKVD agents or not – and also for the OSS, the decision taken first by Britain and then the USA was one of pure military expediency. More German deaths in Yugoslavia would result in fewer Allied casualties in Italy, and it was surely as straightforward as that.

As the OSS memorandum concluded though, American actions would have consequences:

> There would appear to be no doubt that Tito's movement is taking the leadership and influencing other partisan movements in Southeastern [sic] Europe and that such movements will increase in scope and importance as Germany's hold on the Balkans weakens. It would seem wise, therefore, for the United States not to allow itself to be placed in the position of appearing desirous of supporting to the bitter end groups hostile to the Partisans and regarded by them as reactionary, anti-democratic or downright Fascist and collaborating with the Germans in promoting disunity and civil war. If partisan movements on the Jugoslav [sic] pattern represent the quote wave of the future unquote in southeastern Europe, and the best information points us in that direction, we should consider whether our Allies could ride the crest and relegate to us the trough or whether we by our own absence of alertness should find ourselves there in the eyes of the Balkan peoples themselves, who are still exceedingly well disposed toward our country.

Endnotes

1. NND 857146 RG 226 E 146; Box 63, Folder 863.
2. NND 857146 RG 226 E 146; Box 63, Folder 860.
3. NND 843099 RG 225 E 99; Box 55, Folder 5.
4. The Moscow conference comprised talks at which key Allied leaders had met.
5. NND 857146 RG 226 E 146; Box 63, Folder 856.
6. For example, Peter Batty in *Hoodwinking Churchill: Tito's Great Confidence Trick* (London, Shepheard-Walwyn, 2011).

Chapter 11

The Shepherd Conspiracy

What do Roosevelt, Stalin, Churchill, Wild Bill Donovan, Allen Dulles, David Bruce and Bill Casey have in common? The answer is *The Shepherd*.

The "Shepherd" was the codename for one of the most exciting and hitherto secret Office of Special Services (OSS) recruitments of the Second World War, that of Ivan Subasic, the leader of the Croat people before 1941, when the Nazis invaded Yugoslavia, and who was the OSS candidate for the leadership of a free Yugoslav government after the liberation of Belgrade from the Nazis in 1944, and with a plot going back to 1943, before even Fitzroy Maclean had visited Tito that November.

But "the Shepherd", as he was called in all the Top Secret OSS files, was more than that. For he was not only an asset, but also an active agent, spying on both Churchill and Stalin for the OSS, relaying back to Donovan, Dulles and others, including Reagan's future CIA Director Bill Casey and London-based OSS agent David Bruce, on ultra-secret conversations with the USA's two allies, Winston Churchill and Soviet leader Joseph Stalin. He was a figure of some importance, being *Ban* or Viceroy of Croatia before 1941 and then Prime Minister of the Royal government of Yugoslavia in exile 1944–1945, before ending up as Foreign Minister in Tito's victorious government after the war. All this, and a spy for the Americans!

All this is based on declassified OSS material that has not seen its way into print before. Even unofficial OSS histories that mention Yugoslavia barely mention "the Shepherd" and the role that Subasic played in the secret plans of Donovan, Dulles and others to control what happened in the region after the war.

In other words, what you are reading in a book on covert operations in Yugoslavia is, along with the MI3 revelations elsewhere, one of the

159

few major scoops still left on the Second World War: the attempt by the OSS, the direct precursor of the CIA, to pursue a major strategic and foreign policy objective of their own – and with Roosevelt's clandestine approval – without the knowledge of their British ally. Furthermore, it was conducted in a way that had it succeeded would have transformed the Cold War for the better, and created the kind of Yugoslavia for which those who did not want a Communist fate for that country dreamed of.

What is so interesting about Subasic is that in recent years he has been misunderstood not as a US agent but a Soviet agent of influence. When the USA received from a Soviet defector the goldmine later known as the Venona decrypts – the crucial intercepts of Soviet intelligence radio traffic that exposed or confirmed traitors such as Kim Philby and Donald Maclean as Soviet spies – others were also revealed over the course of time as also working for the USSR. One of these was their agent "Ceres" (all their spies had codenames) and research soon revealed that this person was none other than Subasic, who thus appeared to be a Soviet NKVD agent spying for the Russians against the Americans and the British.

This meant that while the Americans did not fully inform their British ally of what was going on, it is more than likely that the Soviets, through the NKVD, knew precisely what the Americans' plans for Subasic were all about, and how they were using him in the negotiations with Tito – about which the British *did* know – to create a multi-party democracy in Yugoslavia after the Allied victory.

There was, however, one vital piece of the jigsaw about which the Soviets were as ignorant as the British. They did not now, what has now been made clear, that Subasic was really an American agent, spying for the Americans on Stalin and Churchill. He was, in truth, a Croat patriot out to get the best possible deal he could for his fellow Catholics and Croats in whatever state emerged from the ruins of Yugoslavia after the war was over, not just against the Nazis but within what was left of the original Yugoslav state as well. Those who know these things, and have seen still highly classified material, are sure that when Subasic spoke to the Americans as an OSS agent, he was telling the truth, and it is always possible that the reasons why some of the "Shepherd" files are still so profoundly secret decades after the war, and many years after much of the "Shepherd" material was slipped almost unnoticed into the National Archives in Washington DC, is that his OSS handlers might not only have known about his links with the NKVD, as revealed in the Venona decrypts, but perhaps even encouraged it. Subasic, as the OSS mole within the NKVD itself, would make him one of the most important spies in espionage history, alongside Penkovsky and Gordievsky working within the GRU and KGB successively for the British.

Croat, Catholic, patriotic: these were the motivations of Ivan Subasic, and these were just the very values that the British writer and some-time SOE agent Evelyn Waugh spent his last weeks in Yugoslavia trying to support, little realising that American spies in the Balkans were singing from the same hymn sheet as he was.

This lack of knowledge of what the American spies in the Balkans were really up to is surprising, since both serious histories of the Balkans, and even fictitious accounts (such as Alistair Maclean-based film *Force Ten From Navaronne* with Harrison Ford and Edward Fox) have plenty to say about the stories of the immensely brave British and American agents who fought the Nazis in the region during the war.

Not only that but histories have simplified the story, since the clandestine side, the adventures of British SOE and American OSS agents, have been left out of the picture. For not only were the Yugoslavs at war with Italy and the Third Reich but at war with each other. The fascist Ustase regime in Croatia, and the equally collaborationist Nedic regime in Serbia, sided with the Italians and Germans, massacred hundreds of thousands of their fellow citizens, with atrocities that even shocked the Nazis.

The Royalist regime of the exiled Yugoslav King Peter was represented by the Serbian-based Cetniks, under their leader General Mihailovic. The Cetniks were originally supported by Britain and the USA, as the heroes of national resistance against the Axis, but the ultra-secret Enigma decrypts revealed them as not fighting as many Germans and Italians as a group that was initially unknown in the West, the Communist-based Partisans under Tito, whose forces were killing far more Axis troops than anyone else. In 1943 Churchill sent a special emissary to the Partisans, Brigadier Fitzroy Maclean, whose postwar book *Eastern Approaches* became not only one of the best-known wartime stories but also one of the most famous travel books of all time – Maclean recommended to Churchill to switch sides and support the Partisans instead. Britain therefore did so, with the result that the Communist Partisans won the civil war against their fellow Yugoslavs, and also the war against the Axis, seizing Belgrade in 1944 and winning the entire country by 1945. Tito was a Croat, with Slovene descent as well, and believed in the whole country staying together as one, rather than being the representative of just one ethnic group. The Cetniks were Serbs, and this too played a major part in British thinking, since Britain also wanted to keep Yugoslavia as a single entity and not have any one group dominate the other.

It was hitherto thought either that many Americans backed the Cetniks, who were zealous anti-Communists, or tried to play both sides at the same time, with one US mission to Tito and the Partisans and another to Mihailovic and the Cetniks.

In fact, the now declassified OSS papers give a very different story. First, the OSS had a major representative in Tito's camp as well as in that of the Cetniks. This was Farish, and he too was exposed by Venona as also having at least links with Soviet intelligence, if not actually acting directly as a spy for them as well as for the West. The top secret OSS reports, put together by brave agents parachuted into the field – or smuggled in by boat – show that many of the OSS were sympathetic to Tito's Partisans, even though they were Communists, and for the same reason as the British, namely that the Partisans were killing more Germans and that they wanted to keep the whole country together without one ethnic group, especially the Serbs, taking control.

But unknown until now, the OSS had their own man at the heart of Yugoslav politics, the last ever *Ban* (or Viceroy) of Croatia, Ivan Subasic.

Most Yugoslav exiles were in London or Cairo. But "Shepherd" was different, as his place of exile was New York, around the corner from both Allen Dulles, who had an office there, and from the regional office of the OSS itself.

Like Tito, he was a Croat, and also like Tito he wanted to keep the country together. Unlike the other Royalists in exile, he could do a deal with Tito, as someone not Communist but who was a leader of the democratic and non-Communist Croat Peasant Party that aimed to run the country as a genuine democracy after Allied victory.

Sadly, troops on the ground counted for more than votes, and despite the agreement with "Shepherd", Tito's Partisans were able to seize full power. But in 1948 Tito broke with Stalin and left the Soviet bloc, Yugoslavia being a neutral country, Communist but "unaligned" and friendly to the West, until it imploded in the 1990s. Many have attributed Tito's successful break with the USSR to the brave American and British OSS and SOE soldiers who risked so much during the war to help the Partisans fight the Axis. Subasic died peacefully in the 1950s, not as Prime Minister any more, but someone who was able to help in the liberation of his country and in its break from tyranny in 1948.

Reading the now recently declassified OSS/CIA files in Washington DC, it is impossible not to be gripped by the sheer excitement of the Donovan/Dulles plot, the ultra-secret reports of "Shepherd" reporting on his meetings with Churchill in London and Stalin in Moscow, and on the brave reports from the field of the OSS agents dropped behind enemy lines with Tito's Partisans. Indeed, the OSS had, in effect, a policy all of its own, sometimes quite independent of the State Department, and which, in both the recruitment of "Shepherd" showed that the OSS was not just finding out what was happening but aiming to control the course of events as well. The now declassified "Farish Report" on Tito completely changed what even Roosevelt thought in time for his meeting at Tehran with Churchill and Stalin.

The "Shepherd" was recruited not in the field, as is usually the case with secret agents, but in New York, through the Foreign Nationals branch of the OSS. On 25 August 1943, at the St Regis Hotel in New York, Subasic was introduced to the OSS founder, General Donovan. Subasic was in refuge there, doing all possible to keep as far away as he could from the mainstream Yugoslav émigrés, many of whom were in Washington, where the exiled Royalists were based.

The majority of the circle around the King were, like young King Peter himself, strongly Serb, and unhappy about the deal done by Prince Paul in 1939 that gave the Croats their long overdue proper place as one of the founding nationalities of the Yugoslav state in 1918. Subasic, as *Ban* of Croatia, was a protégé of Paul's, something that the Americans never fully understood, failing to see that he was an appointee rather than an elected official. Nonetheless he was revered among the Croats both outside the country, especially among émigrés in the USA, and, just as vital, inside it as well. For as Waugh and the OSS both grasped, the Croats might have been nominally on the side of the Axis, but the majority of them had buyer's remorse almost as soon as the NDH (Independent Croatian State) was founded. The idea that most Croats supported the treacherous Ustase regime is, as Waugh was wise enough to know, more Serb propaganda than reality on the ground. If the Croat people changed sides, then victory over the Axis would become much easier.

Initially the OSS was not sure how best to utilise their major new recruit. But within weeks of the secret meeting between the "Shepherd" and Donovan in New York, both Subasic and his handlers had come up with a clandestine plan: the penetration of Yugoslavia, in which Subasic, and his OSS minder, Bernard Yarrow, would be the key. It was a project so secret that when most American wartime archives were de-accessioned, the "Shepherd File" was to remain concealed for decades afterwards, with much of it still withheld by the OSS successor organisation, the CIA, so sensitive and explosive is what was hatched in a hotel room back in 1943.

For while some – notably the State Department officials in the USA, and Serb Royalists in exile and in Yugoslavia – supported the Serbian nationalist leader Mihailovic, despite his deals with the Axis, and the British, as a result of the MI3 decrypts, sympathised with Tito and the Partisans, who were of course drawn from all the ethnic groups in Yugoslavia.

But the OSS understood that one of the best ways to undermine the Germans was for as many Croats to defect back to the Allies as possible. As the OSS put it, the West needed "not only the effective penetration of Yugoslavia but also the winning over of the pro-Axis military forces now acting in that territory. The only man who has the necessary qualifications for such a project is the Ban of Croatia, who is now residing in the United States"; the "Shepherd".

As we note elsewhere, Serb nationalists and their British sympathisers in the 1990s berated British wartime heroes such as Churchill's emissaries Fitzroy Maclean and Bill Deakin for supporting Tito and the Partisans. To such critics, Mihailovic was a martyr, killed by wicked Communists for being a patriot and loyal to his King. But as Maclean, Deakin and both Winston and Randolph Churchill understood at least Tito believed in keeping Yugoslavia together as a single country. He may have been a Communist, but at least he was killing Germans and he was a Yugoslav. For Tito, and his British backers, keeping Yugoslavia together as a single country was just as vital in the long term as was the defeat of the Axis in the short term. This may all have been secondary to the main aim of winning the war, tying down German battalions in the Balkans and thereby helping Allied forces in Italy. But it was in the background nonetheless.

This was also the policy backed by several Americans, including Farish, as we shall see elsewhere, whose rationale was very similar to that of the United Kingdom. But the USA was in fact playing an even more complex game, a very different one from its British and Soviet allies, and one very much of its own. For Donovan, unlike Secretary of State Cordell Hull, felt that the Americans had a real stake in the Balkans and that what happened in Yugoslavia after Allied victory was as important as what was going on in wartime.

So, while Farish was in the field with Tito and the Partisans, another OSS operative, Huntington, was with Mihailovic and the Cetniks, and in New York the civilian Bernard Yarrow was with the OSS' own man, the "Shepherd". He was, according to the secret Donovan plan, "for a federated Yugoslavia and is above party groups and factions" and was the only man capable of "uniting all resistance and fighting forces now operating within Yugoslavia in order to expedite the delivery of his country from the yoke of the German invaders".

Indeed, the OSS spymasters felt that only their man "Shepherd" would be able to win over the army of the NDH in Nazi-controlled Croatia to their side, but also that of the "Serbian Puppet Government" under Nedic as well. Neither of the collaborationist armies would support the Communist Tito, and no Croat would ever support the Serb-based Cetniks. If Subasic were able to deliver on his promises, Yugoslavia would remain a federal state after the war was over, and the OSS would have one of their agents in charge of the newly liberated country. The sooner Subasic could contact resistance groups on the ground in Yugoslavia – including Tito's Partisans, many of whom, the OSS felt, were more patriots than Communists – the better.

So secret was this plan that not even the Royal government in exile was to know about it. This was an OSS plan and while the State Department did not stop it, the diplomats were far from happy with the spies embarking on a foreign policy all of their own. (OSS did cover their hide by logging all their meetings with the State Department, especially since the diplomats continued to support the Serbian nationalist Mihailovic long after everyone else had transferred their support elsewhere.)

Subasic was keen to talk to the OSS, to co-operate with them "when the course of events in Yugoslavia will dictate it". The OSS founder and Director, William Donovan, was to meet Subasic in New York. The thinking behind the OSS willingness to meet him was that as the *Ban*'s prestige was so high in his home country, he would be able to bring the benevolence and aid of the 5 million Croatians with him. The conspiracy had begun.

The meeting took place in secret at the St Regis Hotel in New York, on 25 August. It was between Donovan, referred to as "the General" in the OSS files and Subasic, still called by his Croatian title, 'the *Ban*'. Other members of the OSS were there, including John Hughes. The OSS was still not entirely sure what to do with him, but the idea of weaning 5 million Croatians away from the Ustase regime in Zagreb, and in favour of the Allied cause, was coalescing in their minds.

But by September, various ideas on how to use Allied-friendly Croatians were forming more clearly, as shown in a memorandum for the OSS by John Hughes and Bernard Yarrow, so secret that it had to be kept in an especially safe drawer. It was called *The Penetration of Yugoslavia Project*. It was ambitious from the start:

> This project has as its aim not only the effective penetration of Yugoslavia but also the winning over of the pro-Axis military forces now operating in that territory. The only man who has the necessary qualifications for such a project is the Ban of Croatia who is now residing in the United States.

As the OSS realised, Subasic was not just revered by everyone in Croatia, "but his popularity is great throughout the whole of Yugoslavia". Furthermore, although Croat himself, he was "for a federated Yugoslavia and is above party groups and factions". As King Peter had appointed him as the *Ban*, he was someone who had good relations with the Royalists in Yugoslavia but without being a Serb.

The OSS discovered that after talking to Subasic he was now "willing and ready to assist the OSS not only in penetrating effectively Yugoslavia at this moment, but also in uniting all resistance and fighting forces now operating within Yugoslavia in order to expedite the delivery of his country from the yoke of the German invaders".

Subasic, the OSS planners thought, was in a unique position. He could win over his fellow 5 million fellow Croats (that number occurs frequently in the OSS files) from the Ustase collaborators, gaining a possible force of 200,000 people to accomplish this. On top of this, he could overthrow the other collaborationist regime as well, that of the Serbian quisling, General Nedic, based in Belgrade. The *Ban* could get the thousands of members of the Croatian Peasant Party to come to his aid as well.

So an initial plot began to come together:

a) An operational base in Bari.
b) A mission, led by Subasic, that would be deliberately Yugoslav (a Serb, a Croatian, a Slovene) and that would also be deliberately non-political.
c) Then contact Yugoslav prisoners of war in Italy, especially the 19 generals among the 1,250 officers.
d) Use these to link up with fighting forces already on some of the islands.

e) Begin talks with the Partisans in some regions, and with anti-fascist groups within Ustase controlled-territory in Croatia.

The OSS felt that they now had "at our disposal the most dynamic force and the most powerful weapon in the personality of the *Ban* to encourage and unite the resistance forces now operating in Yugoslavia".

While everything had to be kept quiet in order not to jeopardise the project, it became necessary for the OSS eventually to share their plans with the State Department. The latter were happy for the *Ban* to go, but not with their blessing or that of the Army. The whole plan was still to be kept completely secret.

Despite the restrictions, the thinkers at OSS continued to ponder how their opening via Subasic could be useful in creating a genuinely national Yugoslav government. On 25 September Lieutenant Patrick Dolan contacted his superior, John Hughes, in the New York office of OSS. The aim was certainly ambitious, namely to "unify the Partisan and Cetnik resistance groups in co-operation with the established OSS-SOE missions in Yugoslavia with Tito and Mihailovich [*sic*] and the direction of Guerrilla [*sic*] operations before and after this unification has been accomplished". Both the Ustase regime and that of the Serb collaborators under Nedic could be overthrown, and the Croatians softened up for an Allied invasion.

The OSS did realise one major brake upon their activities. This was the clearly expressed views of the Joint Chiefs of Staff that whatever the former conspired to do, such activities "should be of such a character as will involve no commitments on the part of the United States. This should be directed solely to assisting the defeat of the Axis." The Joint Chiefs had also asked that the "OSS shows preference among resistance groups or prospective successor governments only on a basis of their willingness to cooperate, and without regard to their ideological differences or political programs".

This was, as we saw, very much how Winston Churchill saw the issues as well when he sent Fitzroy Maclean to see the Partisans. The fact that, to both Churchill and Maclean, a Partisan victory might well lead to a post-victory Communist government in Yugoslavia was strictly secondary to the immediate short-term goal of beating the Third Reich in the war. As we see elsewhere, Churchill was quite prepared to talk to Stalin and allow the USSR to have areas it controlled once Hitler was defeated. However, in the case of Poland, Churchill was to become very anxious that such a brave nation be absorbed into the new Soviet empire.

The Joint Chiefs of Staff were just as short-term in their outlook as the British were over Yugoslavia. The whole controversy between Churchill on the one hand, and Eisenhower and Marshall on the other on the so-called "race for Berlin" demonstrates this. Whereas Churchill, a short-termer in relation to Tito, feared the long-term consequences of a liberation of Berlin by the Red Army, the American generals felt strongly that Germany had to be defeated first before any post-war political solutions could be found. Over the Yugoslav question, both Churchill and the Americans were in agreement – fling the Germans out of the country first, and then worry about the post-war settlement.

This was, as will become evident, not the way in which Evelyn Waugh saw things, very conscious as he was of the long-term implications of allowing Communists both to win the internal civil war (against the Cetniks) and the wider conflict between the Allies and the Axis, with the Partisans on the winning side of both.

The British were being pragmatic. But so too were the OSS, just that they were backing a different group to win the internal battle so that the main war could be won more easily by the Allies. The OSS recognised fully that "the Partisans are the only effective resistance group at present active" and also, very significantly, that the Royalist government in exile had made matters far worse by being both "anti-partisan and pro-Serb".

To the OSS, Subasic and another exiled politician, a Serb from Croatia named Sava Kosanovic, were the two ideal men to lead a campaign that would get the support of all the disparate Yugoslav peoples. The fact that unlike the vast majority of contemporary Balkan politicians the two men were honest was also a major factor in their favour. Not only that, but as the OSS admitted, the "complex Yugoslav political situation has created a tangle of loyalties so involved that even the ablest intelligence officer would, without the help of men such as these, have difficulties". So secret was everything that only a special courier service between New York and Washington DC would be safe – up to this time the OSS had been using the regular post!

The OSS solution was interesting in that they genuinely believed that they were fulfilling the Joint Chiefs of Staff requirement to have a politically neutral solution. But they were overlooking the fact that both of their candidates would have their own political agendas, and seek to install themselves as rulers of the country after the war, though under the nominal command of the exiled King Peter.

But now the State Department started to realise these implications as well. As one of their memoranda – for 25 September – made clear, its author was "disturbed by its implications". Had it been a simple matter of restoring the *Ban* to Croatia that would be one thing. But the OSS were in effect trying to have a national solution, one "heavily weighted in Croatia's favor [*sic*]". Subasic, in the view of the State Department, was individually a fine man, but someone who was both in conflict with the Royalists and also "anathema to the Serbs", and the Serbs were still the most powerful national group within Yugoslavia.

Not only that, but to the diplomats, the *Ban* was rather "optimistic of his prospects". He might have been revered back in 1941, but now, in 1943, the situation in Yugoslavia had changed, which yet again is also an understatement, since, as Maclean and the British realised, in a way that the Americans clearly had not, that it was Tito and the Partisans who were truly pulling their weight against the Germans.

Above all, the State Department understood what the OSS had not, that there really was no accurate way of finding out on the ground who was supporting whom in the maelstrom of the parallel Yugoslav conflicts, the civil war and the struggle against the Axis. As the diplomats put it:

> This Department has tried very hard to obtain reliable information about the situation within Yugoslavia, and we must confess that we are still somewhat bewildered. We admit that there has been considerable exaggeration of General Mihailovich's exploits, and a measure of truth in some of the accusations against him. We do not accept the denigration of the Partisans on the part of the Serb nationalists, and we are willing to give the Partisans credit for being much more than "bandits", "communists", [*sic* for punctuation] et cetera.

What follows next is interesting, because it suggests that the State Department officials involved in this discussion did not have access to ULTRA, because otherwise they would have known the answer to the legitimate question that they now posed – namely that ULTRA showed beyond peradventure that it was the Partisans who were taking the battle to the German occupying forces. As the State Department concluded:

> At the same time we have never been able to ascertain what were the sources of the splendid information concerning

the Partisan's [sic] achievement which so many unofficial "experts" here in America claim to have.

Had the State Department only consulted those with access to ULTRA, they would have known the correct answer – that such opinions were based upon fact and not surmise. It also seems that the SOE were not sharing much with the Americans through official channels, so it was then imperative, to the diplomats, that the USA started to make enquiries on the ground of their own.

It was then, in October 1943, that the OSS christened their plot the "Shepherd Project", although the files declassified to date do not tell us of the reason for this particular codename. But the idea of Subasic being the shepherd of his peoples is an interesting one, whether or not such a guess is accurate.

The OSS had to come up with an answer to the State Department, and this was now the task of John Hughes to undertake. There was some degree of back-pedalling, with due recognition given to the fact that the "Shepherd" would not be going to Yugoslavia as the official envoy of the US Government or US Army commanders in the region. But the OSS stuck to its original thought that the *Ban* was the only person who had the local standing to get the information needed on the ground to give the Allies the intelligence vitally necessary to rid Yugoslavia of Axis forces. He alone could achieve this, and he had convinced his friends in the OSS that he had no policy thoughts on how Yugoslavia should evolve after the war was over.

This was clearly what the OSS believed, and that this being the case, the Shepherd would genuinely be seen in Yugoslavia as being neutral between all the factions. This temporarily mollified the State Department, so long as it was kept fully informed of everything by the OSS, which, from the correspondence in the OSS files, was something that it is possible to infer that they feared might not happen. Hughes promised the State Department that they would behave themselves, but when one also considers, for example, the shaky relations between SOE and MI6 in Britain, it is obvious to see that established departments were by nature suspicious of the new upstarts that had been created during the war.

Donovan himself became very excited at the prospects offered by the Shepherd Project. He was now keen for it to go ahead as fast as possible, and would be telling no less than the President himself. To make sure that he was fully in the picture, Donovan saw Subasic again at the St Regis Hotel in New York. But he wanted to be sure that it went right. Until his authorisation came (and perhaps also that of the President), all was to be handled with the "utmost secrecy".

So, on 19 October 1943, Subasic was asked to write a memorandum directly for the President, and for Donovan's meeting with the latter. The text is rather flowery, if not gushing, as he declared himself "only a guardian and the first servant of my people ... unencumbered by ambition and material gain". Speaking to Roosevelt's concerns, he wanted for Yugoslavia "all those rights which are attributed to a freedom loving and democratic nation according to the principles of democracy".

Donovan himself was careful to write an accompanying memorandum, on 21 October, recognising that the President had shown "a great deal of interest" in the Balkans. Donovan continued that Subasic wanted to go on behalf of the OSS to make contact with the key players in Croatia, and would do so "merely as a soldier and patriot to assist us in our fight against the enemy". Subasic felt that he could easily persuade the Ustase army over to the Allied side, which of course was quite a claim to make, not that Donovan pointed that out to the President. Subasic also promised to help the USA to "establish liaison with Tito, with whom he hopes to work very closely", though how he aimed to achieve this was also not elaborated by Donovan for the President.

Donovan had to cover the fact that Subasic had steadfastly avoided contact both with the US State Department, and with the USA and Britain's still-official ally, the exiled Royal government under the nominal command of King Peter. The former was apparently to avoid embarrassment and the latter because of the exiled government's rather strong pro-Serb bias. The second was a statement of truth, but Donovan did not deal with what, to the State Department, was the substantive issue, namely that the "Shepherd" had provided no concrete proof that he really was as admired by millions of Yugoslavs as he claimed for himself.

Now that the President was in the picture, or that part of the picture in which Donovan believed, delicate steps could now proceed to set the ball in motion. So, on 20 November, it was agreed that Subasic could go to Italy or North Africa, and there await the authorisation to go to Yugoslavia itself. Subasic was also now dangling before the links with the Partisans, and in an interesting way. It seemed that "some of the men who formerly were very close to him are now with Tito's army". This was in fact a very obvious development. Tito was no Serb, as we saw, but a half-Croat, half-Slovene, and, one could argue, the one genuine Yugoslav both on the ground and dealing with the Germans.

The plot was therefore hatched that Subasic would aim to get to Yugoslavia itself so that he could talk to the various guerrilla groups, including "the Partisans ... in the territory occupied by the resistance forces", with the aim of uniting as many of the Partisans and Croat Peasant Party forces as possible, thus increasing significantly the number of anti-German forces on the ground.

Donovan's aim was for the USA to be a player in putting together a post-war Yugoslav Government. In this, he was up against not only the Serb-supporting State Department, but also the Tito-supporting British and also the wishes of the Joint Chiefs of Staff themselves. The latter had told the OSS that their Balkan activities "should be of such a character as will involve no commitments on the part of the United States. They should be directed solely to assisting in the defeat of the Axis", and that in choosing their local allies to accomplish this, the OSS should "show preference among resistance groups or prospective successor governments only on a basis of their willingness to cooperate, and without regard to their ideological differences or political programs".

Here the OSS was proving to be very different to the leading members of the American military, such as Army Chief of Staff Marshall in Washington DC, and soldiers in the field such as Eisenhower. For them the key priority was winning the war – the details of the peace could be sorted out afterwards. Towards the end of the war, as his memoirs reveal, Churchill was to begin to think long term, especially about the fate of Poland and its likely oppression by the Soviet Union. This was despite his priorities regarding Yugoslavia in 1943, in which only Allied advantage mattered rather than the fate of the Balkan peoples after the defeat of the Axis powers.

But to concentrate only on victory, rather than give a second thought to how the map of Europe would appear after Allied triumph was, Donovan felt, with a not inconsiderable degree of merit, a very short-sighted policy, since the shape of Europe after the war mattered a very great deal. Indeed, he understood, as we have seen, that people could simply be substituting one kind of tyranny for another, which would be of no good to anyone.

The OSS realised that while short-term objectives were all very well, they agreed fully with Maclean and SOE that the Partisans were "the only effective group at present active" against the Germans. Nor was the Royal government under weak and exiled young King Peter any good either: the Royalists, in being Serb nationalists, alienated the Croats, and in being anti-Tito they were alienating the only local guerrillas actually doing any good: Peter and his cronies had thus "aggravated both disputes".

So to the spymaster Donovan, the one answer was someone who was a Croat, appointed to high office by King Peter, who also had links with and vital credibility with Tito and the Partisans, and Subasic, the *Ban* of pre-war Croatia, was just such a man. The sooner, Donovan felt, that the "Shepherd" could get out to Yugoslavia the better.

Indeed, so excited was Donovan that he went over the heads of everyone in Washington DC, from the Secretary of State through to the Joint Chiefs of Staff, and straight to Roosevelt himself. He had already begun to excite the President about his various ideas for Balkan strategies, plans that would give heart-failure to the more cautious minded military commanders such as General George C. Marshall.

Donovan now persuaded Subasic to write a memorandum for Roosevelt, not to get the US involved in dangerous escapades, but "merely as a soldier and patriot to assist us in our fight against the enemy". Subasic would go under OSS auspices to Yugoslavia, to find out what was really going on in the region, to win over as many Croats as possible to the Allied cause, and "to establish liaison with Tito, with whom he hopes to work very closely".

Donovan did not hide from Roosevelt his disagreements with the State Department. He reminded the President that Susbasic had spurned the representatives of the Yugoslav Royal government in exile in the USA, and that Susbasic believed that the Royalists were "in the power of Pan-Serb groups, who think in terms of Serbs only, and not in terms of a federated Yugoslavia in which all groups, Serbs, Croats and Slovenes, are equally represented".

Donovan hoped that the President would want to meet the man himself. While Roosevelt did not agree to do this, he did, however, give his spymaster full *carte blanche* to go ahead on the project, which then proceeded with full vigour.

Then, as Subasic was about to fly to his clandestine assignation in the Balkans, the situation changed – the King was now prepared to speak to him, and a whole new range of possibilities opened. This would, as the OSS realised, now make their task much easier.[1]

It was now possible that Subasic could be a conduit between the Royal government in exile, under King Peter, and Tito's Partisans in the field, the only guerrilla group that was both effectively fighting the Germans, as the British realised, but would actually try to keep the country together after the war, the wish of the OSS.

Now it becomes interesting, because not only did the OSS want to get Tito on their side but they also now needed – since Tito was a Communist – to appraise the Soviets of their intentions. This involved telling Andrei Vishinsky, the Deputy Foreign Minister, and the former notorious prosecutor for Stalin's show trials in the Great Purge before the war. Since the OSS did not know from their own secret intelligence sources what the outcome would be, they felt that they had to clear the project now with both Partisans and Soviets, to make sure it worked.

It is also interesting because, as we saw at the beginning, as well as being an OSS spy as the "Shepherd", Subasic was also a Soviet intelligence source, through the NKVD, as "Ceres". Were the OSS, in telling Tito and Vishinsky, informing them about someone about whom the NKVD already knew? Somewhere in the CIA, in files so secret that they are still guarded under lock and key, may be the answer.

If Subasic, or agent *Ceres* to Stalin's spies the NKVD, was a pivotal part of the Soviet plan, the USSR took its time. Not until January 1944, some three months after Subasic was ready to hop on the first available plane to Yugoslavia, did the Russian authorisation come through. As for Tito, still ideologically in step with Stalin at this time, the Partisan leader also took time to reply.

But on 15 February 1944, came the reply for which the OSS had been waiting. This came via an interesting source – the OSS agent to Tito, Major Linn Farish, who was tragically to die in a plane crash in the Balkans later that year. It was, as we saw, his report in 1943 that had persuaded the USA, not just the OSS, that Tito and the Partisans were serious players, and that as Maclean had told Churchill, the Partisans were not only genuine Yugoslavs who wanted to keep the country together but were also killing far more Germans than the Serb nationalist Cetniks. "Tito … will be glad to see [Subasic] at his HQ for conversations" came the message, with an added note that at the age of fifty-two he might be too old to be parachuted in, which meant that he would have to be infiltrated by sea. This was good news; Subasic's period of waiting was now over.

But was this one Soviet NKVD agent helping another? Or was it two loyal OSS agents coming together? For while Farish was one of the most important OSS agents during the Second World War, and and one of the most influential – his report on Tito was quoted by Roosevelt at the crucial Tehran conference in late 1943 between the President and Churchill and Stalin – Farish's name also appears in the Venona decrypts, as NKVD agent "Attila".

Either way, Subasic and his OSS minder were soon off to London, where they met with the young King Peter, who was in the process of marrying a Greek princess (a cousin of Prince Philip, then a young officer in the Royal Navy). Here Subasic's luck changed, going from a *persona non grata* with the Royalists to being someone now considered as a future Prime Minister of the exiled government.

The State Department, composed of supporters of Mihailovic and the Cetniks, were furious at this, since Donovan and his fellow spies had, in effect, overturned official US policy. But their protests were to no avail. The legendary spymaster had won the turf wars and the President's ear.

On 3 May 1944, Subasic, Yarrow and a Colonel Buxton met in Donovan's own office; there would be no clandestine meetings in hotels any more for the OSS' prize recruit. Now the fact that Subasic was simultaneously the "Shepherd" for the OSS and "Ceres" for the NKVD becomes interesting. He was about to go and see the King in London and then go on to see Tito in Partisan-controlled Yugoslavia. What he told Donovan would also have been good news for those wanting a non-Communist post-war outcome for Yugoslavia. The British, Subasic told his handlers, had made two mistakes in the war. First, they had been too friendly with Mihailovic, and encouraged him much too much, and now they were compounding their earlier error by doing the same thing "in regard to Tito". As the Royalists were so weak, they were dealing exclusively with Tito, and thereby encouraging the latter and his Partisans to think of themselves as the people who would run the country after the war.

He, Subasic, would change all this. A "strong Government" linked externally to the Royalists but helping Tito on the ground would be the way forward; and the Allied military aid should be funnelled not direct to Tito, as was happening at the moment, but through a new unified Royal exiled government to the Partisans. If Mihailovic decided he would resist the Germans after all, then he too could get Allied aid "in proportion to the resistance exercised".

This would unite all anti-Axis forces in Yugoslavia, and would enable the peoples of that war-torn country to make a genuine choice after the war was over, rather than on the basis of who commanded the strongest resistance army while the fighting on the ground was still in progress.

Donovan had his plan, and his man in place. He then covered himself against Washington enemies by taking the President fully into his confidence.

Come 1944, and the British were also now part of the plan to place Subasic in power. Along with Donovan's assistant Yarrow, Subasic met Churchill in London in that May:

MEMORANDUM FOR THE PRESIDENT

The following report of the meeting on 21 May between the Ban of Croatia and Mr. Churchill was prepared for me by my special assistant, Mr. Bernard Yarrow ...

In view of the secrecy maintained by the British on this conference, apart from this report to you, I am having only the Secretary of State advised ...

The Ban informed me yesterday that he had received a telephone call from Churchill's secretary, requesting him to have dinner with Churchill at the latter's country place ... on Sunday, 21 May ... The Ban, ... accompanied by Mr. Stevenson, British Minister to Yugoslavia, ... arrived there about noon ...

At one o'clock, Mr. Churchill joined them and during the dinner he had the Prime Minister of Holland seated at his right and the Ban at his left. Addressing his guests and pointing to the Ban, Mr. Churchill said: "I want you to meet the next Prime Minister of Yugoslavia." Noticing the expression of surprise on the Ban's face, Mr. Churchill said to him: "Why, don't you know that you are going to be the Prime Minister of the new Yugoslav Government?" The Ban replied: "The King consulted with me regarding the formation of a new government but has not as yet informed me of the fact that I am to be the Prime Minister of that Government and that I will be entrusted with its formation. Mr. Churchill then said: "Why of course. That is the reason I asked you to come here."

Thereafter ... Mr. Churchill stated ... that he consulted, of course, with the President of the United States about the formation of this new government under the premiership of the Ban and was assured of his complete approval.

Turning to the Ban, Churchill then said: "You will form this government and I assure you that Great Britain and the United

States will regard yours as the only government of the Yugoslav people, and within four or five weeks you will get all the support and assistance we can possibly render to your country ...

Churchill further added: "We shall continue to have friendly relations with Tito because he is conducting a vigorous campaign in Yugoslavia, but we shall look to you and your cabinet as the only legitimate government of Yugoslavia."

Churchill informed the Ban that he had informed Tito that, if he is in favor of the new government, his support will be very welcome, but at any rate he must refrain from attacking it and thereby disrupting the earnest attempt which will be made by the new government to unify Yugoslavia. ... He frankly did not know what the attitude of Stalin would be. He expressed the hope that the USSR will join with England and America in giving whole-hearted support to the new government but had no information on that point up to the present.

On the way home Mr. Stevenson spoke to the Ban about the conference with Churchill. The Ban pointed out to him that whereas the Prime Minister took it for granted that he is the future Premier, the King has not advised him as yet that he is entrusted to form the government. The Ban then said that he is contemplating calling King Peter tomorrow, Monday, May 22nd, and informing him of the conference with Churchill so as to bring the matter to a head.

With Churchill's full support, and that of his emissary to the Balkans, Fitzroy Maclean, the Tito-Subasic Agreement was signed on the liberated island of Vis on 16 June 1944, to come into full effect that November. Subasic was to be Foreign Minister of a unity Government, which, the British hoped as well as the Americans, would be the democratically elected and thus wholly legitimate Government of Yugoslavia after the war.

Maclean, in his memoirs, emphasises that Britain kept out of direct involvement with the talks on Vis. But as he fully recognised at the time, Tito held all the cards and that the agreement probably sounded then, and was soon proved later, "too good to be true".

The Americans were also keeping Mihailovic – whose collaboration with the Germans even they believed in – right out of the picture, as a

177

memorandum sent by the OSS to President Roosevelt made plain that August:

25 August 1944

MEMORANDUM FOR THE PRESIDENT

General Donovan (who is presently in London) has asked that the following report of a conversation he had on 21 August with Prime Minister Subasich be sent to you from him:

I talked with Subasich on Monday and he told me the following:

"On August 20 I had a conversation with Adam Pribicevich, Vice President of Draga Mihailovich's Committee. When Pribicevich asked for my help to stop the Partisans' fight against the Chetniks, which is now raging with full intensity and when he asked me whether we could bring about a reconciliation between the Partisans and the Chetniks, I answered:

"If you wish to fight the Partisans as Communists – conscious of the fact that they are sons of our nation – and to this end, accept the help and collaboration of the Germans, you cannot expect anything from the King, the Royal Government or the Allies" …

There has also been received from our representative in Bern the following Boston Series report which is of direct relevance to the matters discussed in General Donovan's talk with Subasic …

During the second week of August 1944, Hermann Neubacher, German special plenipotentiary for the Balkan area, is reported to have made the following comments on Mihailovich and the political situation in Yugoslavia:

"The position of those Chetniks who advocate cooperation with the Germans is strengthened by the fact that the latter may soon be forced to evacuate Serbia. This would be the signal for a show-down engagement between the Communists and the Nationalists. Mihailovich therefore probably intends to cooperate with the German Army while it is still in Serbia, in order to lessen the effectiveness of Tito's Partisans. By emphasizing the common fight against Communism, Mihailovich would obtain as many weapons as possible from the Germans. He feels that he will then be able to take over the German positions easily when the German

178

army leaves. Informal negotiations between Mihailovich and the Germans are said to have been initiated, and may possibly be followed by an official conference at a later date."

By January 1945, not only was Subasic finding negotiations with the Partisans hard-going, but he was dismissed by his supposed political master, King Peter, whose Prime Minister he was now notionally supposed to be. But by March the young exiled sovereign had calmed down, and all was – in theory at least – back in play.

However, Tito now had the Red Army on his side as well as his victorious Partisans. By the end of the war, brute armed strength was all that actually mattered. Predictably, once elections were held in October 1945, the Communists won overwhelmingly, so that any compromise necessary pre-VE Day was now needless. Subasic resigned, and thankfully for him, died peacefully in his bed in Zagreb in 1955, all the American and later British hopes for him dashed by military realities.

But while the story of the Tito-Subasic Agreement is well known, *The Shepherd File* is not, and most of you will probably have heard of it for the first time here in this book. Some of it appears now on the CIA website, but does not start until mid-1944, *after* the Shepherd file closes.[2]

The OSS did have its own policy, but in support of Subasic it was very different from what has been supposed. Intelligence, as Sir Alec Cadogan is reported to have said, truly is the missing dimension of history. Was Subasic a spy for Stalin as well as Venona suggests? Or was he, as some think, just a patriot speaking to all sides to get a good deal for his people? We shall, alas, never discover. But his story is a fascinating one that needs to be better known than it is.

Endnotes

1. An interesting side-view of Allied relations – when OSS received the news, in early December 1943, it was agreed that, "we make sure that neither the British in Washington or in London are appraised" of the plans. They would discover eventually but not until the Americans were ready.
2. https://www.cia.gov/library/center-for-the-study-of-intelligence/kent-csi/vol9no2/html/v09i2a07p_0001.htm accessed 12th December 2014.

Chapter 12

Churchill, Gettysburg and Yugoslavia, 1945

On 22 February 1944 Winston Churchill finally closed the door on aid for Mihailovic and the Cetniks. Although the die had in effect been cast back at the end of 1943, as we have seen, it was not finally until early 1944 that all became public. And as he could not of course mention ULTRA and the real reason for the decision, he quoted the advice he had been given by Bill Deakin when he spoke to the House of Commons. Tito was the hero of the hour and Mihailovic was history. The change had been made and the break with Mihailovic sealed.

This is what happened, but understandably, in the light of Mihailovic's execution in 1946 by the new Communist regime in Yugoslavia, there are those who wish it had been otherwise.

But can you argue from a might have been instead of an as it actually occurred? This takes us into interesting territory, or "counterfactual history".

Alternative or counterfactual history is no modern invention. In 1932 Sir John Squire edited a book titled *If It Had Happened Otherwise* and there is a chapter in it on Gettysburg by none less than Winston Churchill. Not all historians agree that counterfactual history is a legitimate historical tool: there is much debate in academic life on its merits and disadvantages. Professor Sir Richard Evans, the former Regius Professor of History at Cambridge University, has written against it, while the well-known columnist Niall Fergusson, who now teaches history in the USA, has edited books of counterfactual history and defends it intellectually.

The purpose of our book has been to describe what actually happened, rather than the what-ifs or might-have-beens of counterfactual history. Tito took power in 1944–1945, was a loyal satrap of Stalin until 1948, and then, uniquely as we saw, switched Yugoslavia from being a subservient Soviet satellite behind the Iron Curtain into being a nation that while still Communist became officially neutral in the Cold War, becoming known in 1954 as the Non-Aligned Movement. For this he was savagely attacked in print by no less than James Klugmann, by this time a faithful member of the pro-USSR Communist Party of Great Britain, for whom Tito's declaration of independence was ideological anathema.

Those are the facts.

So why is counterfactual history relevant for us at all, especially if it is, according to Professor Evans and others, more entertainment than serious academic history?

The answer is surely that the basic premise of the conspiracy theorists is that if Britain had continued to side with Mihailovic, Yugoslavia would never have gone Communist. This is given in the eyes of the revisionists and conspirators.

However, all of this is counterfactual history with no basis in what actually took place at all. When Churchill and Maclean had their infamous chat in 1943, they presumed that the Partisans would win the civil war in Yugoslavia anyway. And remember it was the Soviet Red Army that liberated the capital Belgrade on 20 October 1944. Many Partisans helped, but it was Soviet heavy weaponry that completed the deed and defeated the Wehrmacht.

Let us therefore explore the counterfactual – British support for Mihailovic – but do so in what one can surely argue is a far more realistic way than the pro-Serb revisionists, both in the 1940s and again during the second civil war, in the 1990s.

Let us look first at the reality as it was when the war ended. Tito was so strong that although the Red Army played a major role in establishing the Communist leader in power, he was able to make it appear that he took power himself.

This idea of doing it alone was of course an exaggeration, but there was enough of a grain of truth in it to give him a unique degree of legitimacy among the Communist-imposed regimes of Central and Eastern Europe after 1945. No other Communist leader – except for perhaps in Albania – could claim to have played a major military role in the defeat of the Axis. Tito could be so bold, and in 1948, when he quit the Soviet bloc, he was then able to remember the British contribution, however slender, to his margin of victory in 1945. Deakin and Maclean's actions in 1943 were now recalled positively, instead of being ignored at the expense of the Red Army's actions in 1944.

This does not ignore the savagery of the years 1945–1948, when Tito, as a follower of Stalin, massacred thousands of his own people, including many family members of Croat friends of the author, who lost relatives in that period murdered on Tito's orders.

What is different is that because Tito was the national hero of Yugoslavia in 1948, he was able to crush any pro-Soviet resistance in the country, and defeat attempts by Stalin to launch a counter-coup that would have installed a pro-Moscow lackey who would do the USSR's bidding. Tito, unlike all the other Soviet bloc dictators, was not installed as a puppet of Stalin but as an independent man, loyal totally to Communist ideology but without the need for Soviet troops to keep him in power. One could put it this way: Communism *yes* but Stalin *no*. Not a few authors have pointed out that Tito's claim is distinctly exaggerated, but the fact is, that is how he was perceived. This was still very much so in the 1970s, when his powers were on the wain, and the idol was seen very much to have feet of clay. Yet, as one anti-Communist Yugoslav put it, at least Tito kept the Russians out.

To return to the illustration we saw earlier, given by the friends of mine whose family was eliminated after 1945: Yugoslavia was still a cage, but a very big cage. During Tito's lifetime, there was no genuine democracy of any kind in Yugoslavia, and dissent was strongly frowned upon. But the kind of heavy brutality of Romania or East Germany was unknown. After hundreds of thousands of deaths in the civil war of the 1940s, the extraordinary thing is that peace lasted not just until Tito's death, but for several more years thereafter. All this was possible because while most Yugoslavs were probably not personally Communist, the fact that Tito had liberated them from the Soviet bloc in 1948 and kept the USSR out of their country was, for them, something to cherish.

How different things would have been had Yugoslavia, in 1944–1945, been like Poland or Romania or East Germany, countries in which Communism was ruthlessly imposed not by popular will but by the tanks of the Red Army. Cities in Czechoslovakia and Hungary would have Second World War Soviet tanks displayed in prominent places, and vast memorials to the dead of the Red Army, to remind those now under Communist rule that they had been, to use the usual phrase, liberated from fascism by the blood of the Soviet Union. To be anti-Communist was to be pro-fascist, therefore implying that millions of

Red Army troops had sacrificed their lives in vain. Conquest, therefore, legitimised Soviet rule.

But Yugoslavia was different.

While the Red Army helped, the key point is that in terms of legitimacy, that laurel unquestionably went to Tito and to the Partisans. Soviet tanks destroyed much of the Wehrmacht, but ordinary people felt that it was the forces of their own nation that had liberated the country. Tito was the hero, not Stalin and his legions.

However, had Tito been crushed by the Cetniks during the war, as the revisionist/conspiracy theory buffs would have preferred, 1944–1945 would have been radically different, and in several ways.

So, we can suggest some new and quite separate counterfactuals:

a) The Red Army would have "liberated" Yugoslavia in 1945 in the same way as they did with other parts of Eastern/Central Europe.

b) The civil war that paralleled the war against Germany 1941–1945 *might* have resumed in 1945, with bloodshed as terrible as that of 1945–1948 and the 1990s in real life.

The point about both these counterfactuals is that neither of them ends up with a Serb-ruled Yugoslavia. The first presumes that Yugoslavia would still have become Communist, and the second that the slaughter would still have happened, only differently, and that Yugoslavia could have broken in pieces in the 1940s rather than, as actually happened, stuck together until the 1990s.

Would Stalin have been happy to have King Peter restored, and Mihailovic installed in Belgrade as the heroic and Serbian leader of post-war Yugoslavia? In Romania King Michael (a cousin both of the Serb king and of Britain's George VI) was already in Romania in 1944 when he deposed the pro-Nazi local fascist regime and surrendered to the Soviets. He was unable to resist being deposed by the Communists in 1947, the Red Army being in occupation of his country. Similarly, the coup against a democratically elected Government in Czechoslovakia shocked the world, and led the next year to the creation of NATO. But there was not much that the then-oppressed Czech and Slovak peoples could do to resist Soviet conquest since its armies had captured the country in 1945. So, the idea of a Yugoslav monarchy, bolstered by triumphant Cetniks, in 1945, is surely a complete fantasy.

The point about proper counterfactuals, from the viewpoint of those who regard them as academically respectable, is that they have to be realistic. This is what distinguished legitimate counterfactuals from, say, alternative history, that has aliens invading earth, more like *Doctor Who*, than serious attempts to consider different outcomes to real events. The idea of the USSR allowing the return to power of the Serb-dominated pre-1941 regime surely falls into the category of something that could, given Stalin's power and actual behaviour in 1944–1945, never have the remotest chance of being able to happen.

If the Soviets had imposed Communism in Yugoslavia legitimacy would have been with them, and Tito would have vanished in 1948 rather than consolidating his hold on power. In terms of the Cold War, the Soviet bloc would then have enjoyed several warm water ports on the Adriatic, which in reality were denied to them after Tito's declaration of independence. That would have made NATO's task harder and given the Warsaw Pact a considerable strategic advantage.

Second, in real life Tito's popularity – or at least his status – was able to keep the First World War creation of Yugoslavia together, right down to the 1990s. Perhaps significantly it was not until the collapse of the Soviet bloc in 1989 and then the demise of the USSR itself in 1991 that saw Yugoslavia disintegrate, for although that country had escaped Stalin it had remained Communist, and it was Communism that lost all popular legitimacy in the years 1989–1991.

But suppose Mihailovic had taken power and restored the King in 1945: would the Croats, Bosnians, Slovenes and the other national groups within Yugoslavia ever have agreed to a Serb-ruled Yugoslavia? Even if Tito himself had gone, there would have been plenty of people from the non-Serb majority for whom this would have been totally unacceptable. To presume acquiescence from all of the other nationalities, especially after the horrors of war, is surely delusional thinking. The much stronger likelihood is that the civil war would have broken out all over again, and with the same degree of carnage that we saw in the 1990s. The chances of a Mihailovic-backed Yugoslavia staying together as a single coherent entity are arguably around zero.

In Greece, Churchill's percentages agreement/naughty document deal with Stalin made in Moscow in 1944 gave Britain hegemony over events in Greece. But in Yugoslavia the bargain was 50/50: both Britain and the USSR to have equal influence. With large-scale fighting, mayhem and civil war raging in Yugoslavia it beggars belief that Stalin would not have got involved, by backing a faction favourable to the USSR – in a way that he agreed not to do with the civil war in Greece.

British intervention in the Greek civil war was not at all popular, including with the USA, who thought that to back a reactionary monarchy was not the best solution, although the USA was equally opposed to a Communist seizure of that country. But would anyone have supported active British involvement in a Yugoslav civil war after 1945? Brave British soldiers killed in defence of King Peter – and so soon after VE Day and the end of the war against Germany? Here too it seems highly unlikely, and the idea that Attlee's Labour Government would have sent British troops to get involved in a conflict that not even the Germans could win seems improbable in the extreme.

In other words, Yugoslavia would have broken up, and much earlier than was in fact the case. Thousands would have died and it would be impossible to say how the post-destruction borders would have lain in such an instance. In the *Sporazum* of 1939 some of the territory given to the enlarged Croatia had non-Croats within its borders, and the state we now call Macedonia was an invention of Tito, which in our counterfactual world might therefore not have come into being.

Even if the USSR would not have been involved in such fighting it is hard to believe that the Bulgarians and Greeks, both of whom regarded much of Macedonia as theirs, would not have intervened and turned the civil war into a new Balkan war, with all the savagery that we saw in the two real Balkan Wars prior to 1914. The Yugoslav civil war could rapidly have become international, with all kinds of dire consequences.

In the real world, Tito spared the world all such horrors – Warsaw Pact naval bases on the Adriatic, a Balkan conflagration and likely massacres stemming from a Yugoslav implosion. The time he spent as a Soviet vassal 1945–1948 was bad enough but a world with no Tito would have had consequences far direr and considerably longer lasting.

So Communist Yugoslavia, if one considers realistic counterfactuals to the rather sunny but fantastical alternative of the conspiracy theorists, was the least bad option. He postponed the civil war that was rumbling beneath the surface and gave his part of the Balkans decades of peace. He kept together the artificial creation that we call Yugoslavia in ways that would have been impossible for anyone else, and, as many non-Communists would reflect in his lifetime, he defeated Stalin and kept the Soviets out, because of the legitimacy that he had earned during the war.

Not only that, but well-meaning revisionists, such as the late Michael Lees, or the more recent author Peter Batty, while naturally decrying Communist tyranny in Yugoslavia, overlook the general strategic picture of the whole war after 1941. Our book has emphasised the importance of Italy and of the Allied campaign there to Balkan strategy in particular. But the other thing totally neglected is the fact that from 1941–1945 Stalin was our ally, however vicious his USSR most certainly was. Of course, this made the war much more morally ambiguous than has hitherto regarded as having been the case. Wonderful new books by BBC producer Laurence Rees or by historians such as Norman Davies and Timothy Snyder have reminded us that in 1939–1941, under the Nazi-Soviet Pact of August 1939, the Wehrmacht and Red Army invaded Poland and massacred countless thousands of the inhabitants; the massacre of Polish officers at Katyn was a Soviet crime not a German one. But in 1941 *Barbarossa* changed everything, as Churchill, a long-term anti-Bolshevik, knew all too well.

On 22 June 1941, the German invasion of the USSR swiftly became the single largest military campaign in history. No fewer than 85 per cent of German casualties in the Second World War were on the Eastern Front, between the USSR and the Third Reich, something we all too easily forget in the West with our concentration on D-Day and the war in North-West Europe.

That same day Churchill broadcast the following message:

> No one has been a more consistent opponent of Communism for the last twenty-five years. I will unsay no word I have spoken about it. But all this fades away before the spectacle which is now unfolding. The past, with its crimes, its follies, its tragedies, flashes away ... The Russian danger is therefore our danger, and the danger of the United States, just as the cause of any Russian fighting for hearth and house is the cause of free men and free peoples in every quarter of the globe.

As he also put it privately: "If Hitler invaded hell I would make at least a favourable reference to the devil in the House of Commons."

The new and much better way of looking at the Second World War, pioneered by Laurence Rees in his BBC documentaries as well as in print, is to remember that comparatively speaking the Western Front – D-Day onwards in particular – was a minor sideshow compared to the carnage and existential struggle between the two dictatorships. The death toll at Stalingrad alone by far outstrips the total casualties of Britain and the USA combined, a fact that we are only now remembering.

The new view also makes clear that we were in alliance throughout 1941–1945 with a tyrant who had been an effective ally of Hitler's from August 1939 (the Molotov-Ribbentrop Pact) down to *Barbarossa* in June 1941. Ours was not therefore an exactly virtuous ally. Stalin, having carved up Poland with Hitler in 1939, effectively reconquered that unfortunate nation in 1944, and the Poles spent the next forty-five years under the Soviet yoke. But the Soviet Union was our ally after 1941 against the Third Reich nonetheless.

Furthermore, the more we read about the *Bloodlands*, to use a new term of Timothy Snyder's for the part of Europe in which tens of millions died in the 1930s and 1940s, the more we discover that until 1941 Stalin had slaughtered countless more people than even Adolf Hitler. The Nazis were of course eager to make up for lost time! Had Goering's *Hunger Plan* become reality, no fewer than 40 million Slavic peoples would have been deliberately starved to death. And we need no reminding of the Holocaust …

But on 22 June 1941 Stalin became our ally: acquiring an endearing, and wholly inappropriate sobriquet of "Uncle Joe". Communist guerrilla groups all over occupied Europe – from France and Italy to the Balkans – became fighters on Britain's side as well. The agents of SOE knew this full well, whatever their own individual politics. To be friends with Communists was not always in tune with their own feelings or politics. It was an operational necessity nonetheless, a necessity not lost on men such as Fitzroy Maclean (a Conservative MP) and Bill Deakin, no left winger either.

With so many countries free after 1989 of foreign Soviet tyranny, it would be wonderful to read such joy backwards. Emotionally it is easy to empathise with those who would have wished otherwise back in the Second World War. But is it good history?

When it came to Yugoslavia Churchill was a pragmatist. In his 1944 'Naughty Document' with Stalin he persuaded the Soviet leader to make Yugoslavia a 50/50 neutral state. So, when Tito left the Soviet bloc in 1948, Stalin kept his word to Churchill and did not send the Red Army to reconquer the country. Churchill's necessarily Faustian deal with Stalin saved the day for Tito in a way that would not otherwise have been possible.

So, obviously for most of us, Communism is never a solution and in that sense the emotions of writers such as Lees and Batty are wholly comprehensible. But nice options were unavailable for the peoples of Central and Eastern Europe 1945–1989, and in Tito, from 1948, the

West had someone benignly neutral in power in one of that part of the world's most strategic locations. Tito remembered his vast debt of gratitude to the British, and their decision in 1943. Churchill and the Chiefs of Staff in London, with the support of Fitzroy Maclean and Bill Deakin on the ground, had made that move for wholly British reasons, but Tito was the beneficiary because of his willingness to take the fight to the Germans, and so the gratitude became long term and mutual.

The reality is that Churchill and Maclean were prophetic, without realising it in 1943, about life in post-war Yugoslavia. Having made a short-term decision to save British lives they ended up making the correct long-term decision after all. Theirs, along with Deakin and others, was the right call.

Appendix

Sample Sigint Communications

From Major David Talbot Rice MI3b, 21 January 1943:

Operation *Weiss*

1. Most Secret Sources report that the Italians will begin an operation under this name against the Partisans in Croatia on January 20.
2. The operation will be conducted by the Italian V Corps (HQ Susak) which is part of the Second Army of General Roatta. Three Italian divisions will take part. As far as can be discovered no German land forces will be engaged, but the Luftwaffe will support from the air.
3. 13 Re Division from Gospic will take up a line Vhrovine-Gospic.
4. The objective of this operation is presumably the Partisan forces, which have been operating in all directions from their centre in the Grmec Planina.

From Major David Talbot Rice MI3b, 28 January 1943 to DDMI:

DDMI (I)

An attempt is being made to clean up the Partisans in Croatia. Four German and three Italian divisions are to take part and the GAF is to assist.

The activities of the Partisans must be causing the Germans considerable annoyance, if it has been found necessary to amount an operation on such a large scale during winter.

MI3 29 January 1943 to DMI:

DMI

The plan in broad outline is for three German divisions to proceed South-West and West from the general line of the SAVA and for one

German division and three Italian divisions to operate North-Eastwards from the mountain range ... The activities of the Partisans in this part of Croatia must be causing the Axis a good deal of trouble if they have decided to mount an operation of this scale at this particular moment. It is believed that it is intended to be completed by about mid-February.

From DMI (I) 31 January 1943 to VCIGS

VCIGS

The Axis are staging a strong operation to deal with the Yugoslav "Partisans" (Communists), who have for a considerable time been very active.

DMI 1 Feburary 1943

Operation *Weiss*

Later Information Most Secret

1. Little change in the general situation appears to have occurred since 7 February. Mopping up of the Partisans on the Grmec mountains is continuing, but the advance of the SS Division Prince Eugene south-eastwards from Petrovac is meeting with strong resistance, and the supply route of 369 (Croatian) Infantry Division between Bosanska Krupa and Petrinja is threatened by Partisans operating from the woods.
2. Information from MSS sources show that the Germans are not entirely confident that, even if the operation is carried out according to plan, the Partisans will not stream back into the cleaned up areas after the German troops have passed on. There appears to be a shortage of Axis troops for the occupation of these areas and the Germans show a distinct lack of confidence in the ability of Croat troops to maintain order, even if these were available. The information received suggests that the Germans are dissatisfied with the co-operation so far received from the Italian Second Army. This anxiety on the part of the Germans testifies to the skill of the Partisans in evading "mopping up", even when a very considerable Axis force (seven divisions, with air support) is engaged on a methodical operation against them.

MI3b

14 February 1943

From DMI to CIGS and VCIGS ([both] told 3 March)

1 March 1943

MI3b to DMI

5 March 1943

1. No further evidence about Operation Weiss 2 is forthcoming except that it seems probable that units of German 718 Division and Italian 15 (Bergamo) Division, two of the formations designed to take part in Weiss 2, are already engaged with the Partisans. Reports of the 9th and 12th February, however, speak of the re-appearance of small Partisan groups in areas allegedly combed out by Operation Weiss 1.
2. Meanwhile both the Germans and the Italians are concerned by the threat to the bauxite area near Mostar. The partisans captured Imotski on 10/2 and followed this up by taking Prozor and Bradina on 18/2/ The capture of the last-named interrupts the road and railway communications between Mostar and Sarajevo. The Italian General Negri on 9/2 announced that if things became serious he would, disregarding the Croats, employ "Cetniks" against the Partisans, and on 22/2 he informed the Croat Government that the situation demanded the employment of about 5000 Montenegrin "Cetniks". These would presumably be potential supporters of Mihailjovic, whom the Germans distrust completely. Most Secret Sources comments: "The menacing consequences arising from this cannot be foreseen".

From Major David Talbot Rice MI3b to DDMI (I)

10 March 1943

> Grave disquiet is being aroused at German HQ by the Italian employment of Cetniks (i.e. followers or potential followers of Mihailjovic) against the Partisans. They have declined to regard them as Italian auxiliary troops and continue to point out that such Cetniks are their avowed enemies. Mihailjovic, they state categorically, has ordered his men to fight the Germans, and the Germans themselves are under orders to fight them though not to provoke conflict. They therefore request the Italians to withdraw all Cetniks before any chance of German-Cetnik clashes can arise.

Partisan resistance continues to be strong and their threat to the bauxite zone is unabated. The introduction into the already complex situation of Cetniks who are prepared to fight Germans, Croats and Partisans alike while preserving their understanding with the Italians, opens up every kind of possibility.

Bibliography

The majority of the research for this book was done in the Deakin Archives at the Churchill Archives Centre at Churchill College Cambridge. I am beyond grateful to the Winston Churchill Memorial Trust for making a second by-fellowship at Churchill possible in 2016 in order to research this treasure trove of archival material. As well as his own SOE archive, Deakin aided the official history of SOE in Yugoslavia that never happened, and so accumulated hoards of declassified and recently classified material from the War Office, including the invaluable files of MI3, which I have used in this book, along with material from the Cabinet Office, GCHQ and some of those SOE archives that survived much of the shredding in 1945 when SOE was disbanded.

The OSS Archives in Washington DC are invaluable for the relevant chapters in this book, and they include the Donovan Papers of OSS's founder and wartime director Bill Donovan.

The Winston Churchill Memorial Trust in 2010 gave me a grant not only for the OSS material but also for the Fitzroy Maclean Papers that are held by the Alderman Library at the University of Virginia. Maclean kept not only Second World War material but also papers in the 1990s concerning the resurrection during the break-up of Yugoslavia on controversies of fifty years earlier.

Churchill College Cambridge has Churchill's own Chartwell Papers. Many of these replicate documents in The National Archives in Kew, in Greater London, and I have extensively also therefore used the PREM files of Churchill as Prime Minister, which are Crown Copyright.

Limited numbers of SOE files and Bletchley Park decrypts are also to be found in The National Archives.

Books and Articles

Andrews, Geoff. *The Shadow Man* (London, IB Tauris, 2015)

Bailey, Roderick. *Intelligence and National Security*, Vol. 20, No. 1, March 2005, 72–97, 'Communist in SOE'

Bailey, Roderick. *The Wildest Province: SOE in the Land of the Eagle* (London, Jonathan Cape, 2008)

Batty, Peter. *Hoodwinking Churchill: Tito's great confidence trick* (London, Shepheard-Walwyn, 2011)

Bennett, Ralph. *Behind the Battle: Intelligence in the War with Germany 1939–1945* (London, Sinclair-Stevenson, 1994)

Bennett, Ralph. *Ultra and Mediterranean Strategy 1941–1945* (London, Hamish Hamilton, 1989)

Bennett, Ralph, Sir William Deakin, Sir David Hunt, Sir Peter Wilkinson. *Intelligence and National Security*, Vol. 10, No. 3, July 1995, 527–9, 'Mihailovic and Tito'

Catherwood, Christopher. *The Balkans in World War II: Britain's Balkan Dilemma* (Basingstoke, Palgrave Macmillan, 2003)

Cripps, John. 'Mihailovic or Tito? How the Codebreakers Helped Churchill Choose', in *Action This Day*, ed. by Ralph Erskine and Michael Smith (London, Bantam Press, 2001), pp. 237–63

Davidson, Basil. *Special Operations Europe* (London, Gollancz, 1980)

Deakin, F.W.D. *The Embattled Mountain* (Oxford University Press, 1971)

Hastings, Max. *The Secret War* (London, Collins, 2015)

Hinsley, F.H. *et al.*, *British Intelligence in the Second World War, Volume 3, Part 1* (London, HMSO, 1984)

Lees, Michael, *The rape of Serbia: the British role in Tito's grab for power, 1943–1944* (San Diego, Harcourt Brace Jovanovic, 1990)

Mackenzie, W.J.M. *The Secret History of SOE* (London, St Ermin's Press, 2000, with introduction by M.R.D. Foot)

Maclean, Fitzroy. *Eastern Approaches* (London, Jonathan Cape, 1949 and London, Penguin, 2009)

Stafford, David. *Britain and the European Resistance 1940–1945: A Survey of the Special Operations Executive with Documents* (Basingstoke, Macmillan, 1980)

Sweet-Escott, Bickham. *Baker Street Irregular* (London, Methuen, 1965)

Index

195